THE PONY CLUB
MANUAL OF HORSEMANSHIP

BOOK 1
FUNDAMENTALS

The Pony Club
Lowlands Equestrian Centre
Old Warwick Road
Warwick
CV35 7AX

www.pcuk.org

First published in 2026 by The Pony Club, in cooperation with Kenilworth Press, an imprint of Quiller Publishing Ltd.

British Library Cataloguing in Publication Data.

A catalogue record for this book is available from the British Library.

ISBN 978-1-907279-17-1

Design: Becky Bowyer

Cover photograph: Pete Morris Photography

Printed in China

Distribution by
KENILWORTH PRESS
An imprint of Quiller Publishing Ltd
The Hill, Merrywalks, Stroud, GL5 4EP
Tel: 01453 847800
email: info@quillerbooks.com
web: www.quillerpublishing.com

Appointed GPSR EU Representative: Easy Access System Europe Oü, 16879218
Address: Mustamäe tee 50, 10621, Tallinn, Estonia
email: gpsr.requests@easproject.com
+358 40 500 3575

THE PONY CLUB
MANUAL OF HORSEMANSHIP

BOOK 1
FUNDAMENTALS

An Essential Guide to Riding and Pony Care

Dr Joanna Winfield FBHS

KENILWORTH
PRESS

THE PONY CLUB

EST 1929

Introduction

Riding is one of the most rewarding sports, enjoyed by people of all ages and abilities. At its simplest, it's a way of getting from one place to another, but at its best, it's about forming a strong bond with your pony and working together as a team.

The journey of learning never really stops, and that's what makes riding so exciting – there's always something new to discover! This is the first of three books which will form the new Manual of Horsemanship, providing you with the fundamentals of riding and pony care.

Horses and ponies are remarkable creatures – powerful yet graceful, strong yet kind and gentle. You will quickly come to appreciate their generosity and learn that, with the right approach, these animals will always give their best. In return, it is our duty to listen, learn, and care for them with respect and understanding.

This book is for anyone who loves ponies and aspires to become a true horseperson. Being a good rider is not just about skill in the saddle – it's about building a partnership through patience, training, and respect. Every pony is unique, and each one has something valuable to teach.

The first section of this book covers the essentials of working with a pony, guiding you as you create a safe and happy environment for you both. You'll learn how to care for your pony properly, helping you to build a relationship based on trust.

Later chapters focus on riding skills, teaching you how to communicate clearly with a pony both on the ground and in the saddle. The better your communication, the better the pony will understand you, and the more enjoyable and rewarding your riding will be.

Whether you've grown up around horses or are just starting your journey, this book will help you to develop the skills and confidence you need. The Pony Club is here to guide you, ensuring you learn in a safe and structured way that always puts the pony's welfare first.

As you progress, you'll not only become a better rider but also a more responsible and resourceful person around your equine friends. Taking care of a pony teaches patience, resilience, and teamwork – all valuable skills that will stay with you for life. Most importantly, you'll experience the joy of riding well and developing a true partnership with your pony.

There's a whole world of adventure ahead of you in The Pony Club – so let's get started!

Sarah MacDonald
The Pony Club Chair of Training

Contents

Chapter 1

Classification and Identification

Classification and Identification

Where do you start when you want to talk about a favourite pony? What do you say when your friends or family ask you to describe him?

Whenever you talk about a pony, you'll need to know the right terms and language to describe him. You should know his size, colour, gender and any markings. This can help you find him on the stable yard or in a group of ponies that might be turned out in the field.

Purchasing your pony

How a pony is built is referred to as his 'conformation'. Good conformation makes a pony easy to look at, and it's far more important than a pretty colour or how long his mane and tail are. Good conformation means that the pony can move and work better, will be more comfortable to ride, and is likely to stay strong and have fewer physical problems. Overall, a pony should look balanced, with all the parts of his body fitting well together. No part should look too big or too small for him.

How a pony naturally behaves is referred to as his 'temperament'. A pony that is easy for you to manage on the ground and when ridden is very important for you as you develop a happy relationship with each other. Some ponies are naturally quiet, and others are more excitable, and this can relate to both their breed and their age. It is important that the temperament of a pony is suitable for the person who is going to ride them, and a safe, even-tempered pony is a pleasure to have around.

When purchasing your pony, it is important to have him vetted by an independent veterinary surgeon to determine his health and well-being. Part of this process is identifying the specific pony correctly, so that he can be recognised. Once vetted, your pony is issued with a veterinary certificate as proof of the examination, and it will also state for what purpose the pony has been vetted.

Points of the pony

Figure 1: Points of the pony – see inside front cover.

Passports

This legal document has the pony's description and markings on it. All equines (horse, pony, donkey, mule, ass, zebra) must have an individual passport. Other pages in the passport carry information about vaccinations and any medicine/drugs administered to the pony by a vet. If any equine is issued a passport for the first time they will also be microchipped, as this is a legal requirement. The vet will fill in all the pony's details on the passport.

Height and size of a pony

The traditional way to measure a pony is in 'hands'. One hand is equivalent to approximately 10.16cm (4in); there are 4 inches to a hand. Therefore, a pony that measures 14.2 hands high (hh) is 14 hands plus 2 inches. Modern practice now measures in centimetres so that a pony may be 143cm (14hh) or 148cm (14.2hh). Shetland ponies, being small, are measured in inches. There are some small differences between the metric (cm) and the imperial (hands) measurements, with the metric producing a slightly higher measurement, e.g. a 14.2hh is slightly smaller than its equivalent 148cm standard. This is important as some competitions are restricted to certain heights and classifications. Knowing the height of a pony is an important part of being able to describe him accurately, which is useful at the point of sale or purchase or in the purchase of tack and equipment to obtain the right sizing.

A measurement is taken from the ground to the pony's wither (the highest point).

hh	*cm*	
10.0	101.60	
10.2	106.68	
11.0	111.76	
11.2	116.84	
12.0	121.92	
12.2	127.0	
13.0	134.62	
13.2	137.16	
14.0	142.24	
14.2	147.32	PONY ↑
14.3	149.86	HORSE ↓
15.0	152.40	
15.2	157.48	
16.0	162.56	
16.2	167.64	
17.0	172.72	
17.2	177.80	
18.0	182.88	

Figure 2: Table of conversions from cm to hands (pony and horse).

- The pony should be measured on a smooth and level surface – concrete or tarmac being ideal.
- A specific measuring stick is used. To improve accuracy, it will have a spirit level on the cross and upright bars.

- The pony must be measured when standing equally balanced on all his feet. His front feet must be together, and his head lowered to the point that the poll comes onto a horizontal line with the withers.

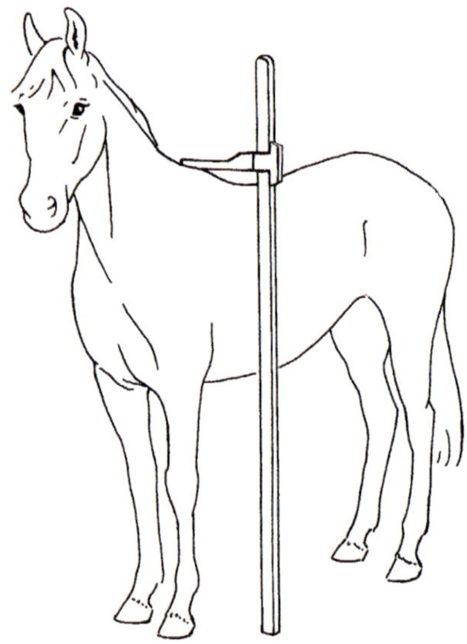

Figure 3: Measuring a pony with a measuring stick.

A measurement for life status within the Joint Measurement Scheme certification requires that the pony be measured without him wearing shoes. For Pony Club requirements, it is accepted that a margin of 12mm (½in) is made if the pony is wearing normal shoes.

Life Measurements are required for ponies competing in restricted height competitions. Two conditions must be met:

- The pony is over six years old (has finished growing).
- The measurements are taken by a panel member of the official Joint Measurement Scheme.

How to describe your pony

Figure 4: Rathnagrew Jacksie (Captain) is an Irish Cob piebald gelding born in 2018. He stands at 160cm (15.3hh) and has a white blaze down his face, along with a half wall-eye on his nearside. Captain possesses a good temperament, is well schooled, and competes regularly in dressage. He enjoys training, attending camps, pole work, some jumping, and hacking.

A formal description

Ponies and horses

A pony and a horse initially appear very similar. The main difference is in the height. Ponies are generally up to and including 148cm (14.2hh), while a horse is anything above this measurement. Some terminology does not change between a pony and a horse, for instance:

- Foal – a newborn until the first day of January the following year
- Colt – a young male up to three years (at birth, a colt foal)
- Filly – a young female up to three years (at birth, a filly foal)
- Yearling – in the year after birth
- Two-year-old – in the second year after birth
- Gelding – a castrated male (at any age)
- Entire/stallion – an uncastrated male of over three years
- Mare – a female over three years of age.

Types of pony

Ponies can be divided into many categories, but one of the first things we do is assess their breed.

Breeds

To belong to a named breed, a pony or horse should be registered with the specific breed register. Registered ponies and horses may be referred to as the type, e.g. New Forest type, where the full parentage isn't always known. There are several native breeds in the United Kingdom, but many of our ponies are 'crossbred', meaning a mixture of two or more breeds, providing hardiness and robustness. Breeds of pony in the UK include: Connemara, Dales, Dartmoor, Exmoor, Fell, Highland, New Forest, Shetland, Welsh Mountain pony Section A, B, C, and D.

Terms related to breeds

- **Pure-bred**: A pony classified as pure-bred will have known parentage, which may go back several generations. For example, all Thoroughbreds will have a minimum of eight generations registered with the Wetherbys' General Stud Book.
- **Half-bred**: One parent is a Thoroughbred.
- **Part-bred**: A cross between one pure-bred parent and one not pure-bred.
- **Warmblood**: A horse bred in a European country that is generally slightly heavier than the English Thoroughbreds but lighter than a cold-blooded horse (Draught pony, Shire or Clydesdale). They are now predominantly bred for type and purpose rather than a

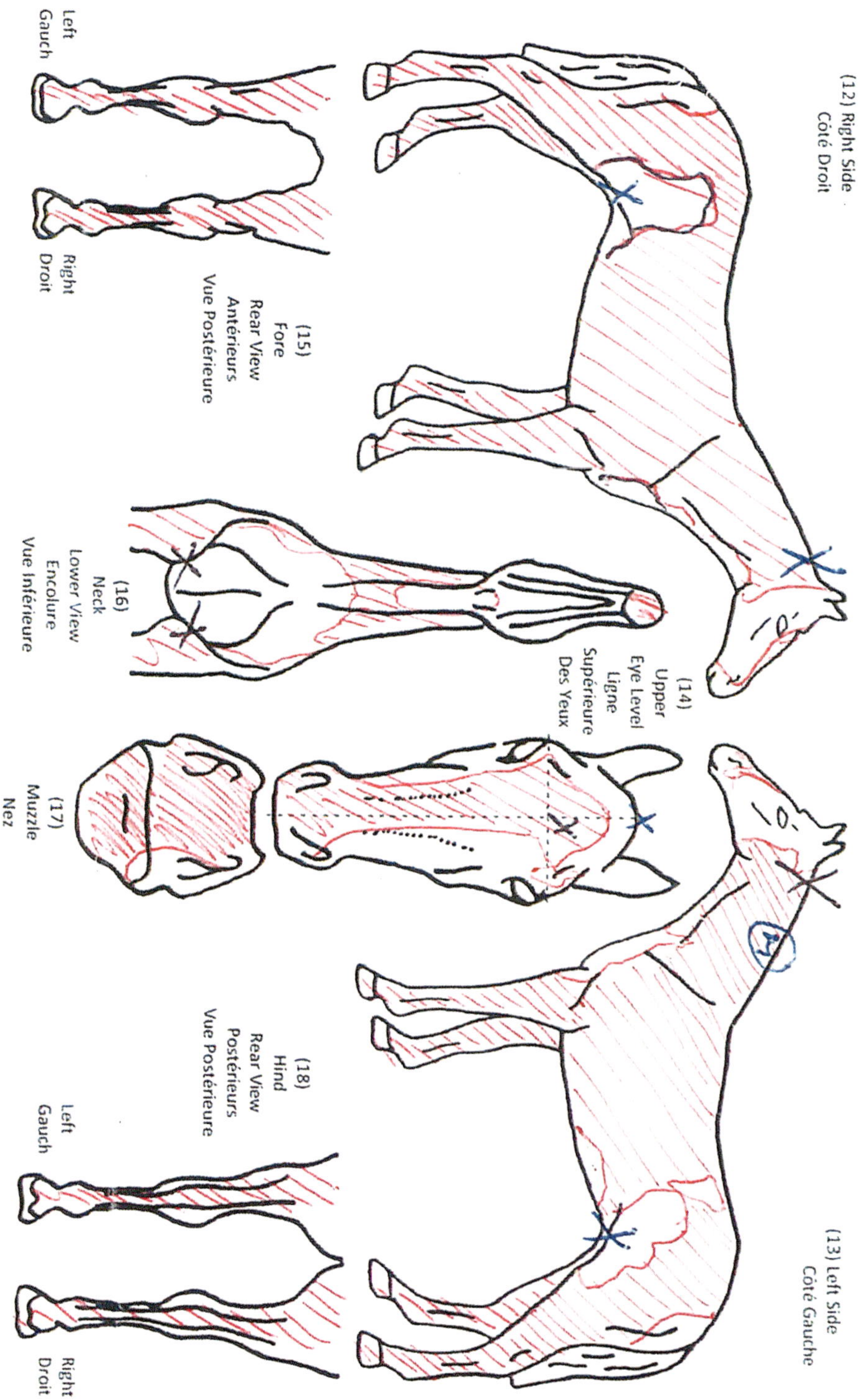

Figure 5: The passport identification chart for Rathnagrew Jacksie (Captain).

specific description. Warmbloods are not a breed, but stud registers exist, such as the British Sports Pony Register and British Warmblood Society.

- **Cob**: A cob is a sturdy, compact, and versatile breed of horse known for its strength, calm temperament, and adaptability. Typically, it has a muscular build, short legs, a deep chest, and a kind, intelligent expression, making it ideal for riding, driving, and various equestrian activities.

Types

Category of types: These relate to the purpose and use of a pony rather than the breed, e.g. a hunter, hack, sports pony, polo pony or cob. These are actual descriptions as opposed to specific breeds and may fall into the three build categories:

- **Heavyweight**: is a horse with robust build and a significant amount of bone (a term that measures the circumference below the horse's knee). They would be very solid in type. A hunter of 15.2hh with good bone would measure 21.75cm (8.5in) around the base of the knee.
- **Middleweight**: is generally lighter than heavyweight and has a more athletic conformation and build.
- **Lightweight**: one that is very fine and may have a Thoroughbred or Arab in its breeding.

Colours and markings

Ponies come in many colours. When we describe them, we refer to the colour of their body, head, tail, and mane. There can be many different shades and variations.

The base colour is the primary colour of the pony's body and skin. Some ponies may have markings over the base colours, such as dapples, a stripe down the back, or dark spots. If the pony has white markings on his face and legs, it does not change the colour but helps you to describe him in more detail.

The **points** of the pony are the tips of the ears, nostrils/muzzle, mane, tail and lower leg. The colour of the points is important in helping to complete a full description.

- **Black**: is a black pony, with a black body with black points and, most specifically, has a black muzzle. There are very few true black ponies.
- **Brown**: is dark brown or nearly black, with brown points, i.e. brown legs, mane and tail.

- **Bay**: is a brown pony with a brown body. There are various versions of light and dark bay, but they would all have black points, i.e. black legs below the knee and the hock and a black mane and tail.
- **Chestnut**: is ginger or reddish-brown over the body, usually the mane and tail are the same colour as the body. Sometimes, a pony will have a flaxen mane and tail, which is a lighter colour than the rest of the pony's body. There are variations of chestnut, called 'light' 'dark', and 'liver'.
- **Grey**: a pony with black and white hairs occurring throughout their body, and the skin is black. As grey ponies age, they often lose their dark colouring and look nearly white, although their skin remains black. Regardless of their age and any changes in coat colour, a grey is always called grey and never 'white'. There are various types of grey pony.
  - **Dappled grey**: has light grey patches on its body on a dark background.
  - **Flea-bitten**: this is a pony with dark hair in little tufts all over the body.
  - **Light grey**: this pony has a predominance of white hairs throughout the pony's body.
  - **Iron grey**: is where the colour is dark grey over the whole body and legs. It is usually seen in a younger pony, and this colour is likely to change and get lighter as the pony ages.
- **Dun**: is tan or mouse-coloured coat with black points. Often, a black line runs from the wither along the back to the tail (known as an eel mark, a list or dorsal stripe). The pony may also have zebra-like marks on the limbs.
- **Roan**: the pony has a solid coat colour but has white hair going through the body to give it a mottled appearance. Variations of roan are:
  - **Strawberry roan**: has a chestnut coat with white running through.
  - **Red roan**: has a bay coat with a white coat running through it.
  - **Blue roan**: the pony has a black/brown coat with white running through it.
- **Piebald**: has black and white patches throughout the body and legs.
- **Skewbald**: has large patches of white and any other colour (often chestnut) except black.
- **Coloured**: this is a pony that does not conform to any specific standard colour.
- **Appaloosa**: this is an American breed known for their colourful spotted coats. They are described by the patterns of colours and spots over their bodies. These are ponies with a base coat with spots of different colours over the body. There are three main types of spotted pony:

- **Leopard**: have spots of any colour on a light- or white-coloured base.
- **Blanket**: these ponies have a white rump on which spots are of any colour.
- **Snowflake**: these have white spots on a foundation of any colour.

- **Palomino**: is the colour of a pony and is sometimes confused as a breed. The body colour is golden and may change in its shading and its intensity. The mane and tail are usually lighter than the body and can be nearly white.

Markings

Figure 6: Head markings.

To describe any individual pony, we need to be clear on our terminology (see How to describe a pony).

Head markings should be described from where they start and finish.

- **Star**: a white mark on the forehead.
- **Stripe**: a narrow white mark running from the pony's eyes down towards his nose.
- **Blaze**: a broad white mark that extends down the face and may extend into the pony's nose.
- **Whiteface**: the amount of white will cover the pony's forehead, eyes and nose and maybe part of the muzzle.
- **Snip**: a white mark between the pony's nostrils that may extend into the muzzle.
- **Wall-eye**: an eye which shows white or pale blue colouring in place of the pony's normal eye pigment. Some ponies may have one or both eyes that are this colour.

- **Whorls**: these are usually circular changes in the direction of the hair and are generally found around the pony's brow.

Legs

To describe a pony's legs accurately, any white marking should be defined and referred to within the pony's anatomy. For example, a pony may have a white pastern, white to the fetlock, or white half-way up the cannon bone. Ponies can be described as having socks and stockings. Traditionally, the word sock applies to any white colour as far as the fetlock, while the word stocking would be for any white marking that goes as far as the pony's knee or hock. Ermine marks are small black spots on the top of a white sock and would usually be seen around the coronet and pastern area.

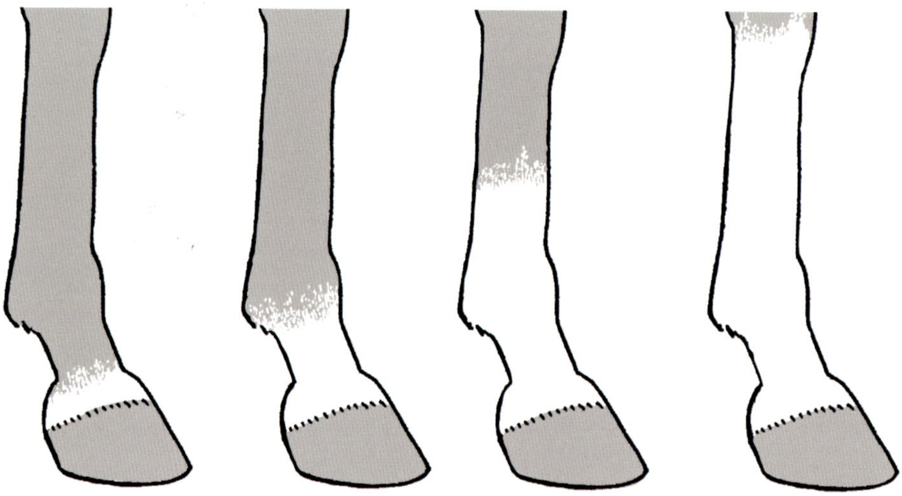

Figure 7: Leg markings.

Whorls

These are usually circular changes in the direction of the hair and can be found anywhere on the pony's body where the coat changes its pattern. They can be clockwise or anticlockwise in how they form. Normal places are on the forehead, between the eyes, the chest, the neck and the crest. The whorl should be marked on the identification page of the pony's passport, registration papers or veterinary certificate as proof of identification.

Brands

Pure-bred ponies and horses are often branded as a form of identification for the breed. This is practised in the UK with native pony breeds. In Europe, warmbloods are branded according to their breed and grade. In Australia, New Zealand and America, they are also used to identify the stud farm and year of birth. Brands are normally located on the quarters, shoulder or saddle region. Some ponies in Great Britain are freeze-branded as a means of personal identification, and this is normally seen on the saddle area or shoulder. Even without a freeze brand, the formal description should contain enough information to identify most ponies.

Ageing a pony

The best way to age a pony is to look at the passport information. However, this is only accurate if the pony was issued a passport at birth and the exact date was known. Failing this, the age of a pony is usually determined by assessing the condition and appearance of the teeth.

Ageing is covered in more detail in Book 2.

A four- to six-year-old pony is often described as young as he is inexperienced and not suitable for beginners or novice riders. A pony in his prime is between six and sixteen years. From sixteen years onwards he may require more specialist management, and may need a reduction in his workload.

Official birthday

As a rule, a pony's age is determined on January 1st. The term 'rising' is used when the horse is officially in his New Year but has not had his actual birthday. So, if a pony was born on 14th April, he could be described as 'rising six' from 1st January of his sixth year until 14th April when he turns six. Ageing a pony is easiest when the pony is very young (below five years old) or older (above twenty-five years).

- Yearlings are very obviously young and ungainly, changing constantly. The limbs are still rather long in proportion to the body. The head lacks the definition of that of a mature pony. The mane and tail are generally untidy, short and somewhat fluffy. Movement is still erratic.
- Three-year-olds look like mature adult ponies but are usually weaker in development. They have not started any work because they are still growing.
- Very old ponies (geriatric) are usually classified as over twenty years old. They show signs of their age in general, and a lack of body tone. The head may show sunken hollows over the eyes and a more angular bone structure. The area around the lower lip may become loose and floppy. There is likely to be a reduction in muscle tone over the neck and the back, making the wither area look more pronounced too. As

a result, the back can look hollow, with poor muscle tone extending along the back and hindquarters. The joint mobility may be reduced when the pony moves, and he may look stiff. There may be signs of wear and tear on the limbs, with bony or soft enlargements present.

Chapter 2

Safety, Welfare and the Environment

Safety, Welfare and the Environment

Keeping safe in the yard

A tidy yard is a safe yard
Brushes, bags, rugs, headcollars, etc., should all have a place to live when not being used. Tools around the yard should be kept in a safe place as well. Forks, brooms, shovels, and wheelbarrows should be put away neatly when not in use. This stops anyone from tripping over them and a pony from getting hurt if he gets loose around the yard.

Hay, haylage and bedding should be stored undercover, perhaps in a purpose-built hay barn. This is not a place to play and mess around, as it can be dangerous. Hay bales are secured with a heavy twine; this baler twine from hay or straw bales should be put in a bag so no one trips over it. Empty haynets should be left hanging in a tidy manner and not on the ground where you could trip over them. Climbing on a haystack or straw bales is also dangerous. The stacks are not built for people to play on and may collapse.

Safety around the yard

Accidents around ponies and on a stable yard can often be avoided; be aware of the following advice in this chapter …

When handling or leading a pony you should wear stout/solid boots to protect your feet – definitely not trainers! Always wear your riding hat to guard against any unexpected knocks to the head, and lastly some gloves … getting rope burns on your hands from a pony that pulls away from you is all too easy and can be very painful. These three important protective pieces of clothing are known as your PPE, your Personal Protective Equipment. Moreover, even when not handling a pony, it is safest to have long hair tied back and coats fastened.

When you are with a pony in the field or the stable, you must be mindful of both your own safety and the safety of those around you. Pay attention to everything in the area; stay alert, listen and watch, and take steps to stay safe. Even the quietest pony could become startled by many things: the wind, sudden noises, other ponies and general distractions. Learn to be aware of these things by observing changes in his behaviour. For this reason, you should avoid wearing earbuds/headphones, which might mean that you don't hear things going on around you.

Your behaviour will affect your pony and possibly other ponies in the yard simultaneously. If you are silly and rowdy the ponies are likely to pick up on this and become reactive, leading to unpredictable behaviours. So, we should be calm and quiet around the yard to create a nice place for them.

Pay attention when entering a pony's stable. Some ponies like to push past you to get into the yard. Getting squashed by a pony can be very painful and may result in injury, as well as the potential danger of having a loose pony in the yard. It is important that a pony respects you and your voice so that you can quickly and calmly ask him to step back as you enter the stable.

When the pony is in his stable, make sure the door is securely fastened, using both the top and the bottom bolts if possible, as some ponies are very clever at letting themselves out! When the pony is not in his stable, you should secure both top and bottom doors so they are shut or cannot swing loosely, as fingers can become trapped or a head knocked, and ponies can be alarmed too. If you tie a pony next to another outside, think about the distance between them so that they do not get too close to kick or bite each other, and you have enough space to work safely.

A pony should always be tied up before grooming or tacking up. This is particularly important if he is in a strange place that he is not used to. When he is tied up it means that you can walk and work in the space around him, knowing that both you and he are safe. If the pony is allowed to be loose in the stable while you try to work around him – whether it be skipping or mucking out, tacking up or just grooming him – the situation could become unsafe very quickly.

When leading a pony close to others, you must again consider a safe distance to walk past. Not all ponies may know each other, if you are at a rally or camp, for example. You may be very aware of how your pony behaves, but not all ponies will know you and be friendly, so never walk too close behind a strange pony. Other ponies and horses may not be used to having people around them, so be careful when walking close to stable doors, as some ponies and horses can reach out a long way and may nip or bite if you get too close. Always check with the owner before entering a strange pony's stable.

Safety rules when working around the yard

- Speak quietly.
- Avoid sudden movements: do not run around the stables.
- Avoid becoming rough or loud-voiced around ponies and while on the yard.
- Watch out for a pony's feet. He may not always be looking where he steps, and he might step on you by accident. You should wear the correct Personal Protective Equipment (PPE) – strong shoes will give you some protection.
- Avoid walking directly behind a pony unless you are working with him, and even then, do so with caution. It is much safer to approach him and work from the front than from the rear.

Welfare

Introduction

The Pony Club is committed to high welfare standards for all horses and ponies under the care of its Members and its Linked Riding Centres.

The Pony Club acts in accordance with British Equestrian's Charter for the Horse.

Recent research and better understanding have helped us to recognise horses as being capable of feeling pleasure and distress. They have the capacity to feel pleasure, joy, pain and fear, but they will also feel calm and safe when treated kindly.

From this research we also recognise that some of the traditional training and management practices are out of date and no longer appropriate. The Pony Club aims to educate and raise awareness of modern, humane care and training methods.

The Pony Club aims to support Members in giving horses the best possible care to ensure they are in good health, properly fed, adequately sheltered, are free from pain, fear and distress, and can express their natural behaviour, all of which promote their mental and physical well-being.

Aim

The aim of The Pony Club's Welfare Policy is to provide clear guidance for Members, coaches, and supporters (parents, guardians, volunteers, officials and staff) on how we can all meet welfare expectations.

The policy also outlines the support available from The Pony Club.

Objective

To protect the health and well-being of all horses and ponies in Pony Club activities, through educating and training at all levels, and giving welfare-focused guidance and rules.

How the policy is applied throughout The Pony Club

Training

- First and foremost, the Welfare Policy is incorporated into all Pony Club education and training.
- All Members, coaches and supporters must be aware of the actions they need to take to be compliant with this policy.

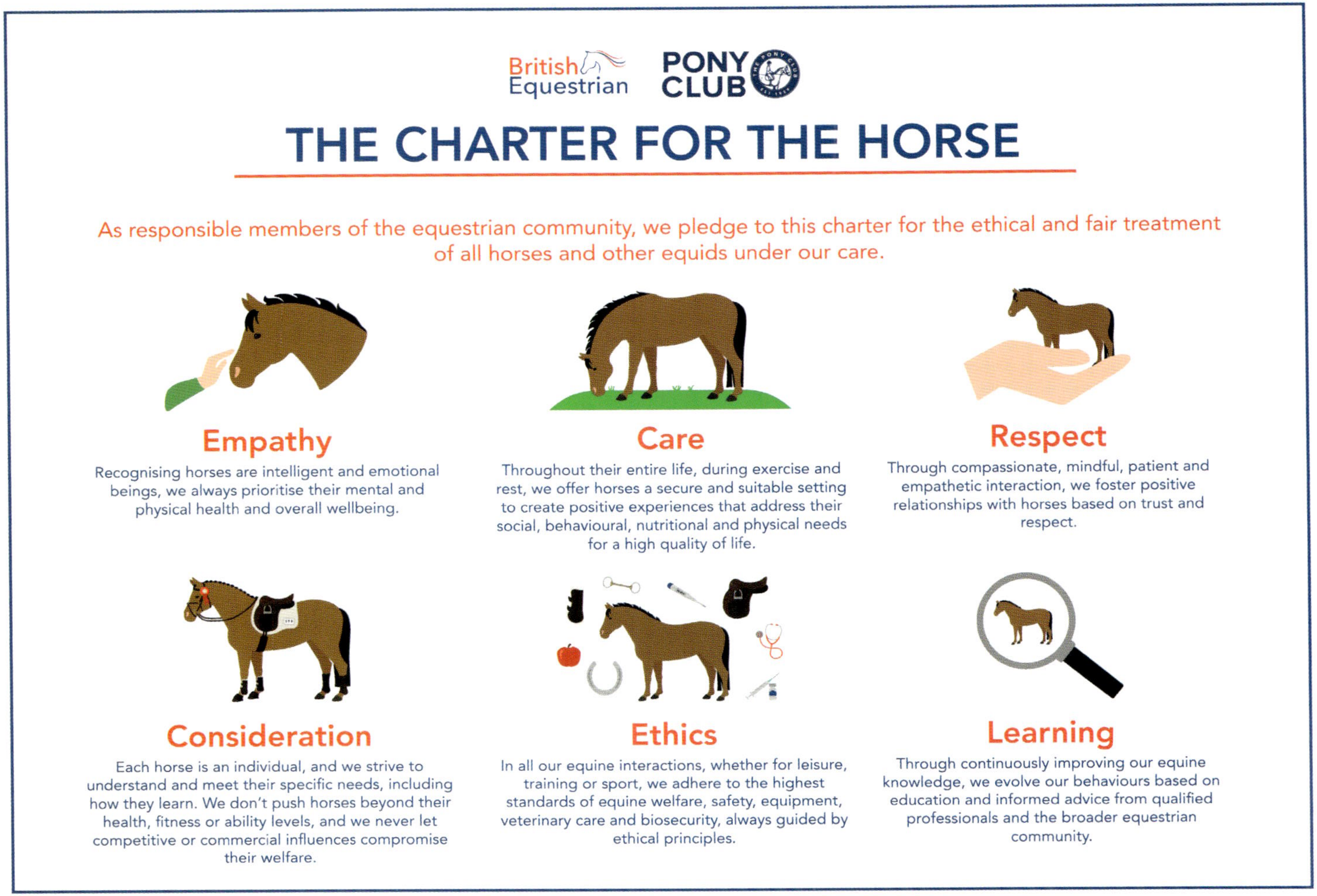

Figure 8: British Equestrian's Charter for the Horse.

- Training and education focus on what is best for the horse, not just for competitive success.
- Members are encouraged to engage in all training, especially those related to welfare. The Pony Club's training and test system is used to educate on all aspects of horsemanship, including several topics that help to develop the knowledge needed to understand the complex needs of horses. Welfare of the horse is more important than competition or personal gain.
- This way of thinking, along with Learning Theory, (the science of how humans and animals learn), is included in all training syllabuses.

Achievement badges

Many badges focus on equine welfare and learning.

The Equine Welfare Badge, developed with The Blue Cross, is awarded after earning 10 Achievement badges that are specifically related to care and welfare of horses.

Codes of Conduct

The Pony Club Codes of Conduct are designed to make sure that Members, coaches and supporters must prioritise equine welfare.

Rules

The Rules of The Pony Club also ensure that at no point is the welfare of the horse disregarded.

They are designed to prevent any actions that might compromise equine well-being.

Meetings and communication

Committees at all levels throughout The Pony Club include welfare as a standing agenda item.

Accountability and intervention

The Pony Club has systems in place for dealing with any apparent disregard for welfare. All officials of The Pony Club are responsible for enforcing the policy.

If a welfare concern is raised, as a training organisation, the initial response would be to provide support and retraining.

Continued breaches may lead to sanctions or exclusion.

Raising welfare concerns

- Concerns are treated seriously, fairly, and confidentially.
- First step, if you are happy to do so, contact your Branch District Commissioner or Centre Proprietor.
- If unresolved, escalate to Area Representative or Centre Coordinator.
- If you wish to contact someone outside your Branch or Centre, please email: equinewelfare@pcuk.org (this can be anonymous).
- Urgent cases: Refer to the emergency contacts on The Pony Club website.

Regular review

The Pony Club's Welfare Policy is subject to regular review in partnership with industry experts and aims for continuous improvement by updating training and literature with the latest research.

The policy is also supported by separate Equine Welfare Guidelines, which, together with the full Welfare Policy, can be found on The Pony Club website.

The Five Domains of Animal Welfare

The Five Domains of Animal Welfare is the most recent evolution of the well-documented five freedoms. The Domains approach animal welfare more holistically, meaning it's not just about meeting animals' basic needs. Their physical and mental well-being should also be considered in decision-making about health and welfare.

1. Nutrition

Nutrition for ponies

All horses and ponies must be fed and watered properly to stay healthy and happy.

Care tips

- **Feed them the right food** for their size, type, and how much exercise they get. Feeding too much or too little can make them sick.
- **Most of their food should be forage**, such as grass, hay, or hay substitutes, and they should always have it available.

- **Grazing on grass** or eating hay is good for their health and makes them happy because chewing and foraging are natural behaviours.
- **Change their diet slowly** if needed, not all at once.
- **Seek advice from your vet** if your horse or pony has any nutrition-related health issues.
- **Use clean bowls and buckets** for their food and water.
- **Always provide fresh water** in the fields, stables, or when travelling. Check it at least once a day.
- **Provide a balanced diet for your pony.** Remember that too much can be as harmful as too little.
- **Ponies shouldn't be without access to forage for more than 4 hours.**

Rules and expectations

- **Water**: Ponies must have water when travelling to events. If the trip is long, ensure they can drink along the way.

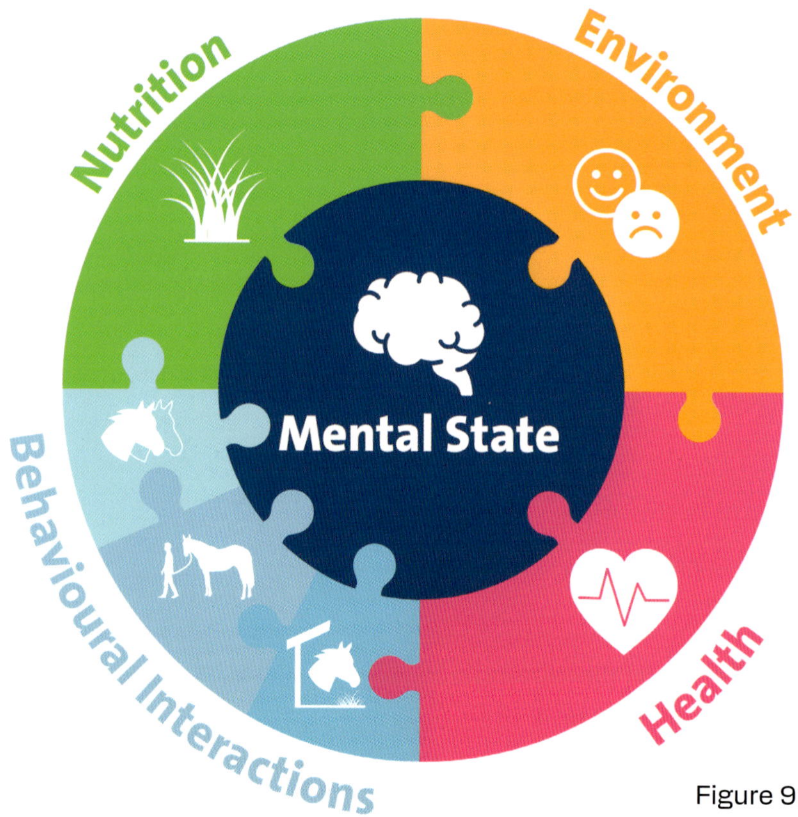

Figure 9: The Five Domains.

- **Food**: If your pony is at an event for more than 4 hours, they must have something to eat, like hay.
- **Weight**: Keeping your horse or pony at a healthy weight is important for their well-being.
- **Stabled horses**: Horses staying in stables overnight need access to food and water, so they don't get anxious or uncomfortable.

Remember, these rules help keep your pony healthy and happy!

2. Environment

Horses and ponies should have an appropriate living environment where they feel safe, are free from danger, and offer adequate shelter. They should also be provided with an environment that gives them the benefit of forage, freedom, and friends. Horses and ponies are herd animals and, as such, need company, which should ideally be from their own kind.

Husbandry and care advice

The environment where horses and ponies are kept should provide:

- A natural environment where they can freely move, graze and forage. If turnout is unavailable, hand grazing or free exercise should be offered.
- The ability to play and socialise, rest and sleep.
- Enrichment.
- Protection from inclement weather.
- Be safe and clear of hazards that could injure them.
- Free from poisonous plants.
- Be of an appropriate size for the numbers using it.
- Fencing should be species specific, safe and fit for purpose.
- Stables should be of suitable size, have good ventilation, be clean, have suitable bedding, and have constant access to forage and water.
- Stables and fields should allow visual access to other horses or ponies.
- Rugs should be used as necessary to give warmth and protection, but care should be taken not to overheat the horse or pony because this can cause unnecessary stress. Rugs should be removed and checked daily.
- Good-quality sleep is essential for the body to rest and recuperate. Horses and ponies sleep for several short periods during the day and night. It is essential to provide a suitable location and bedding, whether inside or outside where horses feel safe, so they can get good-quality sleep.

- When travelling to events, ensure boxes and trailers are safe, adequately maintained and have enough space and ventilation.
- Travelling to an event where there is a substantial change to their normal environment, for example, being stabled for several days, when they normally live out, could have a major impact on stress levels, well-being, sleep, diet, and health. This should be considered when making plans for such events.
- Long journeys should allow regular rest breaks where water should be offered. They should be allowed to recover from a long journey before being exercised or competed.

Rules and expectations

- During camps and stay-away competitions, ensure ponies' welfare and well-being are prioritised and address and manage stress and upsets.
- Always remember to put welfare ahead of competition and personal gain.

3. Health

Preventing disease and recognising signs and symptoms of ill health and pain in horses and ponies is key to keeping them happy and healthy.

Husbandry and care advice

All horses and ponies need routine preventative health care for optimum health. It is sensible to have a health plan which keeps a record of all routine health care. It is a useful way of ensuring their needs are met. This may include:

- Vaccination records.
- Hoof care.
- De-worming programmes.
- Preventive physical care (like physiotherapy and other professional physical therapies).
- Tack checks for both saddle and bridle.
- Dental care.
- Weight monitoring.
- Temperature and respiratory rate checks.
- Pre-existing conditions.
- Regular medicines.
- Feeding schedules.
- Daily routines.
- Cleaning and disinfecting schedules.
- Pasture management plan.

It is strongly recommended to use professional equine practitioners registered with an appropriate professional regulatory body. They will be able to advise you on the frequency of visits required to ensure all preventive measures are put in place to optimise your pony's health and well-being.

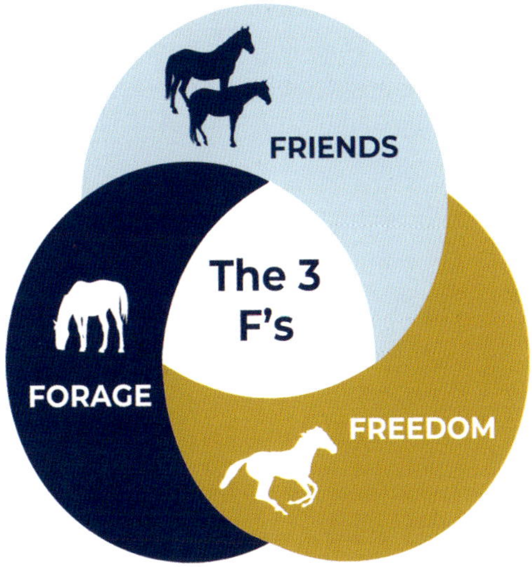

Figure 10: Friends, forage and freedom.

- Recognising signs of stress, pain, discomfort and discomfort-related behaviours can be very difficult as the cues that horses and ponies give can be very subtle and not always obviously related to the source of their discomfort. These behaviours can range from wrinkled nostrils to bucking and rearing, and many others.
- It's important to remember to 'listen to the whispers, so they don't need to shout'. Signs of pain, fear, stress, and discomfort can be easily overlooked. Ignoring these can lead to unwelcome behaviours or learned helplessness, where the person is apathetic to pain and other stresses around them.
- Know their 'normal' movement patterns, appetite, and demeanour.
- Check your ponies at least twice daily if they are kept in the field and ensure they are behaving normally and have not injured themselves.
- It is very important for horses and ponies to be able to have daily turnout or exercise, not only for their physical well-being but also for their mental well-being.
- Prescription medicines, such as phenylbutazone (known as 'bute'), should be carefully considered and only used under veterinary supervision. Their purpose should never be to mask lameness or enable ponies to be ridden when in pain or discomfort. However, if an old pony thrives on having a job and enjoys an occasional trip out to a low-level rally and needs some support to ease some mild soreness to old joints, the use of anti-inflammatory drugs can be beneficial. This should be done transparently with the involvement of veterinarians and Branch DC/Centre Proprietor. This advice does not apply to competition, horses, or ponies in medium or hard work.
- Effective biosecurity at home and when out and about is a key component to keeping horses and ponies healthy.

Rules and expectations

- The combined weight of the rider and equipment, including tack, should not be more than 20% of the horse's weight. For example, a pony that weighs 350kg should not be ridden by someone with a combined weight of more than 70kg, including all tack and equipment, riding hat and boots.
- It is important to remember that it is not an observation of the rider's or the pony's weight; it's the combination of pony and rider that is incompatible. (Refer to sports rule books for weight rules.)
- However, the rider's weight is not the only criterion for a pony to be 'suitably mounted'. For example, the length of the rider's leg on a small pony is also important.
- Do not trim the sensory hairs around the mouth, nose, eyes or inner ear.
- A pony used at Pony Club rallies and events must be at least four years of age on 1st January.
- Do not ride a pony that is lame due to pain, injury or abnormality.
- Do not use a noseband, baton, spurs, bit or any other piece of tack or equipment in a way that leads to injury, stress, pain or discomfort.
- Do not intentionally use any method to cause pain or injury in training or competition.
- A baton, schooling stick and spurs must never be used as punishment or in anger.
- Permission may be required to use spurs, so check with your DC/CP and coach.
- Riders should be taught the correct way to apply spurs before wearing them and have an independent seat with stable legs.
- All horses and ponies must be vaccinated following The Pony Club vaccination policy.
- The Pony Club Biosecurity Policy should be observed, and its advice and guidance should be followed, this is kept current on The Pony Club website.
- Refer to individual rule books for further details on Rules.

4. Behavioural interactions

Good horsemanship extends far beyond its original scope, emphasising what is right, whether horses and ponies are happy and content, whether they understand and are willing, rather than acting through habit, pain, or fear of reprimand.

Care advice

- To learn and understand, horses and ponies need clear and consistent training and expectations of their behaviour. If aids and boundaries are inconsistent, it leads to confusion, frustration and unpredictability.

- Riding and training methods should not involve punishment or cause pain. It should always be humane. Punishment has been shown to frighten and confuse horses and ponies, weakening the bond between them and their rider. A frightened, confused horse or pony can quickly become dangerous and unpredictable.
- Stereotypical behaviours such as weaving, windsucking, crib-biting, or box/fence walking are signs of a welfare problem, so try hard to remove or find a remedy for the stress that is causing it. These undesirable behaviour patterns can be developed from many things, such as stress, boredom, confusion, frustration, fear, isolation, extended confinement, insufficient access to forage, and inappropriate or insufficient exercise.
- Try to keep horses and ponies outside as much as possible, with friends, forage and freedom. If there is no alternative, enrichment methods can be used to improve their well-being.
- Some alternative ways of housing horses and ponies that are considered to meet their mental and physical needs better, are group housing with group turnout, herd living, or a surfaced track system. While these systems may not suit all horses, ponies, or their owners, they can be good alternatives if a horse or pony struggles to cope in a more traditional housing environment.
- All horses and ponies should be able to interact closely, be turned out together, or at least be able to groom each other mutually over the fence.
- Allow horses and ponies to show interest in things and explore their environment. Give them time to sniff, look, and touch new things, and allow them time to explore and accept them. This will help build a bond of trust and allow them to explore and understand the world around them.
- Behave calmly around horses. Don't rush a horse or pony who is unsure or get angry and frustrated with them. Remain calm, gently reinforce the desired behaviour and then repeat.
- Outdated terms such as 'lazy', 'naughty', 'stubborn', and 'kick them' should not be used to describe unwanted behaviour or the treatment of horses and ponies. If someone uses these terms, they may be outdated in their understanding and knowledge.
- Regular grooming keeps their coat healthy and is a good way to bond with them and get them used to being handled. Scratching places where other horses or ponies would mutually groom further helps with bonding and creates positive experiences.

Rules and expectations

- Tack and equipment must comply with all sports rules.
- Do not ride in a manner that causes pain, fear or suffering.

- If you think your pony appears stressed, consider why they are behaving this way and try to understand it from their perspective.

5. Mental experiences

As sensitive individuals, horses and ponies can experience positive and negative mental effects from how they are treated and cared for. Understanding this is key to ensuring their continued welfare and well-being.

Care advice

The living conditions and treatment of horses and ponies should not impose mental suffering, instead, they should give them positive experiences and things that matter to them, such as:

- Minimising negative experiences and resolve them when they arise.
- If negative experiences are not addressed, they will, over time, become chronic and may hinder well-being.
- Eating when they are hungry, foraging, and browsing; provide an interesting and stimulating diet. Removing the ability to chew can lead to stress, mental harm, and stereotypical behaviours.
- Drinking when they are thirsty.
- Having space to roam, play and exercise.
- Having company of their kind – it is essential that they can see, touch and groom each other. If they cannot be kept together, grooming over a fence or in the company of another animal is beneficial.
- Feeling safe; a horse or pony alone may be more vigilant, meaning sleep, stress, and relaxation will be significantly affected. If they are kept alone, consider a companion from another species.
- Having shade and shelter when needed, and ideally, the choice of when to use it.

Positive experiences lead to a positive state of mental well-being, meaning ponies are more likely to thrive and cope when a negative experience arises. Train them to face everyday stresses, such as loading, standing, being handled, so that none of these things causes stress.

Training consistently and free from fear and pain will improve mental security and the bond between them and humans. Always end training on a positive note.

Not only should we seek to remove physical and mental suffering, but we should also seek to provide positive experiences and give them a life worth living.

Rules and guidance

- All Pony Club Members, Supporters, Officials, and Staff are expected to follow the Welfare Policy and these supporting guidelines.
- Never has it been more evident that welfare must always be at the forefront of all decisions, training, care, husbandry, and horsemanship, taking a 'Pony-centred Approach' to everything, we do.

Always remember to put welfare ahead of competition and personal gain.

Environmental considerations

Reducing the environmental impact of a pony stabled in the UK involves us having to think about sustainability, waste management and resource efficiency so we can reduce carbon 'hoofprints' and footprints.

Sustainable bedding and manure management

- **Bedding choices**: Choose eco-friendly bedding materials such as straw, hemp, or recycled wood products that are biodegradable and sustainably sourced. Some bedding options can be composted, reducing waste.
- **Manure management**: Properly managing horse manure can significantly reduce environmental impact. The compost can be used as a natural fertiliser for gardens and fields.

Energy efficiency in stables

- **Lighting and heating**: Use energy-efficient lighting such as LED bulbs in stables.
- **Water conservation**: Find ways to collect and store rainwater (such as barrels or water troughs connected to the roof gutters) and use it for watering and cleaning the horses/ponies.

Responsible pasture management

- **Pasture management**: Proper pasture management, including rotational grazing and maintaining healthy grass cover can reduce soil erosion and improve the soil. This also helps maintain a healthy ecosystem for horses.

Reducing, reusing, and recycling horse-related waste

- **Reducing waste**: Minimise waste by buying in bulk to reduce packaging and opt for products with minimal or recyclable packaging. Encourage the use of refillable containers for supplements and other stable supplies.

- **Reusing materials**: Reuse items like feed sacks for storage or as bin liners. Old blankets, rugs, and equipment can be repurposed or donated to rescue centres rather than discarded.
- **Recycling**: Set up recycling stations in the yard for paper, plastic, and metal. Recycling used materials reduces the need for new resources and lowers waste production.

Managing horse-related waste responsibly

- **Waste separation**: Separate organic and non-organic waste, like manure and bedding. Compost organic material and recycle or responsibly dispose of non-organic waste.
- **Hazardous waste**: To prevent environmental contamination, hazardous waste, such as veterinary medicines, must be disposed of following local regulations. Never put medications down the drain or dispose of them with regular waste.

By adopting these practices, we can significantly reduce the environmental impact, promoting a more sustainable and eco-friendlier stable environment.

Figure 11: Spot the dangers on the yard.

Chapter 3

How Horses Learn and Behave

How Horses Learn and Behave

When you're working around the stable with your pony, especially if it is your first time handling him, it's really important to have someone experienced with you. This could be a coach, a parent who knows about ponies, or someone who works at the yard. They can show you the right way to do things, like how to lead your pony safely, brush him properly, or clean his hooves without getting hurt. Ponies can be gentle, but they're still big animals and can act unpredictably if they get scared or excited. Having someone who knows what they're doing means you can learn safely, feel more confident, and enjoy spending time with your pony even more.

Primary: flight and fight response

Ponies make great use of their senses: eyes, ears and noses to notice everything around them. A pony's eyes are on the side of his head, allowing him to see all around him. If you approach a pony from behind, he may find it less easy to see you. He may become startled and react because his attention is focused elsewhere. It is a good idea, therefore, to call his name or talk to him as you approach him. This is discussed in greater length later in this chapter.

One of the first things to understand when working with ponies is that they can quickly become scared or frightened of things we think are normal. That is because when they are in the wild their first instinct is to run away if they are startled by anything they think is strange or dangerous: this is called the 'flight instinct'. If a pony does get scared and can't get away from something, he might bite or kick to defend himself.

Ponies have a highly developed social instinct. In their natural state, they live in herds and love each other's company. In the last chapter we discussed the need for ponies to have companions: we know that ponies who can physically touch each other will have lower stress levels than those with no company. Providing ponies with friends so that they can touch and see each other is very important.

When handling a pony, always be aware of the look in his eye. We can also look and feel for tension on his body as a helpful sign of how relaxed or tense he may be. This will help you to understand his thoughts and anticipate his movements. You can tell from his eyes and body language whether he is calm or excited. Understanding and identifying with a pony's character is essential to you both getting on with each other.

A pony is very much a creature of habit and favours the same thing happening at the same time every day. For example, if a pony is brought into the stable at night, creating a routine he expects to follow each evening is comforting for him. Picking out feet, for example, is much more easily achieved if they are picked out in the same order each time. Therefore, it is a good plan to adopt and follow a daily stable routine as much as possible.

Approaching your pony

Always speak to a pony before approaching, handling, or moving him. This is a simple but important lesson. A word frequently repeated soon becomes familiar. A pony will learn from the sound and tone of your voice and how it is used. He soon comes to recognise your voice as the person who feeds him or from whom some kindness is to be expected. For your safety's sake and to keep him calm, speak to him before you do anything else.

It is best to approach a pony from his shoulder rather than straight in front or behind him. Take deliberate steps and never rush. Speak to him as you approach him. To help you make friends with a pony, you could place your hand on his nose so he can sniff it, and then he will learn who you are. He would prefer you to stroke his neck or shoulder rather than try to pat his nose or face.

Behaviours: reward and punishment

'Learning Theory' is the understanding of how ponies learn. We know that ponies have a more simplified level of learning ability than people. You can use your body language to help your pony have good manners. The timing of your behaviour is important for your pony to understand what behaviour you are rewarding or want to change, or stop, or remove.

Rewarding your pony can be done in two ways:

- Giving them something nice, such as a treat, or scratch on their favourite scratchy spot (ponies prefer a scratch to a pat), or
- Removing something uncomfortable, such as pressure on the reins or from your legs.

Examples of things a pony can be rewarded for doing

- Standing still to mount.
- Walking up to you when catching him in the field.
- Walking straight into the trailer/lorry.
- Reacting quickly to leg aids.
- Picking up feet, etc.

Understanding how ponies learn is essential for communicating with them. Expecting them to think and react the way that people do is neither wise nor helpful.

Ponies learn from what we do all the time, not just when we think we are training them. Ponies will not know instinctively what you want them to do. They learn by trial and error. They will keep trying behaviours until they understand which one it is that you want.

For example, imagine you have two fields next to each other. A gate connects the fields at one end. When someone calls the pony, it doesn't know where the gate is. The pony must walk along the fence, back and forth, until they find the gate. After doing this a few times, the pony learns exactly where the gate is and goes straight there when called. People are different. If you tell someone where the gate is, they'll understand immediately. Ponies need to figure it out by making mistakes and learning from them. This is why ponies and people learn in different ways.

Handling and control

LEADING AND HANDLING

pcuk.org

Putting on a headcollar

The headcollar

This is made of leather or synthetic fabric, with a buckle on the nearside cheekpiece. A short strap connects the noseband and throatlash. They may or may not be adjustable. The lead rope is usually attached to a ring in the centre of the back of the noseband.

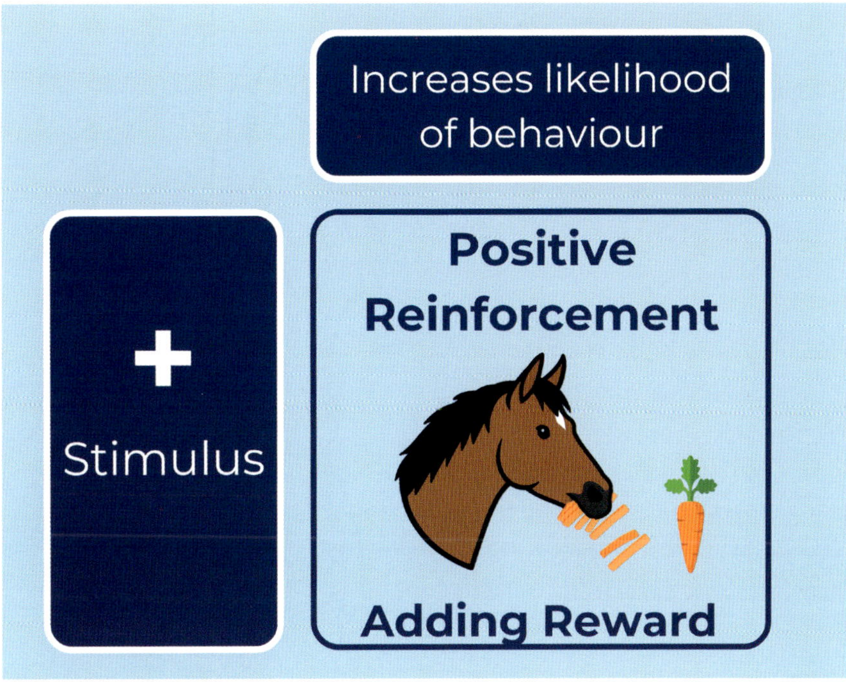

Figure 12: Positive reinforcement.

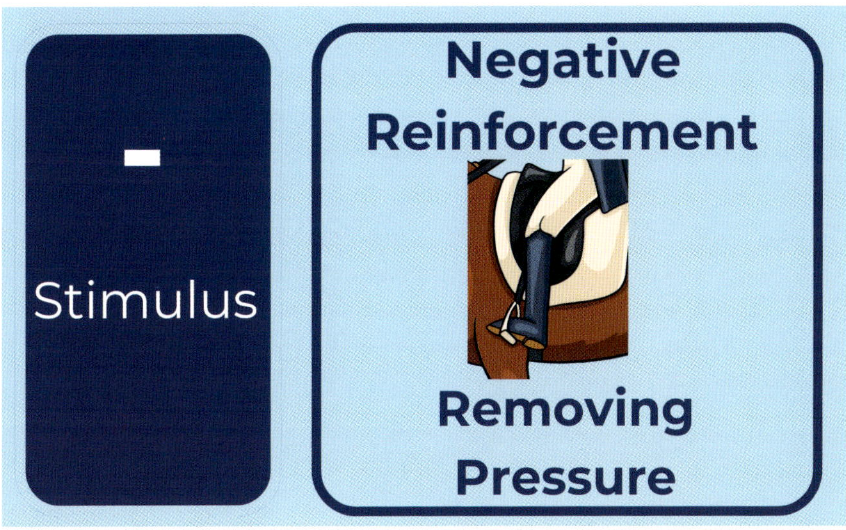

Figure 13: Negative reinforcement.

When you go into a stable it's unlikely that the pony will be wearing a headcollar. Talk to him as you approach and enter the stable, and he should turn his head towards you.

- Before putting on the headcollar, unfasten the buckle on the nearside cheekpiece.
- Walk in and stand by the pony's left shoulder, facing forward.
- Put the lead rope around his neck.
- Place the noseband over his muzzle, and in your right hand, take the headpiece over the poll behind his ears.
- Then, fasten the cheekpiece.

Figure 14: Putting on the headcollar.

Tying up your pony

- Make sure that the lead rope is attached to the metal O-ring at the back of the headcollar.
- Use a quick-release knot.
- The lead rope should be passed through a small loop of string **(of a strength that would break in an emergency)** attached to the securing ring, rather than through the ring itself. This will secure the pony for normal purposes but will give way should he panic and struggle hard to free himself. There are also various safety tie up fastenings available on the market.
- The pony must be secured by a quick release knot, so you can undo it quickly and safely should you need to. There are several ways of doing quick-release knots and you should become familiar with at least one of them.
- For safety, it is always best to tie a pony in a stable or enclosed space if you are going to be working with him, for example, when grooming or tacking up.
- Beware of tying up to an unsafe wall or rail, which might give way before the string.
- Haynets should always be tied up separately.
- Never tie a pony to a haynet.

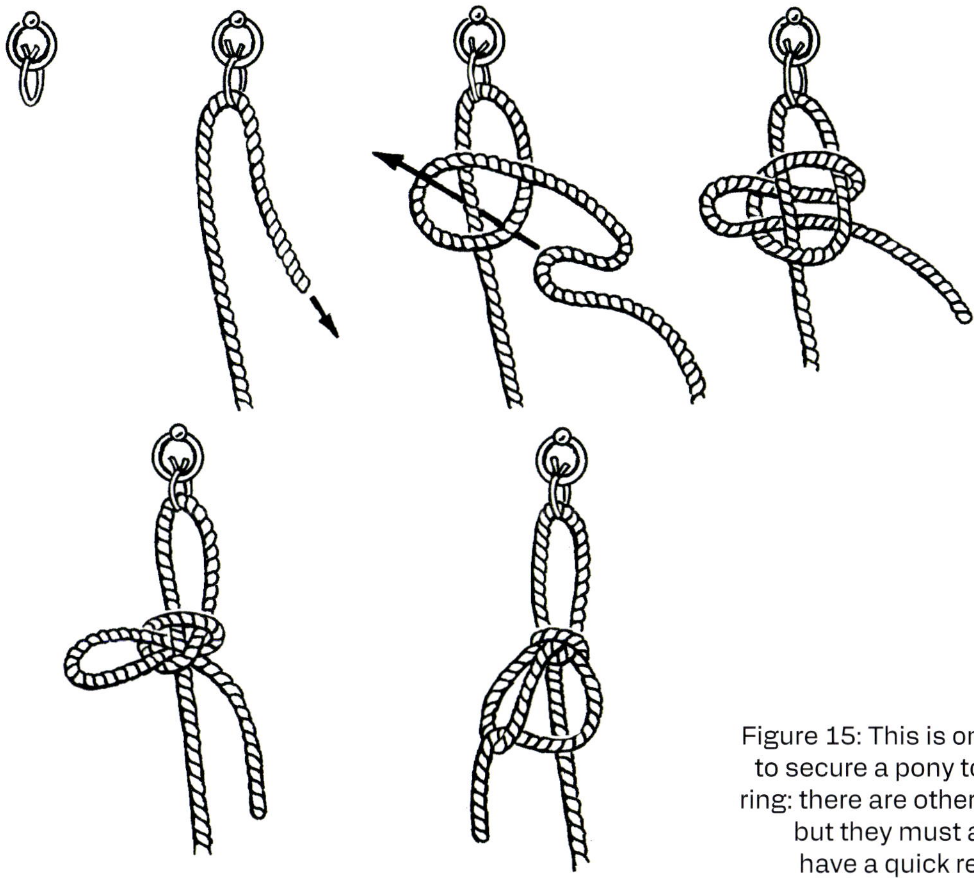

Figure 15: This is one way to secure a pony to a tie-ring: there are other ways, but they must always have a quick release.

Cross-tying

- This is a way of securing the pony using two lead ropes or chains rather than one.
- Your pony is positioned between two walls or stout posts roughly 2m (6½ft) apart with the ropes or chains fastened to the D-rings on each side of his headcollar.
- Chains may be permanent fixtures on appropriate posts or walls in barns or stables where cross-tying is normal.
- If you use a lead rope, one of the ropes securing the pony should be a quick release at the wall.
- Cross-tying is also used when transporting a single pony in a double trailer without a partition.

Figure 16: Cross-tying a horse.

Leading

Leading is when a person on the ground leads a pony without a rider. The pony can be led either by the reins if he's wearing a bridle or using a lead rope if he's wearing a headcollar. A pony should be accustomed to being led from either side, but most ponies will expect to be led from the left (near) side. If a pony is strange to you, you should always lead him from the nearside.

In Britain, when leading on the road (public highway) the pony must travel in the same direction as the traffic, and the person leading him must always be on the right (off) side, to be between the pony and overtaking traffic. For further information, see The Highway Code. You should also wear a hi-vis jacket or similar so that you can be seen, even in broad daylight.

Figure 17: How to hold a lead rope.

Figure 18: How NOT to hold a lead rope.

Occasionally, it is advisable to lead a pony in a well-fitting snaffle bridle. This is useful for additional control if the area is busy or the pony is too strong to handle in a headcollar. If you are on a road (public highway), a bridle must be worn for control and insurance purposes.

Leading your pony in a headcollar

- Hold the rope with one hand a short distance from the headcollar or halter, keeping the free end in the other hand.
- Never put your fingers through the headcollar's D-ring or wrap the rope around your hand. Both can be dangerous.

Leading in a bridle

Pass the reins over the pony's head. Hold them with one hand a short distance from the bit, with one finger dividing them. Hold the buckle end in the other hand.

A pony should not be led with the running martingale still attached to the reins. If the bridle is used with a running martingale, the buckle on the reins can be undone and the martingale can be knotted back to the neckstrap to lead.

Figure 19: Leading in a bridle.

Leading a pony tacked up (saddle and bridle)

- Using the snaffle with the reins straight to the hand.
- The far rein passed through the ring on the side of the snaffle nearest you. This will prevent the bit from turning backwards in your pony's mouth if he hangs back as you lead him.
- Running martingales should be detached from the reins and secured to the neckstrap.
- The stirrup irons should be run up to prevent them from coming loose.

Catching a pony in a field

- Take someone with you and make sure you are wearing your hat, gloves and suitable shoes.
- Call his name as you walk into the field.
- Check that your pony has realised that you are there and walk up to him.
- Be aware of other ponies in the field and their behaviour.
- Approach him towards his shoulder.
- Give him a scratch on his neck and put the lead rope around his neck so you can hold him still where you put the headcollar.
- Put the headcollar on as described earlier.
- He may not like to leave his pony friends in the field, so you may need to be firm with your reinforcement and release to encourage him to leave.
- Do consider the behaviour of another pony if he is left in the field on his own, it may be best for both to be caught and taken out of the field at the same time.

If the pony starts to walk away before you get to him, it is best to stop and wait; avoid following him. Call his name again and hold out your hand. If he is alone in the field, it is okay to offer him a treat, as this will help teach him to come when you call him.

Note: Do not take treats or a bucket of feed into a field with other ponies, as this is unsafe. It is easy for the ponies to get close to you, but they may become pushy. If a pony is tricky to catch, it is a good idea to go and see him, sometimes give him a treat, and then let him go again. This way, he will learn that being caught means nice things and not always going to the stable or away from his friends. If you still have problems catching him, get some advice from an experienced person.

Turning a pony out in a field

Ensure the pony is suitably prepared for going out into the field. This is a similar process for catching him.

When taking a pony out to the field, you need to ensure that you are suitably prepared with your hat, gloves, and suitable shoes and that you are leading the pony in a headcollar, ready to turn out.

- As you approach the field, you will lead the pony from his left side. Put the lead rope into your right hand while you undo the gate.
- Open the gate with plenty of room to walk the pony through.
- As you walk into the field, turn the pony around so that you face the gate.
- Make sure that it is firmly shut.
- Walk into the field and turn the pony back to face the gateway. This is because some ponies will turn away quickly when released, and you may get knocked over or kicked as they do so.
- Undo the headcollar and quietly slip the noseband over the muzzle.
- Give the pony a treat if it is safe as a reward for not rushing away.
- If the pony is strong to lead when turning out, or it is a windy day, you may need help leading him or opening/closing the gate.

Standing up in hand

Ensure the pony looks alert, stands still, and shows his conformation to the best advantage. Stand directly in front of him and face him, holding one rein in each hand. He should be standing with his front legs 'square' (level with each other) to balance himself, and some ponies will naturally stand with all four legs 'square', which is ideal.

Showing a pony and leading in hand

The object of this is to show off the pony without a rider, either at the halt (which is called 'standing up in hand'), or while moving as freely as possible at the walk and trot ('running up in hand'). This procedure is used during veterinary inspections.

Trotting up in hand

You may be asked to do this for several reasons, such as for a vetting, when showing and to check your pony's soundness.

- It is usual to lead from the left side.
- Run or walk as requested, looking straight ahead and not at your pony.
- Your pony should be moved directly away from the person inspecting him, then turned as described above and led straight back.
- The person inspecting him will step to one side if they wish you to carry on past him.

- It is most important for the rein or rope to be slack enough to allow the pony to carry his head naturally.
- He should be encouraged to move confidently and well.
- The pace should be active but not hurried or unbalanced.
- If the pony hangs back, avoid pulling on the lead rope. Either carry a baton or stick in the outside hand and move it behind your back, tap his flank, or ask a helper to move behind him.

To back up

There are many times when you need your pony to back up. This might be when handling him in the stable, around the yard, or leading him. Also, the better a pony backs up the better they slow down and stop when leading them.

Teaching your pony to back up when you are leading him:

- When he is standing still, turn round and face him.
- Then, take a step forward, applying pressure to the lead rope to guide him to step back.
- When you do this, as your pony takes a step back (even a small one), release the pressure on the lead rope/reins as a reward.

Moving forwards, turning and stopping

- It's important that the pony is polite and responsive to you and has good manners when he's being led from the ground.
- You may need help from an experienced person to show you how to do this.
- A pony should be able to stand quietly, waiting for you to ask him to move forward without fidgeting.
- This is useful for any inspection, such as by a vet or farrier or when showing.
- When required, it is important that your pony moves forward and maybe backward in case you need to move him around the stable yard.
- It is also important that your pony should walk and trot in hand so he can be checked for soundness and any other reasons.
- It is good practice to lead your pony from both sides.

To move forward

- Push your leading hand (usually your right if leading from the left) to apply forward pressure on the lead rope/reins.
- As soon as the pony starts to move forward, release the pressure – remember that the release of pressure tells them that moving forward was the correct response/answer.

- Look at something ahead of you to help you walk straight; avoid looking at him.
- A trained pony will walk forward readily alongside you.

To turn

- Before turning, ensure the ground is safe, and avoid slippery surfaces, drains, or uneven ground.
- If you're trotting, gently slow down to a walk before making the turn.
- Then, you can turn them away from you.
- Push your right arm to the side to help your pony turn, leading his chin away from you.
- As soon as he turns, release the pressure a little so he knows turning was the right response/answer.
- Keep yourself on the outside of the turn so you do not get stepped or trodden on.
- This will also help him to stay balanced and under your control.

To stop

- Apply light backwards pressure on the lead rope or reins.
- If he does not want to stop, apply stronger pressure.
- If he still does not stop or tries to pull away instead of standing still, use short little tugs.
- As soon as he halts release the pressure on the lead rope; remember this is his reward for doing the right thing.
- You should be standing by his shoulder when he comes to a halt.

In time, you can work on teaching your pony to stand square. This is when all four feet are flat on the ground and evenly spaced underneath his body, and he stands quietly and relaxed.

Handling the legs

Lifting a foreleg

- As you approach the pony, first speak to him so he knows where you are.
- Place a hand on his neck and turn to face his tail.
- Run your hand down over his shoulder, elbow, back of his knees and tendons.
- On reaching the fetlock, gently squeeze the joint.
- As he lifts his leg, with your free hand, catch his toe and hold it with your fingers; less weight falls on your arm when you hold the foot at the toe rather than at the pastern.
- If your pony does not lift his foot when spoken to, you may encourage him to do so by leaning against his shoulder and pushing his weight onto the other leg.

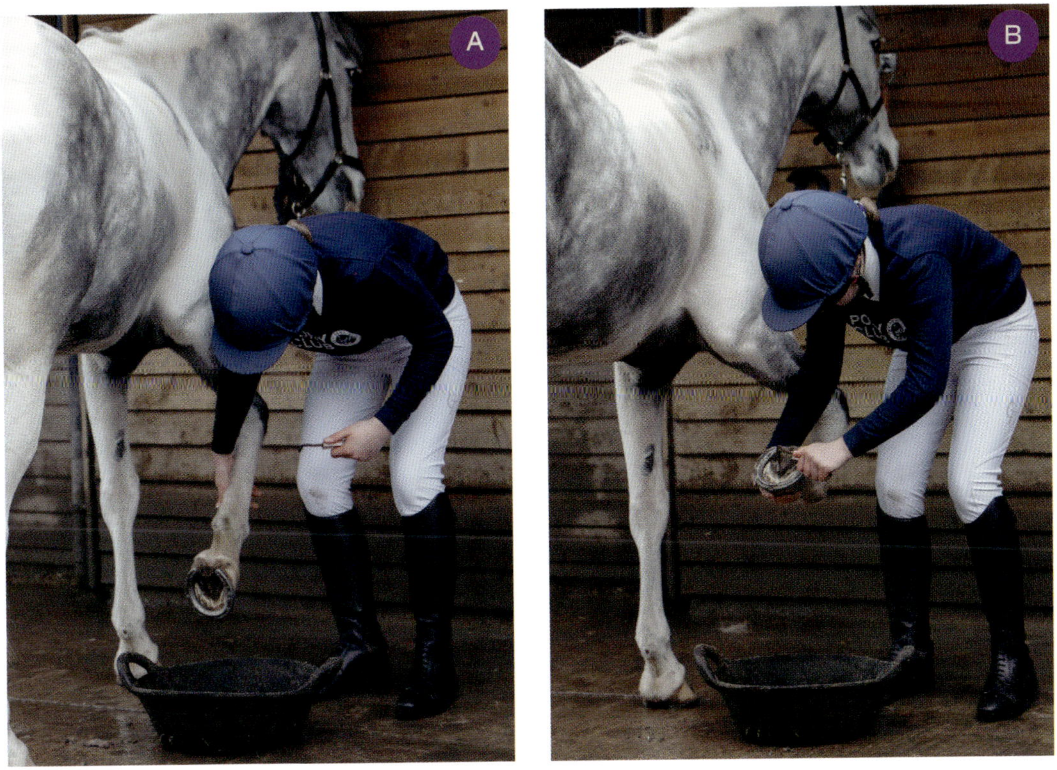

Figure 20: Picking out ponies' feet.

Lifting a hind leg

- As you approach the pony, first speak to him so he knows where you are.
- Then, stand beside his hip and face his tail, placing your hand nearest your pony on his quarters.
- Run your hand down the back of his leg as far as the point of the hock.
- Move your hand to the front of the hock and run it down on the inside front of the cannon bone.
- When you reach the fetlock and the pony raises his foot, move the joint slightly backwards and then slide your hand down to encircle the hoof from the inside.
- Do not lift it high or carry it far back, as this may upset his balance.

Figure 21: Picking out a hind limb.

Chapter 4

Caring for your Pony

Caring for your Pony

Keeping your pony at grass or stable

Requirements for keeping your pony at grass

Grazing land: hectares (acreages)
It is impossible to lay down any hard-and-fast rule about the acreage needed to support a pony, as so much depends upon the quality of the grass, the drainage of the land and the nature of the soil. If several ponies are at grass together, about 0.5 hectares (1 acre) per pony is adequate.

One acre for a horse or pony on its own may be insufficient, especially if the paddock is used all year round by a horse rather than a pony. In this case, alternative grazing must be found so that the paddock can be rested and treated for a few weeks, at least once a year, to keep it in good condition.

Water in the paddock – see also Chapter 5: Nutrition, Watering and Feeding

Field troughs
Self-filling automatic troughs

- These are ideal but need checking daily and cleaning regularly. They should be approximately 1–2m (3–6ft) long, about 38cm (15in) deep, and placed so that the top is about 60cm (2ft) from the ground. An outlet at the base helps when cleaning and emptying them.
- Troughs should be placed clear of trees so that leaves do not accumulate in them. The ground should be well-drained so that the earth surrounding the trough doesn't become muddy in winter.
- The nearer the trough is to the house, gate or road, the better the chance of it being regularly checked. This should be done at least twice daily during frost and snow. Your pony will suffer no ill-effects if the ice is broken up and a large piece removed so that he can reach and drink the water.

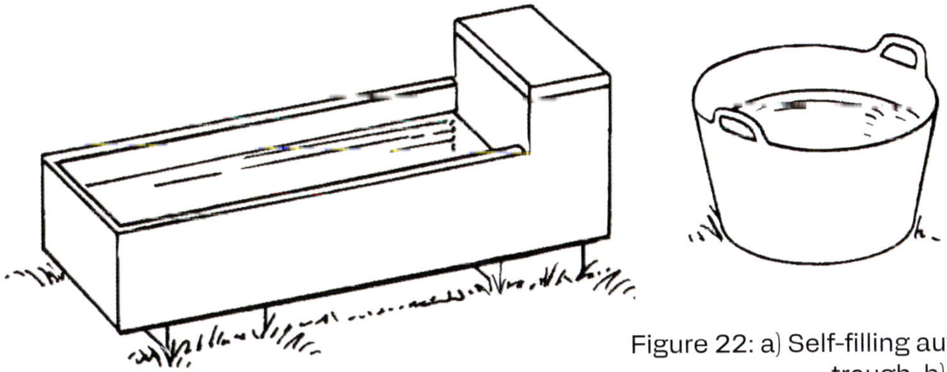

Figure 22: a) Self-filling automatic trough, b) bucket.

- The water must be clear; leaves and other matter floating on the surface should be scooped out daily.

Buckets
If used, buckets must be big enough and filled daily. Ponies and horses drink approximately 22–45 litres (5–10 gallons) daily, depending on weather and exercise.

Rivers, streams and ponds
Rivers or streams with a good approach and water running over a gravel bottom are ideal, but streams with steep, unstable banks or a muddy approach may be difficult or dangerous for ponies to reach easily.

Streams should always be checked for water sources that could be polluted. A suitable stream will have a stony bottom, as sand or mud can cause colic.

Ponds should be avoided, if possible, but if they are in your field, they must be fenced off. The water is usually stagnant, and animals could get stuck if they are deep.

Old baths should be avoided where possible, as their edges can be sharp and could cause injury, and they are difficult to clean properly.

Shelter

- When in the field, a pony needs shelter all year round from the weather, whether it be rain, sun or wind. Natural shelters may be in the form of hedges, banks, walls, or trees.
- Man-made shelters should be open-access field shelters that allow the pony to stand inside, away from poor weather or flies, or provide a windbreak.
- If there are several ponies in the field, the shelters must be big enough to prevent a pony from getting boxed in or bullied by others who do not let him come to the shelter.

Access

- Getting to and from your field is an important consideration so you have easy access to the entrance all year round.
- The tracks to the field from the stable yard should be wide enough to allow you to lead your pony safely.
- Tracks and gates must be wide enough for vehicle access to maintain the fields throughout the year.

Company

- As ponies are very sociable, a pony will be much happier if he can be turned out with others in a group so that they can share their time through mutual grooming and friendship.

Field checks

Your field or paddock should be checked daily; this includes the following:

- The boundary fence is safe and secure.
- There is clean, fresh water.
- There are no poisonous plants.
- If your field is close to a road, track, or footpath, there should be no rubbish that may come into the field.
- Droppings are picked up daily in small paddocks.

The pasture

The food value of the pasture depends on the time of year and the weather, whether the grass is growing actively, flowering, going to seed or dying back, and on the grass's type, variety and quality. Good grazing should have a variety of grasses (also known as 'sward'). Well-established pastures usually contain a mixture of plants in the sward helping it to withstand different weather conditions and providing the pony with a range of nutrients.

Conservation

Keeping a pony at grass requires careful and sensible use of land. Ponies are among the most wasteful grazing animals. In their search for the most palatable grasses they trample down and destroy potentially valuable food. Furthermore, portions of the field eventually become so tainted with droppings that the grass turns coarse and sour and is no longer acceptable as food. During wet winters, some fields become badly trampled, especially if your pony is shod. Mud is not a good environment for ponies.

It may be possible to fence off the muddy areas, or feed and water the ponies in a fresh part of the paddock. Otherwise, they should be brought in or moved to a well-drained area. This will also conserve the grazing in the wet area for future use.

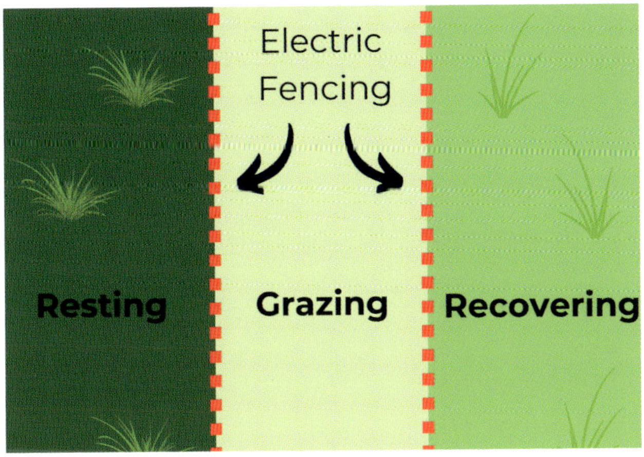

Figure 23: How to split a field or restrict grazing.

Dividing the field

On limited acreages, even in the best growing periods, the grass will be eaten right down and will only have a chance to recover and regrow if the field is rested. It is sensible to subdivide the field, preferably into three or four sections, and rotate them so that each receives a period of grazing followed by rest and/or treatment.

General management

Managing the droppings: while ponies are present, the daily removal of droppings by shovel and barrow is recommended. It conserves the pasture and limits the parasites. In large paddocks, the removal of droppings may not be practical. Harrowing is an alternative. Worms thrive in damp conditions, so if the droppings are scattered by harrowing in dry and sunny weather, they will dry out, and the worm infestation of the paddock will be reduced.

A pony turned out at grass should be visited by a responsible person at least twice a day. He should be checked for injuries, the condition of his feet and/or shoes, and general indications of health.

In warm weather the coat should be glossy and lying smooth. If it is dull and standing up (staring), it could mean that the pony is in poor condition, or cold, or sometimes both. Seek expert advice; the pony may need a turnout rug or more adequate shelter or extra food.

While checking the pony, you should also check the gate, the fence, and the water supply and make sure that everything is as it should be.

Whether the pony is being ridden or not, it is advisable to catch him every day, as this will ensure that he will be caught easily when required for work. You can take a treat in your pocket, such as pony cubes or slices of carrot or apple. This will encourage the pony to move towards you. To catch him, approach him quietly towards the shoulder, or let him come to you, and avoid jerky or sudden movements that might frighten him off.

Before work, pick out the feet and brush the pony lightly, ensuring the areas where the saddlery will lie are free from mud or dried sweat. In warm weather, sponge the eyes, lips, nose and dock.

If the weather is warm, sponge off the sweat marks on return from exercise.

Avoid excessive grooming, which could remove grease from the pony's coat, which is nature's way of protecting him against the wet and cold.

An unclipped pony is unlikely to have dried off completely on return from work but will probably roll and is less likely to catch a chill if turned out straight away than if left to stand in the stable to dry off.

Advantages

Under this natural system and if properly managed, many ponies will thrive, saving considerable time and money.

In the growing seasons of spring and early summer, if the acreage is sufficient to provide the required feed the grass will naturally supply the pony's total diet. In this case, a salt lick and fresh water will be the only additions needed.

The grass-kept pony generally exercises himself enough to keep healthy, and because he is not restricted, he is less likely to be over-fresh when ridden. Because his legs and to some extent his lungs are being constantly exercised, he is less likely to suffer injury to wind and limb than a stabled pony.

Disadvantages

There are, however, some disadvantages to looking after grass-kept ponies, particularly in the winter or when it's cold and wet!

They are not always near you when they are needed, and may be very dirty and wet. The field may not be nearby, and your pony may not be easy to catch. If you leave a well-fitted headcollar on, make sure it is made of leather, which is more likely to break than a synthetic type should it catch on anything. It is important that the headcollar can break if it catches on anything.

Another disadvantage of a purely grass-kept pony is that it is difficult to regulate his diet. The pony may become overweight in early summer, with a belly which is too grass-fat for fast and strenuous work. On the other hand, additional feed, which may be extra hay or a small hard feed, will be needed during the winter months and in the summer, too, if the grass is inadequate or your pony is working. Whether he is stabled, at grass, or kept on the combined system, the pony will need regular exercise to be fit enough for hard work.

Rolling

The grass-kept pony has a great advantage over his stabled counterpart in that he can indulge in a hearty roll in unrestricted conditions whenever he feels like it. Why ponies roll is by no means clear. In springtime, it undoubtedly helps to shift the winter coat. After work, it is probably because those parts of the skin are subjected to pressure under the saddlery and need a rub. Rolling helps a pony to cover any wet parts of his coat with dust, thus speeding up the drying-off process. Ponies at grass frequently have a layer of mud on their backs from rolling; this helps to keep out the cold and wind and to retain warmth. Rolling is also an act of sheer enjoyment and should be encouraged as natural, healthy, and relaxing.

Living out in a rug

After riding, ensure your pony returns to the stable (or somewhere he can dry off, if there is no stable), and is as dry as possible. If, for some unavoidable reason, he is wet on his body, rub him down until he is warm and comfortable, ensuring his ears are dry. He can then go out in his turnout rug. After a few hours, check that he is comfortable and change the rug if it is damp inside. Many modern rugs can 'wick' the sweat away from the pony's body if he gets warm in the field after exercise.

Under this system, the turnout rug comes into its own, as it overcomes the problem of turning out a clipped or thin-skinned pony in winter or poor weather. In the summer, some ponies will be worried about flies and other biting insects, so you may need to put fly repellent on them to keep them comfortable. Fly spray should be used carefully, not around your pony's eyes, and always wash your hands after using it. Protective equipment can also be used on ponies to make them more comfortable, including fly sheets and face covers such as face nets.

The combined system

This is a routine whereby a pony is turned out to grass for a portion of each day. It is a compromise between stabling and keeping him at grass, making the best of both methods.

It is a system well suited to ponies. It is useful if a pony is in light work where peak fitness is not necessary, and time for regular daily exercise is not always possible. However, ponies on this system can become extremely fit if exercised and managed appropriately.

On the combined system, the pony is turned out to grass by day and stabled at night, except during summer heat and when flies are particularly troublesome. Then the procedure can be reversed: the pony is out at night and stabled by day. In winter, a pony can be turned out after his morning feed (if he needs one) with part of his hay ration. The rest of the hay and the balance of his concentrates can be given when he comes in. This arrangement ensures that a pony is stabled when required and provides a suitable place for grooming and feeding. When several ponies are turned out together, ensure there are enough hay piles to reduce bullying and so that every pony can get some hay, that means more hay piles than there are ponies and well-spaced out. If there are four ponies in the field there should five or six piles, so the ponies can rotate to a pile if another pony moves in and stops them sharing.

The stabled pony

When stabling your pony, the following priorities apply:

- Keep to a regular routine: as a minimum, they should be checked twice a day.
- Companionship: as when in the field, it's important that ponies are happy in their environment; they thrive when they're together and are, ideally, close enough to see and touch each other.
- Grazing: it is best that they spend some daily time in a field or paddock.
- Regular feed times: see the rules of feeding.
- Clean, fresh water is always available: see the rules of feeding.
- Daily exercise and/or turnout is essential and must be considered in the light of work expected (camps, competitions, rallies, etc.).
- Daily grooming: see grooming.
- Mucking out.

Daily care and cleanliness

Stable routine:

- Provide your pony with fresh, clean water.
- Provide your pony with suitable forage so that it is available constantly.
- Provide adequate rugs according to the weather.
- Do a visual check for injuries and treat any promptly.
- Pick feet out before leaving the stable.
- Muck out the stable daily and skip out at intervals to keep clean.
- Sweep the area outside the stable and the yard.

Tools

A variety of equipment is needed to manage the stables and keep the yard tidy:

- Wheelbarrow
- Fork suitable for the bedding you will be working with
- Broom

- Shovel
- Skip.

Bedding
Some form of bedding material is necessary for the stabled pony to allow them to lie down and rest, to encourage them to stale, to provide insulation, and to prevent their feet from being jarred during long hours standing on a hard surface.

Rubber matting is widely used on stable floors but should be used with some form of moisture-absorbing bedding on top.

Straw: The straw should be dry, clean and dust-free. Wheat straw is ideal. A pony shouldn't eat an excessive amount of straw bedding; if they do you will need to change the bedding.

Alternatives: Shavings make a good, relatively dust-free form of bedding; wood pellets, paper and cardboard (amongst others) are useful if a pony has respiratory problems.

Mucking out and bedding down
Mucking out: Each day, the droppings and the wettest part of the bedding should be removed and the floor swept.

Bedding down: When relaying the bed, add fresh bedding as necessary. Place the used bedding down first, then add fresh, clean straw/shavings; or you might prefer to mix the old and new. Banking the stable with the bedding material around the walls of the stable protects the pony from getting stuck (cast) if they roll against it. A good, deep bed provides comfort and is more economical in the long run.

Finally, the floor should be swept, and the bed made neat.

Throughout the day, droppings should be cleared away each time you visit the stable. Lift them from underneath the bedding and tip them into a muck skip.

Deep-litter
The bedding method known as the deep-litter system is often used when time for a full muck out is short. Under this system, which may use straw or shavings, droppings should be removed whenever possible, and fresh bedding added to the existing deep bed when necessary. However, deep-litter beds can become smelly and wet; care must be taken to ensure that the pony's feet are kept clean, dry and healthy.

Muck heaps
A muck heap or pit must be kept tidy and be cleared frequently.

The seasons

Early summer

Some ponies, particularly small ponies, tend to grow too fat during the summer months. Excess weight can be dangerous because of the extra effort the pony must make to move and carry his rider. A fat pony is not always easy to ride as any exercise can become an effort and lead to physical problems. Laminitis, which can be very serious, is often a result of the greedy characteristics of ponies. Any pony who tends to put on too much weight should be moved to a field that offers only bare keep so that he finds less to eat and must move further in search of it.

Hay fields, or portions of the paddock on which hay is made, should be closed off and the grass allowed to grow. Ideally, the hay should be made at the height of the growing season before the grass goes to seed.

Flies are a problem in summer, so the pony should be provided with a shelter shed. Failing that, ensure he has ample shade and the companionship of another pony with whom he can stand head to tail so that each can flick away the flies from the other's face. Though various insect repellents are available and may ease the problem, it should be remembered that flies may be nature's way of keeping a pony at grass active and moving rather than just standing about and gorging himself.

Late summer

An abnormally dry summer may result in grassland becoming barer than at any other time. In extreme cases, the grass may become so brown or burnt up that no keep for the pony remains. When this happens, the pony must either be moved to a better pasture or fed hay temporarily. On sandy soil in these conditions, ponies have been known to suffer from sand colic – the result of ingesting sand along with the poor grazing available. Remember to check water more frequently. Flies may continue to be troublesome at this time of year.

Late autumn

When the food value in the grass is deteriorating, the pony might scavenge from hedgerows and trees. Blackberries are rarely a problem. Crab apples (wild apples) have been known to cause colic if eaten excessively. Beech and oak leaves are slightly toxic. Acorns, sycamore and beech nuts, especially when unripe, can be dangerous, and ponies who develop a liking for them should not be allowed access to oak or beech trees at this time of year.

Midwinter

In the winter months, feeding hay as a supplement to grass becomes necessary. Do not put this off for too long, or the good condition the pony carried from the summer will be lost. A thin pony is also a cold pony. Cold, wet, windy weather causes maximum heat loss and is more debilitating than cold, dry weather. Ponies tend to spend their time sheltering rather than grazing in cold weather. Hardy native ponies are better suited to living out at night in winter than lightweight ponies. Keeping lightweight ponies out all through the winter is not, as a rule, a good idea. However, if it must be done, extra concentrates and bulk feed should be supplied so the ponies have the calories needed to maintain their weight.

Depending on the weather and the state of the grass, hay should be fed at night or in the morning. It is more economical and easier to weigh If fed in a net, but this method is not always practical. If several ponies share a field, hay should be shaken out in heaps, spaced well apart on a circle, allowing more heaps than there are animals. All should be fed at the same time. Feed should be provided in the part of the field where the animals are sheltered.

Snow does not cause acute discomfort but stops grazing, so while the snow lasts, the quantity of hay should be increased by feeding at an extra time or two each day. If the grass is very poor, the pony will depend on his hay ration to survive. In this case, hay should be available most of the day and at night. During the early months of the year, when your pony's coat is at its longest, lice infestation may occur. Any signs of rubbing should be investigated, and action should be taken if appropriate.

Early spring

Hay and concentrates should be continued as supplements until there is sufficient grass to provide a nutritional value which is often not until late May.

Figure 24: Illustration of poisonous plants and berries.

Nutrition, Watering and Feeding

Nutrition, Watering and Feeding

Grazing is the natural feeding method for horses and ponies, and a mix of fibrous plants including grass is their natural food. In nature, a pony eats for prolonged periods, grazing and browsing over extensive areas and occasionally resting but is never too full of food to escape rapidly from danger. How they use the food they eat – their digestive system – has gradually adapted to their way of life. An awareness of their natural habitat and of the way nature has intended them to live will guide you towards feeding them sensibly.

A stabled pony can be helped to thrive in his unnatural environment by, for example, having a daily routine and having access to forage throughout the day and night so he can pick whenever he feels inclined to eat. Naturally, a horse or pony's digestive system is never empty and it is important we try to replicate this when they are stabled.

Rules of watering and feeding

Following the rules of good feeding will help to keep a pony healthy and content and able to do the work required. Be observant and constantly aware of his health so that you can make any necessary adjustments to his diet before things go wrong.

Rules of good feeding

Following the rules of good feeding will help to keep a pony healthy and content and able to do the work required. Be observant and constantly aware of his health so that you can make any necessary adjustments to his diet before things go wrong.

Rules of good feeding

- Keep clean, fresh water available.
- Feed little and often.

- Feed according to work, temperament and condition.
- Feed at the same times each day.
- Feed plenty of forage.
- Feed a balanced diet.
- Do not work hard immediately after feeding cereals.
- Introduce changes in food gradually.
- Feed clean, good-quality feed.
- Feed something succulent every day.
- Keep feed bowls, utensils and water buckets clean.

Keep clean, fresh water available.
A pony's body is made up of 60% to 70% water, and although a pony can lose almost all his body fat and half his body protein and survive, a 20% water loss can prove fatal. As a rough guide, ponies drink 22–45 litres (5–10 gallons) of fresh water daily, but they may need more in hot weather.

A pony should always have access to clean, fresh water. In winter, break the ice on field troughs at least twice a day (morning and evening). In summer, keep troughs clear of leaves and algae. If a pony does not have enough to drink, he may become dehydrated, and this can occur in summer or winter.

Signs of dehydration

- Tiredness – reduced performance.
- Sadness – dullness in the eyes.
- Dry skin and mouth – 'pinch test'.

A pinch test is when you pinch and hold the loose skin on the neck for a second or two. Then when released, the skin should quickly fall back to the neck. If it stays raised (stiff) your pony may be showing signs of dehydration.

Feed little and often

If supplementary feed is needed to ensure your pony maintains their weight, it is important that it is fed in quantities and forms that are sympathetic to their digestive system. Your pony's stomach holds between 8–14 litres (1–3 gallons), which is relatively small for such large animals: roughly the size of a rugby ball. Ponies must have plenty of forage and other high-fibre materials to maintain the health and normal function of their digestive system. Too little fibre in their diet increases the risk of digestive problems, such as colic and gastric ulcers, and they may also lose weight.

By the time the food reaches the stomach, the volume will double due to the addition of digestive juices. Digestion is most efficient when the stomach is about two-thirds full, so large feeds will not be properly digested, and much of the food value will be wasted.

Your pony should receive a balanced diet. A concentrate (also referred to as bucket or hard feed) is a feed that combines different ingredients to provide higher levels of nutrients such as energy and protein, compared with forage. There are many concentrates based on fibre that contain relatively high levels of energy and protein too. Concentrate feeds are often fortified with vitamins and minerals to provide a balanced diet. If they are not fortified with vitamins and minerals then a vitamin and mineral supplement or a balancer should be fed. If concentrates contain high levels of cereal-based feeds, the total daily ration should be divided into as many small feeds each day as is practical to do. Cereals contain high levels of starch which can cause digestive upsets if too much is fed at one time.

A pony's digestive system

Food passes through the digestive system by rhythmical muscular contractions. This requires a reasonably constant supply of food. At most, a pony must never be left for more than 4 hours without forage, so adequate hay or hay substitute must be fed to the stabled pony at night.

Feed according to work, temperament and condition

All ponies require a minimum of 1.5% of their bodyweight as forage each day on a dry matter basis. This is to ensure they receive sufficient fibre to maintain normal, healthy digestive function and is a rule that applies, whatever level of work they are doing. It is beneficial to feed more forage than this if your pony doesn't gain excessive amounts of weight. The amount of supplementary feed is determined by how much support your pony needs to maintain their weight. They may need very little extra if they are a good doer.

Work: As exercise and work increase, more energy may be required to ensure your pony maintains their weight. More protein may be required above what the forage provides to help build muscle. More vitamins and minerals are often also needed as these are involved in energy metabolism and are lost through sweat. If work is decreased, or if your pony has time off through injury or illness, the concentrates should be reduced to avoid excessive weight gain.

Temperament: All ponies are individuals and must be treated as such. Some become excitable on certain feeds and require an alternative form of feed. Sluggish ponies sometimes benefit from more energy-giving foods to encourage them to be more active, but it is also really important to check their diet is balanced first as vitamins and minerals are involved in energy metabolism. It's also very important to ensure the pony isn't overweight, as this can have a significant impact on their energy levels.

Condition: Whether your pony is stabled and working hard or living out on grass, he should be in good condition. If he is not, it may be that he is not receiving the correct amount or type of food, and his diet must be adjusted accordingly. For example, if he is too thin, he may need more food or a more nutritious diet; if he is too fat, he may need less. His well-being may also be influenced by:

- **Age**: Both old and young ponies need specialised feeding. Old ponies may lose condition easily because they can no longer use their food efficiently. They may need more cooked or processed concentrates, which are easier to digest. A concentrate (or bucket or hard feed) is a feed that combines different ingredients to provide higher levels of nutrients such as energy and protein. Concentrate feeds are usually fortified with vitamins and minerals to provide a balanced diet. If they are not fortified with vitamins and minerals then a vitamins and mineral supplement or a balancer should be fed.
- **Type**: Ponies of the same height and weight do not necessarily thrive on the same diet. For example, native ponies thrive on bulk feeds (hay or grass) and may easily get laminitis if they are overweight and their diet supplies too much energy, starch and sugar. Their natural habitat is sparse and, therefore, we should make sure they have minimal access to grass to manage their weight.
- **Climate**: A large part of a pony's food helps him to maintain his body temperature. A pony living out in cold, wet weather will need extra food to maintain their condition and keep warm.
- **Company**: Loss of condition could be due to constant bullying by companions, which may impede eating and resting. However, an animal used to company may pine and lose condition if suddenly isolated.
- **General health**: If a pony becomes poorly, he may require a special diet. Your vet will advise you. If he finds eating difficult, his teeth should be checked by a vet or equine dentist. If he is losing body condition, check if he needs worming, as this is often the most likely reason. Once again, your vet will advise you.

Feed at the same times each day

A pony is a creature of habit. Once established, his routine will help him settle down and thrive. Plan to feed him at times that fit in with your other commitments so you can keep to a regular timetable.

Do not work hard immediately after feeding

Allow time for your pony to digest his feed if you are using cereals in the bucket. As a rough guide, your pony may take 20 minutes to eat his bucket feed, 1½ hours to digest it and then be ready for normal work. Never work a pony fast after feeding cereal-based feeds. Ensuring there is some fibre in the stomach before exercising is beneficial for stopping the acidic contents of the stomach from splashing around when the horse or pony moves. A handful of chaff before exercise or travel is a great way to ensure this is the case.

Feed plenty of forage

Forage as hay or grass should be the basis of any diet and keeps the digestive system working and healthy.

Avoid changing the diet quickly

Any changes in food should be made gradually over seven to ten days to safeguard against indigestion. Gradual changes will allow the digestive system to adjust effectively to the new food. If sudden changes are made, there will not be enough of the appropriate bacteria in the digestive system to break down the new type of food, which, being undigested, will have less value to your pony and might even give him colic.

Feed clean, good-quality feed

Feed clean and good-quality forage and concentrate food only. Musty and dusty food may put your pony off eating and may cause digestive upsets and respiratory issues.

Feed something succulent every day

Regardless of whether your horse is in the field or in a stable, it is a good idea to provide as much alternative enrichment as possible. For example, a succulent such as a carrot or apple that can be added to the feed for your pony to sort through and find. Any succulent should be chopped into thin strips so they are less likely to get stuck in the horse's throat.

Clean any equipment

Keep feed bowls, utensils and water buckets clean. Dried-on food tastes sour, and dirty buckets can put your pony off eating or drinking.

Different types of feed

Forage

Grazing

Grazing freely allows a pony to perform more of their natural behaviours especially if they are in the company of other horse and ponies. Sometimes fresh pasture contains too much sugar and so it becomes unsafe for some horses and ponies to graze on it – even for relatively short amounts of time. Being outside has benefits for a pony's respiratory health and so track systems and woodchip paddocks are ways that ponies can be outside but without access to grass. It is really important that alternative forms of forage are provided to ensure sufficient fibre is consumed to maintain digestive health.

If a pony has to be stabled for prolonged periods then even 10 minutes of grazing in hand (this means leading your pony out to graze in a headcollar or bridle) can be beneficial to help their appetite and maintain an interest in their feed. Many a stale pony has been helped by 'Doctor Green'.

Hay

Hay provides an alternative source of fibre needed if a pony doesn't have access to grass. Plenty of good-quality hay should always be available for the stabled pony and for a pony living out when fresh pasture is in short supply. This can occur at times of drought in the summer as well as in winter.

A good sample of hay will be sweet-smelling, light greenish-brown in colour throughout, crisp, and free from dust. Good hay is made in dry, sunny weather, when the grass comes into flower before it has gone to seed. As our weather and seasons change, it may be necessary to feed this year's hay well before the winter. It is recommended to wait four to six weeks before feeding this year's cut. Hay that smells musty or does not shake free immediately will have been baled when the hay was damp and is bad for ponies.

Meadow hay: Comes from a field permanently laid down to grass. It is soft and contains many grasses such as ryegrass, cock's-foot, timothy, etc., with a bottom of low-growing grasses, and legumes such as clover and herbs. Ponies enjoy well-made meadow hay. It is important to look for harmful and poisonous plants such as ragwort.

Soaked hay: Ponies with allergies to the spores in hay, or those with coughs or colds, will often benefit from having their hay soaked. This is best achieved by immersing a full haynet in clean water or dousing it thoroughly with a hose.

To reduce spores in the hay: Soak the hay for about 30 minutes in clean water. This helps wash away or swell dust and tiny spores (like little seeds from mould) that could make your pony cough or have breathing problems. Some ponies have sensitive lungs, just like some people have allergies! It is really important not to let the hay dry out again before feeding – to be beneficial it must still be wet or damp when the pony eats it.

To reduce the sugar content: Soak the hay for at least 2 hours in plenty of water. The longer soaking time causes sugars and some nutrients to dissolve into the water. This is helpful for ponies that need to lose weight or have certain health conditions where they shouldn't eat too many sugars.

Remember to drain the water completely after soaking before giving it to your pony as the soaking water contains all those things you're trying to remove from the hay.

Haylage: This is grass that has been dried and then wrapped in airtight plastic. If conditions are right the sugar in the grass ferments so that the forage is pickled which helps to stabilise it. The higher moisture content makes it particularly useful for ponies with respiratory issues, but it does tend to be more digestible and therefore ponies tend to do well on it, i.e. gain weight more easily. Once a bag has been opened or the seal broken, the haylage must be used within a few days. Haylage is sold in bags or bales of different sizes, which may make it easier if feeding a lot of horses or ponies in a yard.

When feeding forage (hay or haylage), reduce wastage by using small-hole nets in stables and fields. Give any leftover hay to ponies in a field or one that is less fussy rather than putting it on the muckheap. Don't do this when you're away from home, or if you compete in affiliated competitions as there is a risk of contamination with another pony's medication.

A pony should have access to hay most of the time; restricting it before exercise is not necessary.

Chaff or chop

There are lots of different types of chaff or chop, all of which add fibre to the diet, but some are also very nutritious containing as much energy and protein as cereal-based feeds. Chaffs and chops slow the rate at which your pony eats which promotes better digestion of the feed and helps to reduce the risk of digestive upsets such as gastric ulcers and colic.

Chaffs and chops can also contain added vitamins and minerals and so provide a pony with a balanced diet. Many are molasses free and so are very low in starch and sugar making them ideal for good doers and those prone to laminitis.

Concentrate food

'Straights' is a term used to describe a single type of feed such as barley, oats or maize. If feeding straights then either a supplement or balancer will need to be included, to add a range of vitamins and minerals.

Cubes (or nuts)

Cubes are a carefully formulated mixture of ingredients, which include added vitamins and minerals. A cube is produced by mixing and then pressing a range of components into a cube shape or pencil shape. Many brands and varieties are designed for different purposes (Horse and Pony, etc.). The well-known brands are reliable, and their food value is always consistent. Each feed bag has a best before date, the feed should be used before then to ensure the nutrients declared on the bag are present in the feed. Each product has a recommended feeding rate for different sizes of horse and pony. Feeding less than the recommended amount means you are providing fewer nutrients and so the diet isn't balanced. Cubes can make up all or part of the concentrates in the pony's ration. Before buying them, read the instructions on the bag and choose the right type according to the needs of your pony.

Cubes can also be fed with chaff or chop, which slows your pony down when eating and ensures that the cubes are moistened by his saliva before being swallowed, helping to reduce the risk of choking. Dampening this dry food with a little water before mixing will also help this process.

Mixes

These are made of the same balanced content as cubes but many of the ingredients are included as flaked grains and so can be more easily distinguished. They also have a best before date on the packaging and often look more appealing to us as they look a bit like muesli, but most horses and ponies find mixes and cubes equally palatable. The well-known brands are recommended.

Look for marks of quality – BETA NOPS approval is vital if you are competing in affiliated competitions.

Balancers

- Feed balancers are small pellets containing the essential vitamins, minerals and protein that a horse needs in their diet, without many calories.
- Because they are fed in such small quantities, balancers are ideal for good doers who hold their weight easily as they are low in energy and for those with low starch and sugar needs, such as ponies with laminitis.
- Many ponies are perfect candidates for balancers throughout spring and summer, providing all the nutrients they need without expanding their waistlines!

Mashes

A mash can be fed on its own or alongside a pony's usual feed. Many are fast-soaking and high in fibre so can be useful for adding electrolyte supplements to after competitions, long travelling or during camp. A range of products exist in this category of feeds and have a range of energy levels. Always read the label on the bag so you select one appropriate for your pony's body condition and for guidance on how to prepare the mash.

Dried sugar beet pulp

One of the original forms of mash, sugar beet pulp is a useful source of highly digestible fibre. The name can be a little misleading – sugar beet pulp is the pulp left after sugar has been removed from the beet. The sugar is used in human food and the pulp makes a great feed

Alfalfa.

Quick-soaking beet flakes.

Pasture mix.

Balancer.

Figure 25: Different types of feed.

for horses and other animals. If it is unmolassed, sugar beet pulp is less than 5% sugar. It is palatable and provides plenty of slow-release energy. It is a very popular feed ingredient for endurance horses and ponies.

Sugar beet pulp should be soaked prior to feeding. There are many quick soaking forms of sugar beet pulp. Traditional sugar beet pulp shreds usually require soaking in cold water for 12 hours before being fed to a pony. In its dry state, it can cause choking and swelling in the stomach, probably resulting in colic and so it should be stored in sealed containers – just in case a pony gets into the feedroom! It should be prepared in a ratio of about 3 parts cold water to 1 part pulp. Always read the label on the bag for instructions, as some manufacturers may have different guidelines.

Quick-soaking beet can be made up in small amounts daily. It is made by adding 1 part dry quick-soaking beet to 5 parts water by weight. So ½kg of dry quick-soaking beet would require 2½ litres of water. Add more water to make a sloppier mash to help your pony rehydrate. Leave to soak for at least 10 minutes using cold water. You can prepare this in advance if it is stored in cool conditions and fed within 24 hours of soaking. Always read the label on the bag to prepare the mash.

Succulent foods

Adding succulents to feed encourages horses and ponies to eat and they can also be a natural treat or reward. They should be used sparingly as large quantities can increase the amount of sugar in the diet.

Carrots are highly palatable and some ponies also relish swedes, turnips, beetroots, or parsnips. To prepare any of these root vegetables, first, scrub them well under a running tap. Large finger-shaped slices or whole roots are best. Square or round root pieces must not be fed, as they can become lodged in the throat and may choke the pony. You can hang whole roots around the stable to help provide some enrichment when a horse or pony is stabled for longer periods.

Apples are always especially appreciated, but too many can cause colic. Small apples must be cut in pieces to prevent them from being swallowed whole.

Nutrients in the diet

The food and water that a pony eats and drinks provide him with the nutrients of life. The basic nutrients are water, carbohydrates, fats, proteins, minerals and vitamins.

Water

Water is vital. It is present in every cell in the body and is involved in every chemical and physical process needed to maintain life. Water carries all the nutrients around the body, regulates body temperature, acts as a lubricant, and helps remove waste and toxins. A pony drinks 22–45 litres (5–10 gallons) of fresh water daily but may need more in hot weather.

Carbohydrates

- Carbohydrates include fibre – also known as structural carbohydrate, and non-structural, which includes sugar and starch.
- Fibre carbohydrates are joined together in a more complex way – the microbes such as bacteria in the horse's gut are able to break down these complex bonds. This process releases energy which the horse can utilise as a slow-release energy source. (Humans don't have a sufficient quantity of these microbes to be able to utilise fibre as an

energy source.)

- Sugar and starch are broken down by the horse's own digestive enzymes which is a quicker process, hence the term quick-release energy.
- Carbohydrates provide energy that can be used for body functions also known as metabolism: the fuel for growth and body development, activity and warmth.
- If the horse doesn't use the energy from carbohydrates for immediate energy use, it can be stored either as glycogen in muscles and the liver or as body fat.

Fats and oils

Fat and oil provide a concentrated source of slow-release energy which the horse can use as fuel for low-intensity exercise. If more energy is supplied in the diet than the horse needs, it will be stored. Just like excess carbohydrates, fat and oil will be stored as body fat.

Protein

Protein has many important functions in the body being a component of tissues like muscle but also things like hormones which act as chemical messengers in the body. Protein is made up of amino acids – some of which have to be supplied in the diet and so are termed 'essential' amino acids. These are particularly important for breeding and youngstock as well as performance horses. A lack of protein results in poor growth, performance and condition.

Minerals

Minerals are components of body tissues like bones and tendons but are also involved in body functions such as the immune system. Some minerals are referred to as trace minerals because they are needed in very small amounts – they are still essential nutrients and so are part of a balanced diet. Forages in the UK are often short of essential minerals and so an additional source is needed especially to support harder levels of work.

Vitamins

Vitamins can be classified as fat-soluble and water-soluble. Fat-soluble include vitamins A, D and E – you may already know that vitamin A helps us see in the dark and it's the same for horses and ponies. Vitamin E is an important anti-oxidant which means it helps your horse or pony recover from exercise. This is why requirements for vitamin E increase as a pony's workload increases.

Water-soluble vitamins include B vitamins such as biotin. You may recognise this as a vitamin that is particularly important for producing good-quality hoof horn. This is why looking at your horse or pony from the outside can give a good indication of their general health. If they have a dull coat and poor, crumbly hooves, it often indicates they aren't receiving a balanced diet.

Methods of watering and feeding

The importance of a clean and constant water supply cannot be too strongly emphasised. A pony's health deteriorates rapidly if deprived of water or dehydrated. When he knows that water is always available in his stable or field, he will drink when necessary.

Stabled

Buckets or an automatic drinking bowl are the most satisfactory ways to provide drinking water in a stable.

Buckets

- Fresh water should be available when a pony is stabled, even for a few minutes or overnight.
- Rubber, plastic, or polyethene buckets are best because they are lightweight, noiseless, and will not cause injury. If they have wire handles, make sure they are positioned to the back of the bucket when placed in the stable or they can be held up by a clip to the wall (this is useful if your pony knocks the buckets over).
- Two buckets may be necessary to ensure a constant supply of water.
- Place buckets in the corner of the box, either on the floor or suspended from a special ring-fitting, and away from the manger and the hay (where they may become soiled) and from the door (where they may be knocked over).
- Buckets must be kept clean, and the water must be frequently checked and changed.

Automatic drinking bowls

- Though not all ponies take readily to these bowls, they have their advantages. They must be inspected and cleaned out each day.
- In winter, they may freeze up, and the pipes burst. It is also difficult to tell how much water each pony drinks.
- If the pony uses them confidently, they do ensure that fresh, clean water is always available and carrying heavy buckets is avoided.

Away from home

On long rides, your pony should be watered whenever possible. This is important, especially when the weather is hot and humid. At rallies and competitions or other long days away from home, arrangements must be made for your pony to have access to clean water from time to time during rest periods. To avoid the risk of cross-infection from troughs used by other ponies, take a water container and a bucket with you.

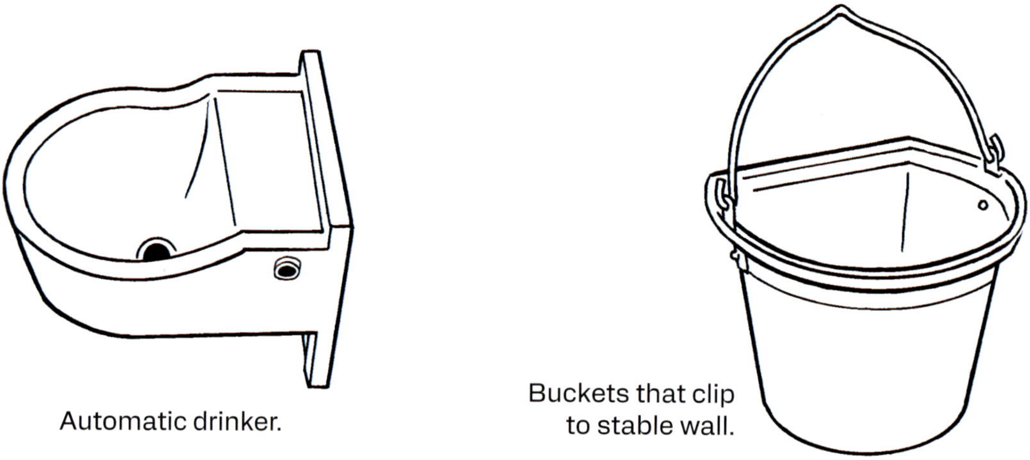

Automatic drinker.

Buckets that clip to stable wall.

Figure 26: Types of drinkers.

After hard work

There is no reason to limit access to water after exercise and, indeed, restricting a horse or pony is likely to make dehydration worse and may have serious repercussions for their health in extreme situations. Horses and ponies tend to prefer slightly warmer water, so if you are able to, providing water between 10 and 15°C will help to encourage them to drink more which will aid their recovery.

How much to feed your pony

How much food does a pony need?

As a rough guide, the (dry) weight of total daily food will be 2–2.5% of body weight. If a pony is overweight it may be necessary to restrict intake but it is also important not to feed less than 1.5% of their bodyweight as forage. Do consider that more can be fed of lower nutritional value feedstuffs, so it is important to evaluate the level of energy (calories) in each part of your pony's ration.

You should consider the fact that every pony is an individual. They differ in type according to their breeding and their ability to utilise the nutrients in the food they are given.

You should feed according to your pony's condition and behaviour and adjust the feeding to suit his needs. A 'good doer' is a pony who will readily eat up all he is offered and will thrive. He

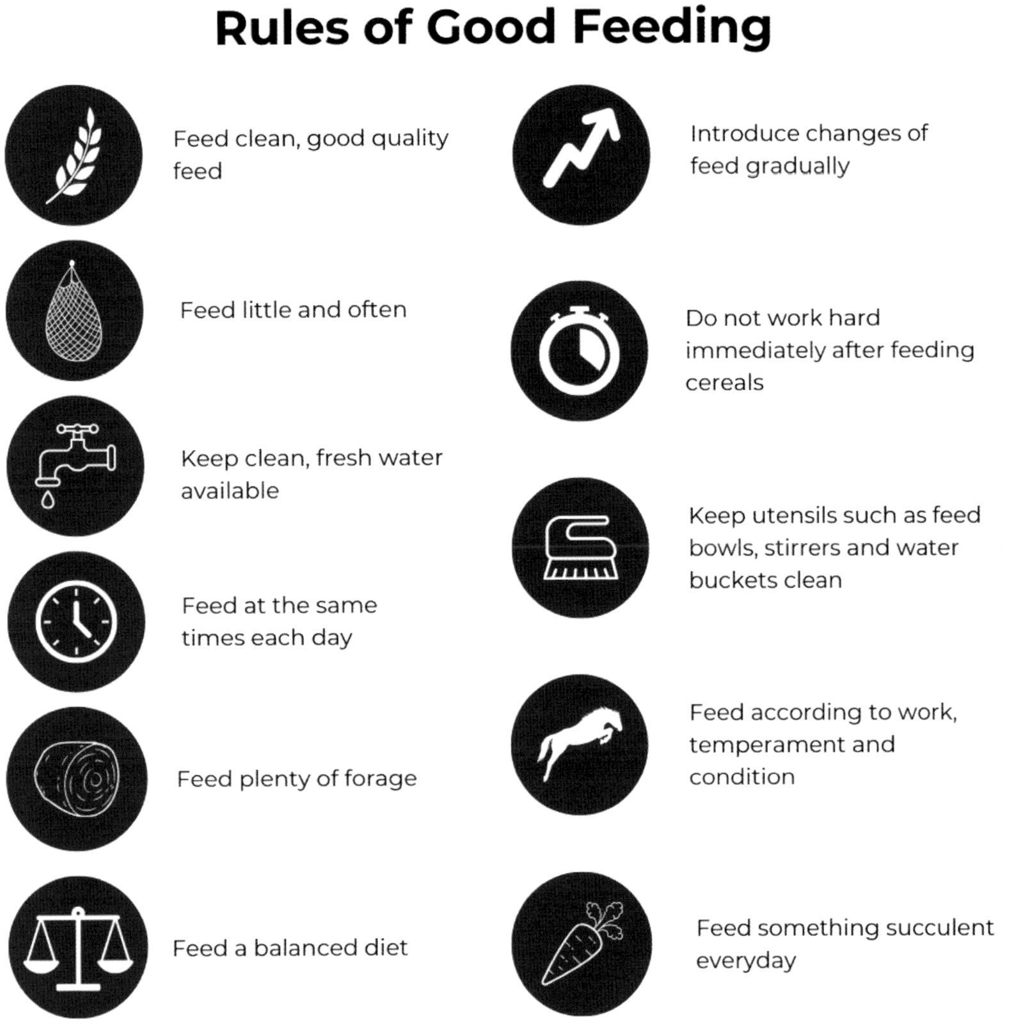

Figure 27: Rules of feeding.

may even be greedy and gain too much weight. A 'poor doer' is difficult to keep in condition despite every care and attention. He may need a diet that is easier to digest or a higher nutritional value. With the help of your nutritionist and vet, you can get to the bottom of any problems and ensure the diet is appropriate. It can take time to achieve results so be patient.

A shy or dainty feeder may have to be tempted by succulents and trying different feeds. Shy feeders sometimes eat best at night when all is quiet. For them, feeding little and often is vital. A late-night feed can, therefore, be beneficial.

Adjusting the diet according to the work required

The diet should be adjusted as work increases or decreases. Forage and high-fibre materials can make a significant contribution to a horse or pony's energy requirements. As workloads increase more vitamins and minerals will be needed to ensure the diet is balanced. Feeds promoted for performance horses and ponies usually contain more vitamins and minerals as well as protein and energy.

The following Levels of Work guide assesses the pony's needs:

Maintenance
This is a term used to describe a horse or pony at rest that isn't being exercised or worked.

Light work
Up to one hour's hacking or schooling daily, mostly walking and trotting with some cantering.

Medium work
This active work might include cantering, jumping, Pony Club rallies and competing at shows.

Hard work
Maintenance plus final fitness programme for participating in:

Pony Club camp, polo, regular mounted games, one-day pony trials, long-distance training.

Where and when to feed

Having decided on a suitable diet for your pony, plan your feeding arrangements according to the Rules of Feeding. Work out a routine that meets the pony's needs and other commitments so that you can feed at the same time each day. He should be given sufficient bulk feed in the daily routine at appropriate times.

If the pony lives outdoors, the same principles apply. It is also recommended that a vitamin and mineral supplement or balancer should be fed to forage/grass-only diets, to balance the nutrients that grass/forage may not be able to supply.

Making up and giving feeds

Feeds should be made up and mixed in a container before being taken to your pony. It is important to know the exact quantities that you are feeding. Weigh your scoop, then weigh each feed type separately to find the weight of each scoopful. Any dry feed (cubes and chaff) should be dampened.

Stabled pony

- A stabled pony is ideally fed from a heavy rubber feed bowl on the floor, which will not tip over easily. This is the most natural way for your pony to eat as it mirrors grazing rather than eating from a manger at chest level.
- This should be removed from the box after your pony has finished his feed.
- Your feed bowl must be kept clean and washed out daily.

Pony at grass

- A pony at grass should be fed either from a bowl on the ground or a manger hung over the fence or gate if the ground is not suitable (muddy or the pony may kick the bowl over).
- If there are two or more ponies in a field there should be one feed bowl for each pony in the field plus an extra one or two placed with plenty of space between to avoid bullying by the other ponies. This is the same for putting out the piles of hay. Bowls should be well apart (out of kicking range) and kept clean.
- If you are feeding your ponies individually, then tie up all the ponies for 20 minutes while they eat their feeds. This will ensure that they eat and that all receive a fair share, but they should not be left unattended during this time.

Feeding hay

Here are three ways to feed hay to your pony:

From the ground

In the stable: Feeding hay on the ground is the best way for your pony. This is how ponies naturally eat in the wild. It lets them keep their head in a normal, low position.

In the field: You can put hay on the ground in dry areas of the field. Do be careful as some might get wasted if it gets wet or dirty.

From a haynet

In the stable: Hang the haynet at about your pony's eye level. This is important so that you avoid hanging it too low where your pony could catch a hoof if the net becomes empty.

In the field: When using a haynet outside, tie it to a fence or tree. Make sure it's high enough off the ground so your pony won't get tangled in it. This saves hay and lets you easily measure how much your pony is eating.

From a hay bin

In the stable: A hay bin is a great choice. It keeps hay clean but still lets your pony eat in a natural, low position.

In the field: Heavy-duty field hay bins are good for keeping hay dry and clean outside. They won't blow away like loose hay and are safer than haynets for some ponies.

Remember: However, you feed hay, make sure your pony can't get hurt by getting caught in anything.

Daily feed for ponies

Ponies normally eat 2-2.5% of their bodyweight as dry matter each day. This should be mainly forage with additional feed to support extra work, promote weight gain or to provide a balanced diet.

Ideal Weight Pony

80% Forage
e.g hay or haylage

20% Bucket Feed
e.g balancer + chopped fibre with sugarbeet pulp

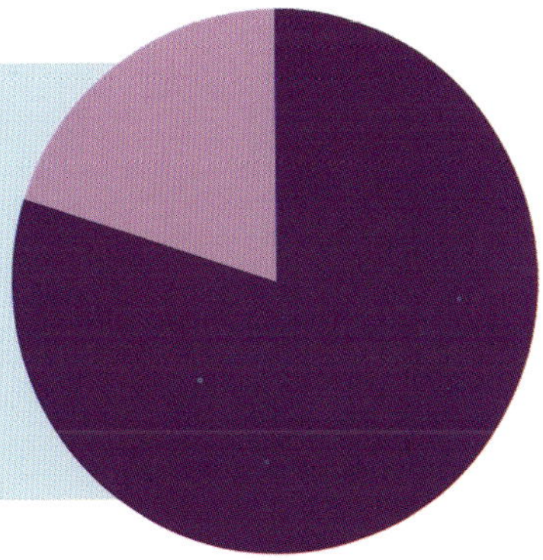

Overweight Pony

95% Forage
e.g hay or straw up to 50%

5% Bucket Feed
e.g balancer + low calorie chopped fibre

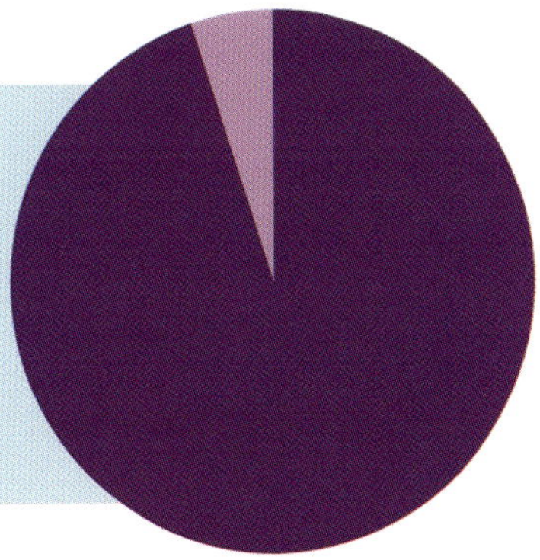

Underweight Pony

75% Forage
e.g hay or haylage

25% Bucket Feed
e.g cereal mix or cube with high-calorie chopped fibre + sugarbeet pulp

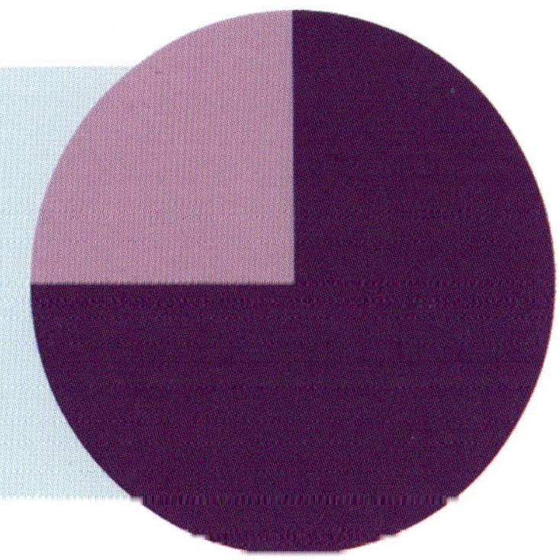

Figure 28: Chart showing diet relating to your pony's condition.

Know your pony

Ponies should be fed according to their exercise levels, temperament and condition.

TEMPERAMENT
All ponies are individuals and must be fed as such.

AGE
Both old and young ponies need specialised feeding. Old ponies may lose condition easily and need extra concentrates. Young ponies also need concentrates to grow and mature.

CONDITION
Whether your pony is stabled and working hard or living out on grass, he should be in good condition and not too thin or too fat.

CLIMATE
A large part of a pony's food helps it to maintain its body temperature. A pony living out in cold, wet weather will need extra food to maintain its condition and keep warm.

GENERAL HEALTH
If a pony becomes poorly, he may require a special diet. Your vet will advise you. If he finds eating difficult, his teeth should be checked by a vet or equine dentist.

COMPANY
Loss of condition could be due to constant bullying by companions, which may impede eating and resting. On the other hand, an animal used to the company may pine and lose condition if suddenly isolated.

WORK
Feed according to exercise and size of the pony.

TYPE
Ponies of the same height and weight do not necessarily thrive on the same diet. Find the feed that suits them best.

Figure 29: Reasons for adjusting your pony's diet.

Clipping, Bandaging and Travelling

THE PONY CLUB · EST 1929 ·

Grooming, Clipping, Bandaging and Travelling

Grooming

Why you should groom and spend time with your pony

Taking care of a pony isn't just about feeding and riding; the routine of daily grooming will also play a big part in their health and happiness. Grooming keeps a pony's coat clean, helps prevent skin problems, and gives you a chance to check for injuries or other issues you might not notice otherwise. The few minutes spent brushing can help to build a bond between you.

When you groom your pony, you're doing something special that helps both of you. Your pony will feel better with a clean coat, and you'll learn exactly what's normal for your pony's body. This way, if something changes or doesn't look right, you'll notice it right away.

Many ponies really enjoy being groomed. It can feel like a nice massage to them. As you brush and clean your pony regularly, they'll start to recognise that you're someone who takes care of them. This builds trust between you, which is super important whether you're riding or just spending time together. Remember, grooming isn't just a chore, it's quality time with your four-legged friend.

The grooming kit

How to groom

- Collect the grooming kit items. They are best kept together in a box, wire basket, or bag.
- Put the headcollar on the pony and tie him up fairly short.
- It is more pleasant to work in a clean area, so before and during grooming, pick up any droppings from around you.
- Remove his rugs. If the weather is cold, leave a rug folded over his loins while grooming the forehand and over his shoulder while grooming the quarters.

Hoof pick

Always begin grooming by picking out the feet. A skip should be placed to catch the dirt so it does not drop onto the bed or the stable yard. Pick up each foot in turn. Remove whatever may be lodged in it with the point of the pick, working downwards from the heel towards the toe; this way, there is no risk of the pick penetrating the soft parts of the frog. Clear the cleft of the frog and pay attention to anything that may be unpleasant smelling as this can be the first

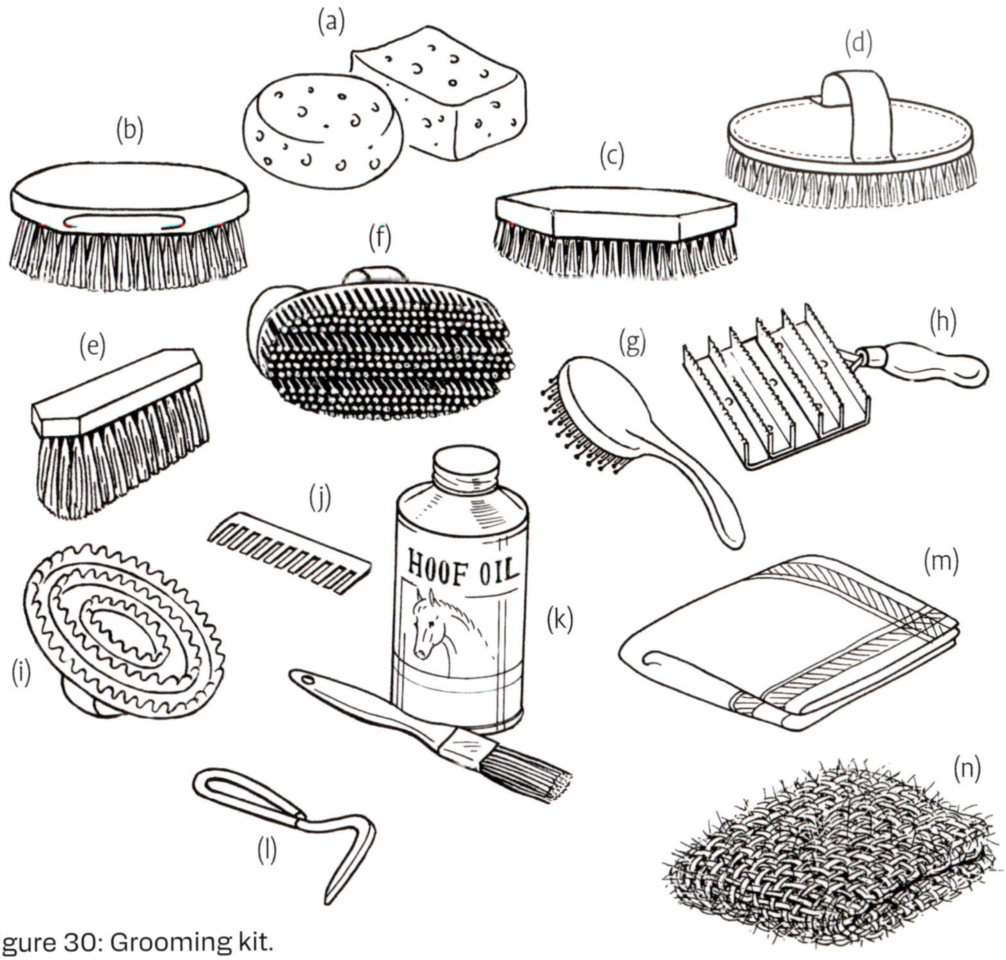

Figure 30: Grooming kit.

a) face and dock sponges
b) dandy brush
c) water brush
d) body brush
e) flick brush
f) plastic curry comb
g) mane/tail brush
h) metal curry comb
i) rubber curry comb
j) mane comb
k) hoof oil and brush
l) hoof pick
m) stable cloth
n) cactus cloth

sign of a condition called thrush. Tap the shoe to see that it is secure. Finally, run the tips of the fingers over the clenches to feel that they haven't risen.

Dandy brush and plastic curry comb

On the grass-kept pony, this is used all over the body. The dandy brush is used only on unclipped areas on the stabled, clipped pony. Rubber or plastic curry combs are sometimes used as alternatives and can help remove the mud from the dirtier parts of the pony's body.

Start at the poll on the left-hand side and work over the whole body and legs. Do not brush too hard over the sensitive parts of the body, but elsewhere you can use a to-and-fro movement to loosen stubborn dirt. The brushes can be held in either hand.

'Cactus' cloth/pad

This can be used as an alternative to the dandy brush on the stabled pony. Its purpose is to loosen dirt, sweat, and scurf. It is particularly useful in sensitive areas where some ponies resent being brushed.

Body brush and curry comb

The body brush is the main grooming brush for the stabled pony and the curry comb is designed to keep it clean. The brush's short, close-set hairs reach right through the coat to the skin beneath, lifting and removing the dirt. It is normal to start on the left side, but you can begin on the right if it is safer to do so, depending on where your pony is tied.

Begin with the mane

- First, throw the mane across to the far side of the neck and thoroughly brush the crest.
- Replace the mane and start working on it at the head end.
- Insert a finger of your free hand into the mane to separate a few locks of hair. First, brush the ends and then the roots to remove tangles.
- Work slowly down the neck, dealing with only a few locks of hair at a time.

Grooming the body

- Begin at the poll region on the left (near) side and gradually work back over the whole body in the same direction as the coat.
- Take the body brush in your left hand and the curry comb in your right.
- Work with a slightly bent arm and a supple wrist and lean your body weight behind the brush.
- Work more gently on the sensitive areas. Use short, circular strokes, finishing each stroke in the direction of the coat's lay rather than to-and-fro.
- After every four or five strokes, draw the brush smartly across the teeth of the curry comb to dislodge the dirt.
- Clean the curry comb by tapping it on the ground or floor of the stable, not against the wall or manger.
- When the left side is completed, pass to the right and repeat the process. When working on the left side, having the body brush in your left hand and the curry comb in your right is easier.

- When working on the right side, having the body brush in your right hand and the curry comb on your left is easier. Exceptions to this are when you groom (a) those parts of the flank and under the belly where the coat lies in the opposite direction and (b) down the back of the hindquarters.

Tail

Take only a few strands of hair at a time. Do this by holding the tail, shaking a few strands free, and brushing the ends clean first with the mane/tail brush. Using the dandy brush on the mane or tail is generally wrong as it breaks the hairs, but an old or soft dandy brush may be used on very thick manes and tails. If loose hairs appear on the brush, revert to the body brush before you ruin the tail!

Face

Untie the pony by unfastening the headcollar and fastening the head strap temporarily around his neck. Use your free hand to steady the head and use the body brush gently and carefully. When finished, replace the headcollar and tie the pony up again.

Sponges and a bucket of water

- Sponging the eyes, nose and dock refreshes the pony, and is appreciated perhaps more than any other part of the grooming routine.
- Keep two sponges of different colours or shapes, with one reserved for use in the dock region. Wring out the sponge so that it is soft, clean and damp.
- Start with the eyes. Sponge away from the corners and around the eyelids. Wring out the sponge again and deal with the muzzle region, including the lips and inside and outside of the nostrils in that order.
- With the other sponge, if the pony is safe, move behind him to clean the dock. If he fidgets, stand at one side to keep yourself safe. Lift the tail as high as possible, gently sponge, and clean the entire dock region, including the skin on the tail's undersurface.

Water brush

- This is used to 'lay' the mane and tail. This term describes how the mane or tail is brushed through to make it tidier.
- Dip the brush into the bucket, shake off the surplus water and apply the brush flat to the mane.
- Brush the hairs from the roots downwards to leave them slightly damp and in the required position.
- Lay the hairs at the top of the tail and either side of the dock similarly.
- At this stage, if you are wanting the tail to look especially neat for something, a tail bandage may be applied.

Grooming ponies who live out

If your pony is living out on grass and without rugs, his skin should be in a thoroughly healthy condition, and it is unnecessary to groom him unless he is being ridden. Under these conditions, grooming should be limited to:

- Picking out the feet and checking shoes.
- Brushing down with a dandy brush or rubber curry comb to remove mud and sweat marks.
- Using the body brush or an old or soft dandy brush to tidy his mane and tail.
- Sponging out the eyes, nose, muzzle and dock.
- Too much grease should not be removed from the coats of ponies living out of doors, as it helps to keep them warm and dry, so a body brush should not normally be used on their coats.

Grooming ponies who are stabled

Full groom

This is usually carried out after exercise and includes the entire grooming procedure. Grooming is most effective when the pony is warm: the pores are open, and the scurf is on the coat's surface.

Light groom

This is basically a quick brush. Give the pony a quick brush all over, using the body brush and curry comb if he is living indoors. This gets rid of dirt and stable stains. If it is cold outside (winter) and if the pony is wearing rugs because it's cold:

- First, pick out your pony's feet to remove any dirt or stones.
- Then fold the rugs halfway back to clean the front part of your pony.
- Fold the rugs forward to clean the back part.
- Brush his mane and tail to get rid of tangles.
- Use a damp sponge to clean around the eyes and nostrils.
- Clean under the tail.

Brush over

In the evening, the pony should be lightly brushed when the rugs are straightened or changed, and the box is 'set fair', with droppings removed and bedding tidied up.

Tail bandages

These should be 7–10cm (3–4in) wide and made of crêpe or synthetic material. They improve the appearance of the tail by keeping the hairs straight and preventing rubbing when travelling. If put on too tightly, an over-elasticated bandage will cause ridges around the tail and discomfort to the pony. Tail bandages should not be used to excess and should never be left on all night or on long journeys.

Applying a tail bandage

- Lightly dampen the tail hair with a water brush. Wetting the bandage is wrong as the material may shrink and injure the tail by cutting off the circulation.
- Stand slightly to one side to make sure you are not likely to get kicked.
- Put your right hand at the top of the tail.
- Unroll about 20cm (8in) of bandage and place this spare piece over the top of the tail.
- Hold the end of the bandage in your left hand and the bandage roll in your right with the roll on the outside.
- Keep your left hand at the top of the tail until the bandage is secured. The first turn is often difficult to keep in place, but you can overcome this by making the next turn above the first. Then, wind in the spare end of the bandage.
- Unroll the bandage evenly around and downwards overlapping the roll above, neatly and evenly, stopping just above or below the last tailbone.
- Tie the tapes neatly in a bow, not tighter than the tension of the bandage and to the side of the tail. This is so that if your pony leans on his tail (against the stable wall or when travelling) he doesn't create any rubs or pressure points.
- Tuck in the spare ends, then bend the tail comfortably.

Removing a tail bandage

Untie the tapes, grasp the bandage with both hands around the dock near the top of the tail, and slide it off in a downward direction.

Hoof oil

For special occasions, paint the walls of the hooves all over with a thin coating of oil to improve their appearance. Used too often, hoof oil may inhibit the absorption of moisture. If your pony has brittle feet, use a feed supplement and/or a hoof dressing, and consult your farrier.

Stable cloth

This cloth removes the last traces of dust from the coat.

Washing

Washing the tail

You will need a bucket of lukewarm water a small amount of shampoo (not detergent), and a clean brush and sponge.

- First, soak the tail to loosen the dirt. If your pony is quiet most of the tail may be immersed in the bucket.
- Any remaining hair may be wetted with the water brush.
- Shampoo and rinse thoroughly, changing the water as necessary.
- Squeeze the water with your hands and swing the tail to dislodge any remaining water.
- Then, using a vertical movement, brush out the tail a few hairs at a time with a clean body brush.
- Finally, apply a tail bandage.

Washing the mane

The mane should only be washed when the weather is warm, and the neck and shoulders can dry without chilling the pony. You will need a bucket of lukewarm water, shampoo, and a sponge.

- Wet the mane with a large sponge from the withers to the forelock, bringing the forelock back behind the ears to join the mane.
- Rub the water well into the roots.
- Dilute the shampoo and, using the sponge, work forward from the withers, taking care that no soap gets into the eyes or ears.
- Rinse well using the sponge until all the soap has gone from the forelock to the withers. Water should not be allowed to run down the face.
- Use the sweat scraper to remove excess water from the neck and shoulders and start the drying process with a towel.

Removing stable stains

Stains can be brushed out, and bent hair can be smoothed back into place using lukewarm water with a water brush or sponge. Then, dry off the areas with a stable rubber or towel. Stubborn stains can be washed with mild soap or specific stain-remover products.

Washing the feet

Generally, frequent washing of feet is best avoided, but after exercise or returning from the field, washing mud off the feet is sometimes necessary. Use the water brush dipped in a bucket of water. Press the thumb of the hand which holds the pony's foot well into the hollow of the heel to prevent water from being lodged there. If you need to wash them in winter or wet weather, it is a good idea to smear some Vaseline into the heel area to lessen the risk of cracked heels or mud fever.

Sponging down
After working in hot weather, ponies who are clipped or have fine coats can be made more comfortable by sponging off the sweat where the saddlery has been and under the elbows and between the hind legs. A pony returning from fast work should be walked around until his breathing has returned to normal and may then be sponged down with lukewarm water. Remove surplus water with a sweat scraper, following the lay of the coat.

Your pony is susceptible to chill in this damp state, so the appropriate rugs must be used and the pony should be led around until relaxed and dry. If the weather is warm enough, rugs may not be necessary, but he must still be led around until he is dry and settled.

Washing the whole pony
This is not recommended. British weather is unreliable, and washing removes the oils in the coat and skin, which provide natural protection against rain, wind and flies. Wetness caused by rain will not penetrate the skin on a pony's back, nor affect the coat under his belly. However, frequent shampooing or prolonged washing will wet the pony through to the skin all over his body, leaving him cold at the time and vulnerable to outdoor conditions for days afterwards. It should be possible to keep your pony clean and healthy by grooming him thoroughly and regularly.

Chilled pony
Suppose there is no alternative to washing him all over for some reason? In that case, he must be dried off completely and not allowed to get cold in the process (so a pony with a winter coat must not be washed under any circumstances). For several days after being washed, the pony will need extra clothing. Even if he does not usually wear a rug, he must be rugged-up for a week until the natural oils have returned.

Clipping, trimming and plaiting

Things to consider when deciding whether to clip your pony. As the days get shorter, ponies and horses develop thick winter coats, which keep them warm during the colder months. However, a pony may overheat if he is ridden with his full winter coat, so many people choose to 'clip' their pony or horse at this time of year. Clipping is a term that we use to describe the process of removing the long hair from your pony during the winter using a mechanical motor (clipping machine), like shearing a sheep.

Clipping can be performed all over a pony's body (e.g. a full clip) or just in specific areas (e.g. a blanket clip). The type of clip chosen should depend on the pony's workload and how much turnout they are having. Ponies that are worked hard and kept indoors most of the time, may need more of the coat to be removed. Whereas ponies in lighter work or those living out will need to retain more of their winter coat.

There are several reasons why ponies are clipped, these are some:

- To enable your pony to work in winter without becoming overheated.
- To maintain condition by avoiding heavy sweating.
- To permit a pony to work longer, faster and better and allow quicker drying off after being ridden.
- To save time in grooming.
- Ponies with thick feathers may need them trimmed to help spot and manage conditions such as mud fever more easily.
- Sometimes older ponies get conditions where their coats grow overlong (such as PPID previously known as Cushing's disease). These ponies often develop thick, wavy coats, which may lead to overheating or discomfort.

When to clip and types of clip

Traditionally, ponies working hard in winter are clipped from late September and every four to six weeks as necessary. Clipping after January may spoil the summer coat, but cat hairs, the long, untidy hairs that sometimes show at this time of year, can be lightly trimmed with clippers.

Full clip

The whole of the coat is removed. A horse or pony with a full clip will need rugs.

Hunter clip

As for the full clip, except that the hair is left on the legs as far as the elbows and thighs, and a saddle patch is left on the back. The coat on the legs protects against cold, mud, cracked heels and injury from thorns, while the saddle patch helps to prevent saddle sores or scalded backs. On a native pony, this has the advantage of making the legs appear less hairy than would otherwise be the case. Ponies with a hunter clip will need rugs.

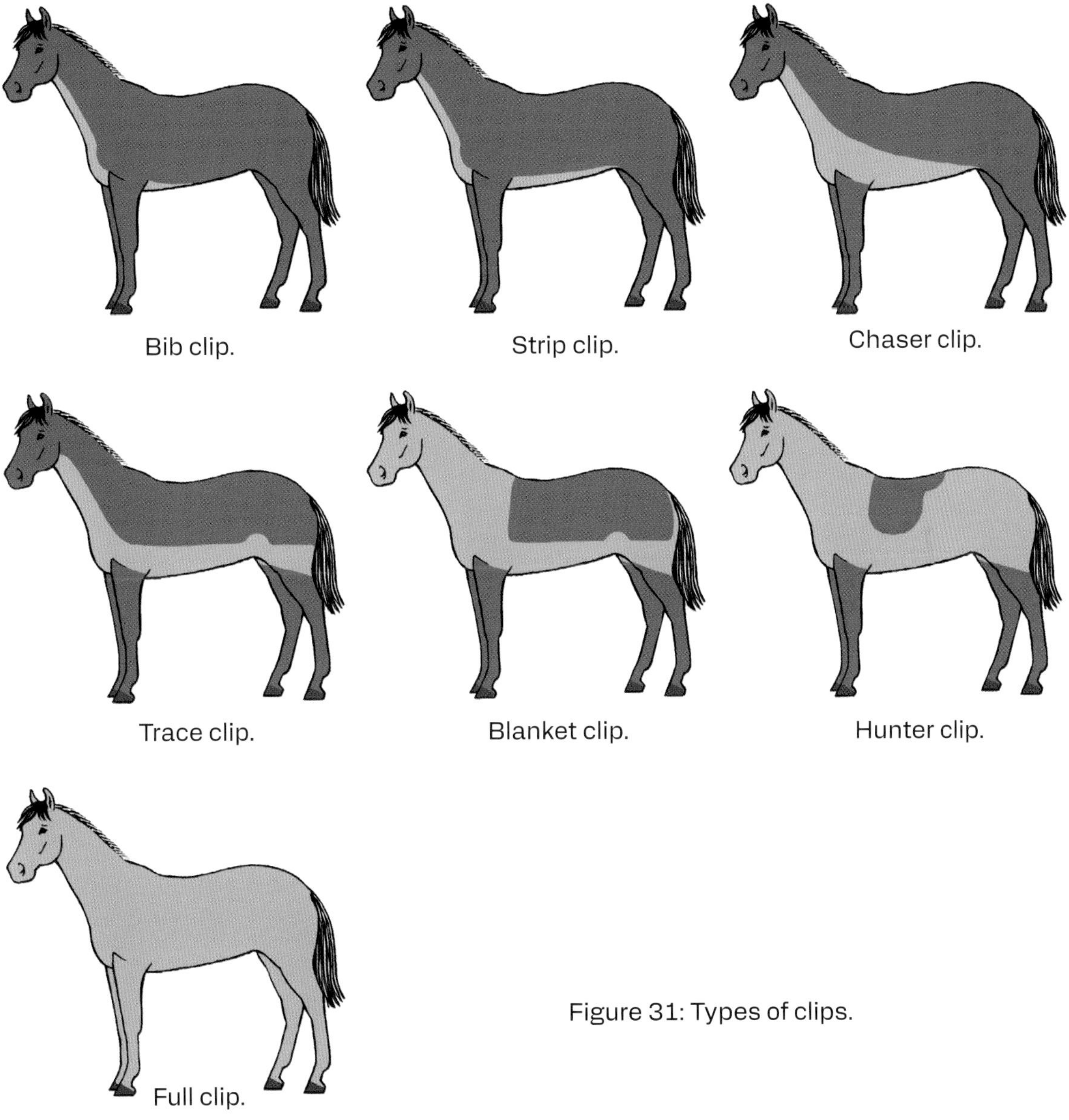

Figure 31: Types of clips.

Blanket clip

The hair is removed only from the head, neck and belly, a patch corresponding in size to that of a blanket being left on the body. This is a useful clip for ponies with fine coats who might otherwise feel the cold. Rugs will be needed.

Irish/chaser/trace clip

The Irish and chaser clip takes off most of the hair from the belly, shoulders and all of the neck; it does not extend around the thighs or quarters. The trace clip is the same but extends over the thighs and around the pony's hindquarters. A pony with this type of clip can live out with a heavier weight rug to help keep warm at night.

Strip, belly, and gullet clip

The hair is removed from under the belly upwards between the forelegs and up the lower line of the neck to the lower jaw. This clip is helpful for native ponies who live out. Many ponies with adequate shelter may not need a turnout rug, but some may feel the cold more than others.

Trimming and plaiting

Trimming is tidying up a pony and includes pulling the mane and tail. The hairs of the mane and tail will pull out more easily when the pores of the skin are warm and open, that is, after exercise or on a warm day. When the hair does not pull easily, trimming scissors and a comb may be used instead. Pull the mane or tail gradually to avoid soreness, achieving the required length or shape over several sessions. Some pony breeds are shown untrimmed with natural manes and tails. Do make sure you ask for some guidance or help before attempting this on your own.

The legs and head

The long hairs under the jaws, down the legs, and at the back of the fetlock joint offer protection from the elements. They may be trimmed on the stabled pony to improve his looks and making him look neater. The comb is moved upwards against the lie of the hair, lifting it so it can be cut. The long hairs growing underneath the jaw are treated the same way on an unclipped pony. The whiskers around the nose and eyes should not be cut or trimmed as the pony needs these to feel where he puts his nose and to protect his eyes and nose.

The ears

The sides of the ears should be gently squeezed together so that the outside edges meet. Then, trim back any long hairs with blunt-ended scissors. Hair from the inside of the ear should not be removed.

The mane

Pulling a mane

A responsible person should advise and help you before pulling a mane.

- To thin a mane that has become over-thick.
- To shorten a long mane.

- To encourage the mane to lie flat.
- To make the mane easier to plait.

The longest hairs from underneath should be dealt with first and removed a few at a time. Do this with your fingers or by winding a few hairs at a time around the mane comb and plucking them out briskly. Never pull the top hairs or any that may stand up after plaiting because they will form an upright fringe on the crest when they regrow and look untidy.

You should not use scissors or clippers.

Hogging
This involves the complete removal of the mane using clippers. It is sometimes done when a pony grows a ragged mane that spoils his appearance. Cobs and polo ponies often have hogged manes. Hogging should be repeated about every three weeks.

Once a mane has been hogged, regrowth can take at least two years to look neat, and even then, the mane may not regain its former appearance. A helper is necessary to hog the mane neatly. By taking hold of his ear, the helper can gently but firmly encourage the pony to lower his head (which will straighten the crest). Remove the whole mane, beginning at the withers and working forward towards the poll on both sides and up the centre. Make sure you leave a tidy line where the mane meets the coat.

Plaiting a mane
This is done for neatness, to show off the neck and crest, and to train the mane to fall to the side preferred (normally the right or offside) of the neck. There should always be an uneven number of plaits along the neck, plus the forelock. There are several ways to plait a mane, but this method is one of the easiest.

Figure 32a: Plaiting the mane.

Plaiting using bands

- You will need a water brush; a mane comb, rubber bands; and maybe something safe to stand on such as a stool.
- First dampen down the mane with a wet brush and divide it into equal parts up the neck. We usually make this an odd number. The number of parts will depend on the length of the pony's neck (so this can be seven, nine or more).
- Now begin the plaiting of each lock of mane, starting behind the ears.
- Having finished a long plait, loop the band several times around the end; then bend under the end of the plait into the required position, folding it as many times as necessary, and loop the band around the whole plait until it is tight.
- Mane plaits should not be left in all night as they tend to pull, are uncomfortable, and spoil the mane.

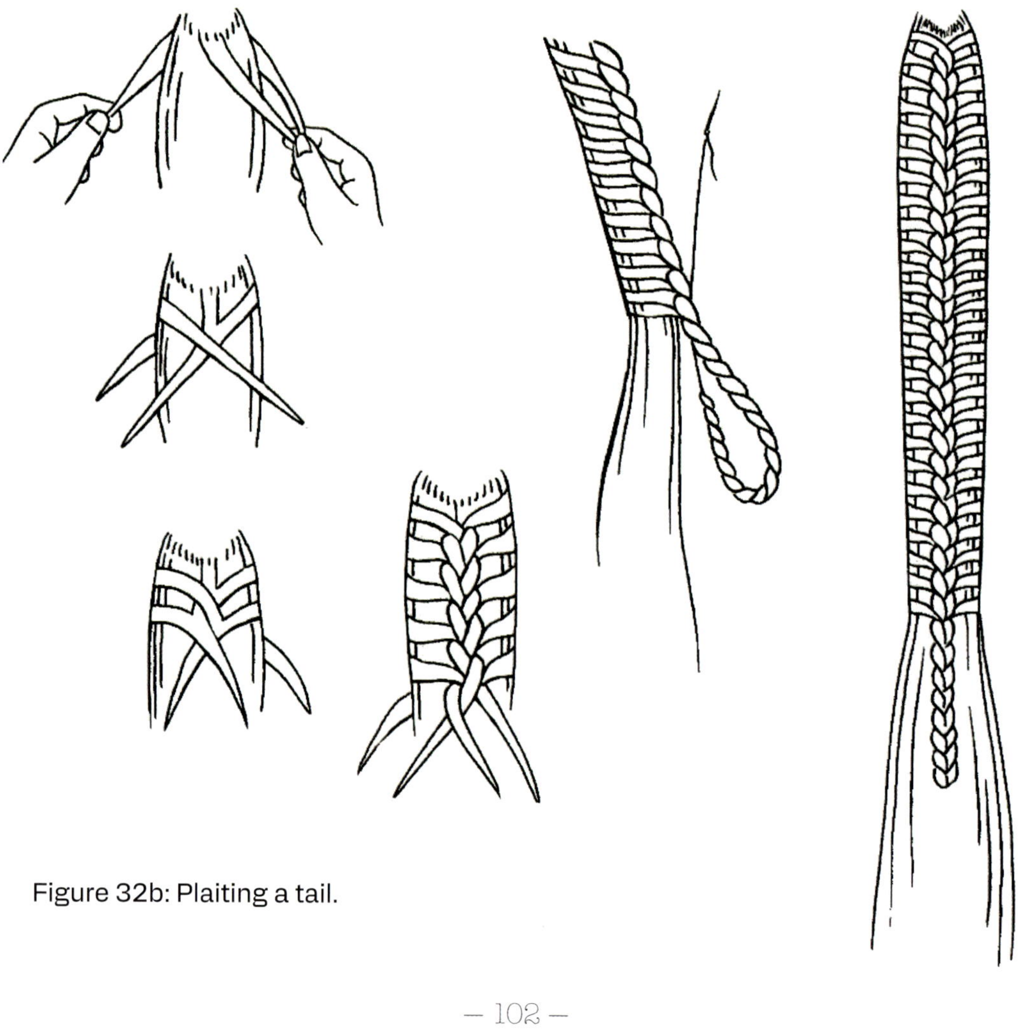

Figure 32b: Plaiting a tail.

The tail

Plaiting a tail

The unpulled hairs of the dock can be plaited to make them look neat for special occasions. Pulling the tail is not always advisable; some ponies don't like it, and only tails with long hairs at the sides of the dock can be plaited successfully. The plaiting procedure is as follows:

- Dampen the hair, then take three small bunches with the finger and thumb from the top of the tail, one on one side and two on the other. If the hairs are sparse or too short, knot them together with thread. The ends of the thread hang down the centre of the tail, and they are used for plaiting small successive bunches (eight to ten hairs) from either side.
- Alternatively, take a small amount of hair from the middle of the dock and place successive bunches from either side with them.
- In both cases, continue plaiting down the centre, adding successive bunches from each side. Work downwards for about three-quarters of the length of the dock. Thereafter, finish plaiting the hairs in your hand.
- When you reach the end, secure it with thread and loop it back under itself, tucking it beneath the plait. Then, sew it firmly in this position.
- The plait itself may lie on the outside or inside of the hair, but the smartest effect is when it is on the outside (laced).
- See Figure 32b on plaiting.

'Putting up' a tail

A tail is put up (tied up) for those activities which may cause it to get muddy and uncomfortable, such as muddy hacks in the winter, or playing polo.

- Begin plaiting as described, but when you reach the end of the dock, divide the whole tail into three bunches, add them to the bunches in your hand, and plait to the end.
- Roll up the plait neatly to the end of the dock and stitch it firmly on both sides to lie flat, directly below the last of the tailbones.

Pulling a tail

A well-pulled and tidy tail adds greatly to the appearance of a stabled pony. A pony living on grass should not have his tail pulled, as this deprives him of natural protection when he turns his hindquarters towards the wind and rain. Clippers should never be used on a tail, nor should a dandy brush be used. A responsible person should advise and help you before pulling a tail.

A 'bang' or trimmed tail

A long tail collects mud, is likely to become straggly, and hides the hocks. To 'bang' the tail, cut the end off the square approximately 10cm (4in) below the points of the hocks. You will need a helper to put an arm under the root of the tail while you cut it; the cut will then be square when the tail is carried naturally. The tails of native ponies should look natural for showing and should not be banged.

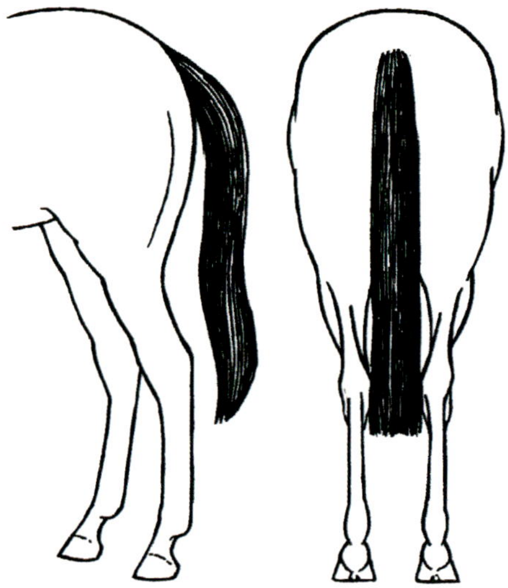

Figure 33: Trimmed tail.

Rugs

In normal circumstances, a pony's coat will keep him comfortably warm, but if he has been clipped or has a fine coat, and is groomed regularly, he will need further protection from the cold.

Most rugs are made from a synthetic fabric. They are light and easy to wash, but some are non-absorbent and do not allow the coat to 'breathe'. These are not recommended because when wearing them, a pony is more likely to break out into a sweat in mild weather or after exercise. The rugs come in three basic levels of warmth, which are light, medium and heavyweight. You should select the most appropriate depending on the pony's needs and the weather.

Rugs are secured by a fastening at the chest and by crossover surcingles. This type is preferable because they do not put extra pressure on the spine. If you think the pony needs extra warmth, you can use an under rug. Do not be tempted to use ordinary blankets, as they tend to slip. Hind-leg straps (or a fillet string) are fitted on some rugs to keep the rug straight. Neck covers can be detachable or integrated into the rug itself these can be for stable, turnout and fly rugs.

Stable rugs (night rugs)

Stable rugs are excellent for warmth and comfort and have a long life. They are light to handle, and the less bulky ones are machine-washable, but they will all flatten out and lose their warmth over time. Night rugs will become soiled when the pony lies down, so it is useful to have a spare. Some rugs will have a hood/neck to protect and keep the pony's neck warm. Under rugs are made of thermal fabrics and can provide extra warmth under the rug at night.

Turnout rugs

These are designed for outdoor use in cold weather and are particularly useful for clipped or trace-clipped ponies. Their special merit is that they protect against wind and rain but are not

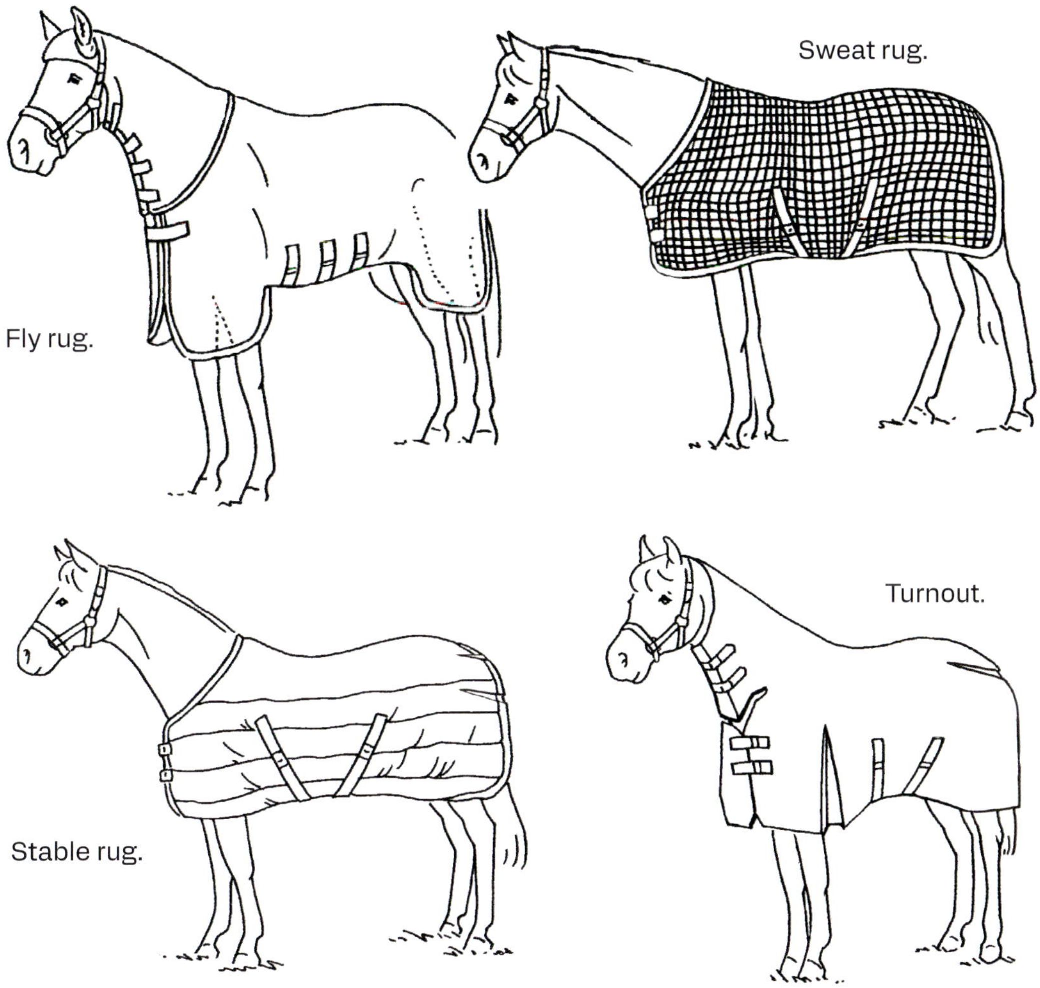

Figure 34: Various types of rug.

intended to be worn in the stable. Rugs made of synthetic fabrics are lighter, hard wearing and will dry out quickly.

- Turnout rugs have various fittings to keep them in place without putting pressure on the spine. Single, sewn-on surcingles are not recommended. Fastenings must be strong and easy to manipulate.
- As the pony will be more active in his paddock than in the confines of his stable, his turnout rug must fit him particularly well. It must stay in place to keep him warm and dry without rubbing him.

When using turnout rugs, remember:

- Before the pony is turned out he must become accustomed to the feel of the rug and its fastenings, particularly if he is unfamiliar with leg straps.
- Ponies living outside in turnout rugs must be checked at least twice daily, and the rugs readjusted as necessary.
- A spare rug must be available for the pony living out, in case the one he is wearing becomes too wet or damaged.

Anti-sweat rugs/cooler rugs

Made of cotton mesh, synthetic materials or towelling, these are used on a sweating pony while cooling, to prevent chills, or on a pony who tends to break out in a sweat on return from work or while travelling. Mesh rugs can be used under a light rug.

Exercise sheets

These short rugs are used in cold weather while the pony is being ridden, to keep the back, loins and quarter muscles warm. They are fitted under the saddle, and all should have a fillet string which passes behind the quarters to prevent the sheet from blowing forward. It is now possible to buy fluorescent exercise sheets, making the pony more visible to drivers when riding and hacking on a gloomy day.

Summer sheets

Made of cotton or synthetic fabric, these protect the groomed pony against dust and flies. They should also have a fillet string to prevent them from blowing about in the wind.

Measurement and fit

Choosing the correct size

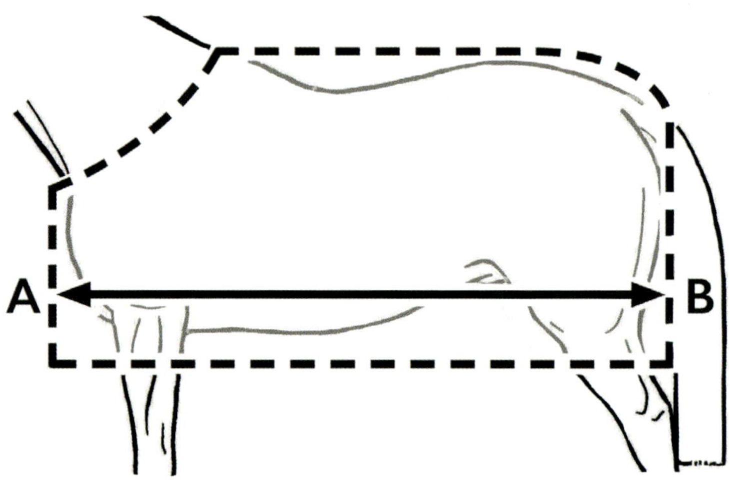

Figure 35: How to measure rug size.

A pony is measured for a rug by taking the distance between the centre of the chest and the furthest point of the hindquarters. The depth of the rug is usually standard, although some manufacturers give a choice of extra depth. Some good-quality rugs follow the curves of the top line of the pony from withers to croup. They must be shaped around the neck and hindquarters to fit properly.

Checking the fit of the rug

- All rugs must cover the pony's back from the front of his withers to his croup. They must be comfortably snug around the chest and deep enough to keep the pony's body warm.
- Turnout rugs must be deep enough to protect the underside of the belly from wind and rain.
- All rugs must be shaped to stay in position without relying on straps or fittings that are too tight.
- Hind-leg straps should be long enough not to pull or rub the pony when he walks but not so loose that his hind legs could be caught up in them when he lies down.
- The projecting parts of a pony, such as withers and shoulder points, must be checked regularly for signs of chafing.

Putting on a rug

- Tie up the pony.
- First, gather up the rug and gently place it well over the pony's back. then slide it backwards into position in the direction of the lie of the coat with the buckles and straps undone.
- Sort out the front part and fasten the buckle, ensuring the clips face inwards to prevent the pony from rubbing or catching them on a fence or haynet.
- Correct the position of the rug. If the pony is known to you and safe, and you are used to putting a rug on, then you can do it from immediately behind. This is one of the few occasions when standing close behind a pony is permissible.
- If you are unsure that the pony is reliable, adjust the rug from the side.

If the rug has crossed surcingles

If the rug has crossed surcingles, move to the left side of the pony and secure them at a comfortable length around the pony's belly. Check that the rug(s) and surcingles are lying flat and comfortable.

If the rug is fitted with hind-leg straps

- Before a rug is placed over the pony, no straps (surcingle or hind-leg straps) should be left hanging loose but should be fastened to prevent them from hitting you or the pony.
- To avoid chafing, hind-leg straps should be crossed through each other. Mind that the pony does not kick you while you are fastening the straps between his legs.
- Finally, check the pressure of the rug around the neck and shoulders and ensure that the mane is lying flat.

Taking off a rug

- Tie up the pony.
- If the rug has crossed surcingles, they should be unfastened and loosely knotted on the right side.
- If it has hind-leg straps, they should each be unfastened and fastened again on the outside to prevent the straps and fastenings from hitting you or the pony.
- Lastly, unfasten the rug's breast buckle and, using both hands, fold back the front portion over the top of the back portion.
- With your left hand on the centre front and your right hand on the centre back, remove the rug in one gentle backward sweep, following the lie of the pony's coat.
- If the pony is wearing more than one rug they should always be removed one at a time, never together.

Care of rugs

- On dry, sunny days, while the pony is out exercising, his rugs can be hung outside to air and freshen up.
- Once a day, the rug worn nearest to the body should be shaken vigorously outside the stable.
- Light rugs should be washed at regular intervals.
- Winter clothing should also be washed before being stored away for the summer.
- Some rugs can be dry-cleaned.
- Any repairs should be carried out, and waterproof clothing should be re-proofed according to the manufacturer's instructions.
- Leather fittings should be oiled with leather dressing and when they are not being used, the rugs can be stored neatly away, in a dry place free from vermin.

Bandages

Before use, bandages must be correctly rolled, with the tapes or Velcro in the centre. If you use tapes, fold them neatly across the width of the bandage, then roll them with the sewn side of the tape inwards. When applying or removing bandages, you should adopt a bending or crouching position at the side of the pony, never sitting or kneeling. You need to be able to move out of the way quickly if your pony moves.

Stable bandages

Stable bandages are made of wool or woollen-type material 10cm (4in) wide, 2.5 to 3.7m (8 to 12ft) long and are supplied in sets of four. They improve circulation, provide protection, and are useful for warming and drying cold, wet legs. In skilful hands, they are very beneficial, but if they are wrongly or carelessly applied, they can harm the pony. Suitable padding such as Gamgee or Fibregee should be used under the bandage to help equalise pressure and to add warmth and protection. Bandages put on too tightly cause ring marks on the legs or, more seriously, damage the tendons. Stable bandages may be used for veterinary purposes. If, for any reason, stable bandages are used constantly, they must be removed and replaced at least once a day.

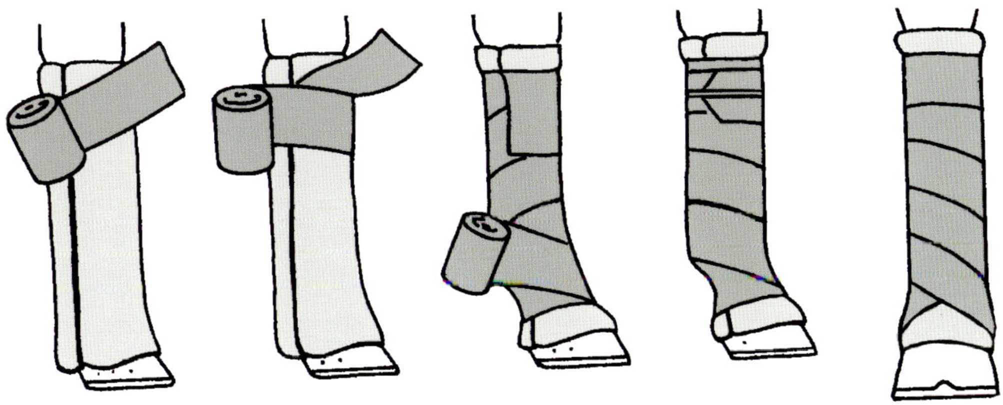

Figure 36: Stable bandages.

Applying a stable bandage

- The Gamgee and bandage should be put on in the same direction.
- Both should follow from the front of the leg to the back (from the cannon bone towards the tendons). So, on the left side the Gamgee and bandage would be placed anticlockwise. For the right legs, this would be in a clockwise direction.
- Wrap the padding around the leg, making sure that it lies flat.
- Then, just below the knee or hock, pass the rolled-up bandage around the leg with even tension.
- Once the coronet is reached, the bandage takes a natural turn upwards.
- The crossover should then occur at the front, just above the coronet.
- Continue unrolling in an upward direction and finish off at the place where you started.
- The tapes must be kept flat and tied so that the knot or bow ties to the outside or the inside of the leg, not in front, where it will press on the bone, or at the back, where it will press on the tendons.
- Tuck in the spare ends or secure with Velcro.

Removing a leg bandage

Unfasten the tapes or Velcro and unwind the bandage quickly, passing the unwound parts from hand to hand. Do not try to roll up the bandage while taking it off. Once it has been removed, run your hand down the tendons to check for any irregularities. Then, hang the bandage up to dry and air.

Travelling bandages

These protect the pony's legs from the chances of injuries occurring in a trailer or horsebox, such as him stepping on himself, or a companion treading on him, or any other knocks that come from travelling. They are put on as described above, but the padding and bandage should be continued lower down to protect the coronet band.

Travel boots

These are used to prevent injury while on a journey. Usually made of synthetic fibre, they encase the legs from above or just below the knee or hock down to the coronet. They are usually fastened with Velcro. The size must be correct for the horse or pony. They should only be used for short journeys as they tend to slip down.

Tail bandages

These should be 7 to 10cm (3 to 4in) wide and made of crêpe or synthetic material. They improve appearance by keeping the hairs of the tail straight and preventing rubbing when travelling.

If put on too tightly, an over-elasticated bandage will cause ridges around the tail and discomfort to the pony. Tail bandages should not be used to excess and should never be left on all night or on long journeys.

Applying a tail bandage

Lightly dampen the tail hair with a water brush. Wetting the bandage is wrong as it may shrink the material and injure the tail by cutting off the circulation. Put your right hand at the top of the tail. Unroll about 20cm (8in) of bandage and place this spare piece over the top of the tail. Hold the end of the bandage in your left hand and the bandage roll in your right with the roll on the outside. Keep your left hand at the top of the tail until the bandage is secured. The first turn is often difficult to keep in place, but you can overcome this by making the next turn above the first. Then, wind in the spare end of the bandage. Unroll the bandage evenly around and downwards, stopping just above or below the last tailbone. Tie the tapes neatly no tighter than the tension of the bandage. Tuck in the spare ends, then bend the tail into a comfortable position.

Removing a bandage from the tail

Untie the tapes, grasp the bandage with both hands around the dock near the top of the tail, and slide off downward.

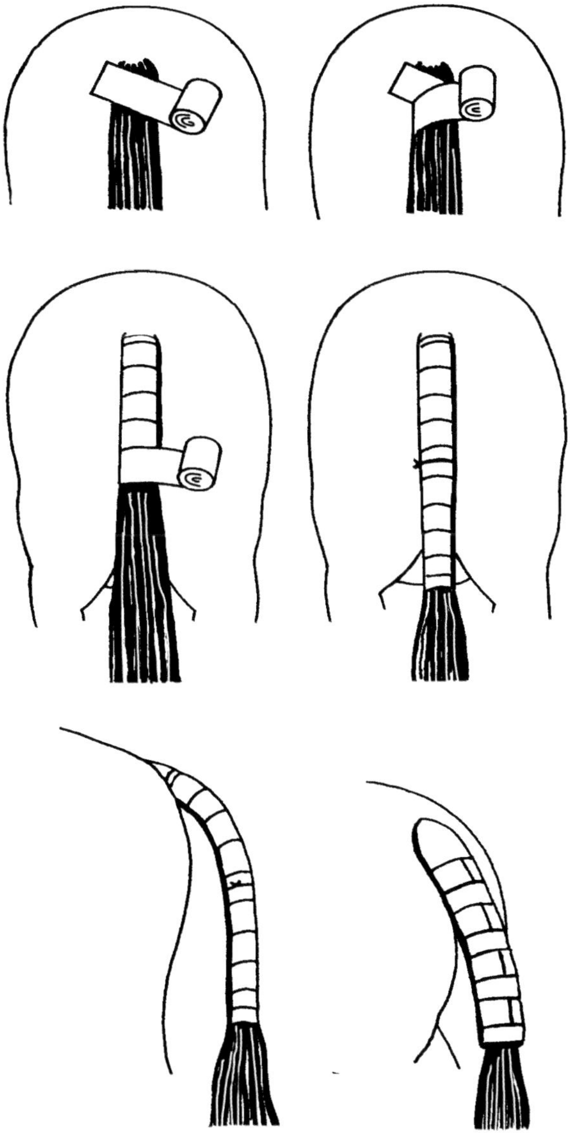

Figure 37: Tail bandage and tail guard.

Tail guards

These protect the pony's tail when travelling. Sometimes used over tail bandages, they may also be used independently. There are several types. Some are fastened around the tail with tape or Velcro, and others zip up and stay in place independently.

Travelling

Types of vehicle

If you use, borrow or hire any vehicle for transporting a pony, the following information should be considered.

- The height, width and length of the space allocated to the pony must suit his size.
- Single-axle trailers are not recommended.
- From time to time, check that the floorboards are not showing signs of rotting, that the tyres are in good condition and that the brakes are sound.
- Keep the metal fittings oiled and ensure they are secure and easy to operate.
- If your box or trailer has floor matting, make sure it is suitably bedded with straw or shavings.
- Incorrect tyre pressures and faulty springs can cause towing problems and discomfort.
- The towing hitch should be the correct height for the trailer.
- Before using the trailer, check the coupling, ramps, side doors, legs and lights (including indicators).
- Check that the horsebox or towing vehicle is taxed, insured, and in sound, roadworthy condition and that the brakes, lights, etc., are working correctly. See that it has oil, water, and enough fuel for the journey.
- Ponies travel more contentedly if they have something to eat. Tie up a haynet ready for him when loaded unless you travel to a rally, competition, or other function where the pony must work hard within an hour or so of arrival.
- Remember to take the pony's passport whenever he travels. This is a legal requirement.

Travel equipment

Preparing your pony

Rugs

The number of rugs needed, if any, will depend on the weather. Remember that a pony generates much heat in a confined space and may also sweat with excitement. Anti-sweat rugs that wick the sweat away from the skin help counteract this. Designed for use under a rug or sheet, they allow the free flow of air while keeping the pony warm; used on their own, they do not serve this purpose and can easily tear. The sweat rug should be secured at the front. The day rug or sheet can be folded back from the chest and secured with a roller. The pony should never be left to travel in a rug secured only at the chest because it could slip round, down, and under his feet.

Figure 38: Dressed ready for travelling.

Protective clothing

The following items will all help to prevent injury:

- Leather headcollar.
- Suitable rug for the weather and length of journey.
- Tail bandage and tail guard.
- Travelling bandages or travelling boots.
- Some ponies may need poll guard.

Note: Some ponies will not tolerate the high hind-leg boot protectors and will need correctly fitted bandages instead. If you use a trailer with a partition and unload through the front ramp, the pony should not be saddled up, as the saddle might get caught as the pony is unloaded.

Travelling tacked up

For short journeys, a pony can travel partially or completely saddled up. If he is in a bridle, always put a leather headcollar over it, with the reins over his neck. The reins should be twisted around each other under the throat and secured by passing the throatlash through one of them. You can loop them behind one or both stirrups if they are very long. Never transport a pony in studs other than road studs.

Loading

- Never ride a pony into a trailer or horsebox.
- You should always have a responsible adult with you.
- They should always take care to avoid being positioned directly behind a pony or in any position where they could get kicked or squashed.
- Always use a leather headcollar rather than a synthetic type. Leather is more likely to break in an emergency, which is a good thing. This also applies when leaving a headcollar on a pony turned out to grass.
- Remember to wear your PPE, hat, boots and gloves when handling and loading your pony. This applies to any helper, too.
- Never wrap the headcollar rope around your hand.
- Position yourself and the pony some way from the ramp, then lead him straight up it.
- Look straight ahead yourself and avoid looking round at the pony.
- If the pony hangs back, keep your body position by his shoulder and encourage him to walk up alongside you. He is unlikely to want to move forward if you pull at him. Remember to use little pulls and releases of the lead rope to encourage him to keep walking.
- Cross-tie, when transporting a single pony in a double trailer without a partition, this is done by securing him to both sides of the compartments, which will prevent him from trying to turn around.
- If there is a partition in the centre, put him on the right side of the trailer or box, as he will travel more smoothly on the crown of the road.
- Only tie your pony up when the bar, the breeching strap, or the ramp are in place or, in the case of a box, until the partitions around the pony are secure.
- Tie him up relatively short with a quick-release knot.
- Beware of any ramp which could accidentally fall on top of you. Always stand at the side to lift or lower a trailer ramp. If necessary, find someone to help you to stand on each side rather than risk an accident.

Training a pony to load willingly

Do not try to do this by yourself; a knowledgeable and experienced adult should always be with you.

Figure 39: Loading into a trailer.

When introducing an inexperienced pony to a trailer, a vehicle with two ramps is preferable. You can open the front and create an open space for him to see that he can walk through the narrow space of the trailer.

Always allow plenty of time when introducing this activity to your pony so that the process is calm. To ensure everyone is calm and relaxed, assess the space before asking him to walk into the trailer.

Lower the front ramp of the vehicle and remove the partition so he can follow the person leading him up the back ramp and see out via the front.

This process can be repeated several times, giving him a reward while he stands inside.

It is helpful to load the pony and then feed him in the box or trailer without moving off for a few days to gain his trust and confidence.

Ponies that are reluctant to be loaded

There are many degrees of reluctance, but if the pony has not previously had a fright, your success in coaxing him into a box or trailer depends largely on his confidence in his handler. Consider how to adjust your methods of loading accordingly. Is it fright? Is it unwillingness to leave stable companions?

The following are some of the methods that may help, and you should select those most likely to overcome the resistance of the pony in question at the time. You will almost certainly need assistance.

- Make sure that you are being shown what to do by a responsible person.
- Move the back of the partition to one side, thus making the entrance larger or remove the partition altogether. Do what you can to make the interior appear light and spacious.
- Lower the front ramp of the vehicle if it has one. A shy pony will sometimes enter if he can see the way out.
- Park your vehicle alongside a wall, a hedge, or another lorry. This makes the horsebox or trailer look less forbidding than if parked in an open space, and it also provides a wing.
- If the ramp is steep, lessen the angle by backing the box or trailer up against higher, level ground and lowering the ramp onto it. The end of the ramp must be firm and level.
- Load another pony first to provide a lead.

- The helper should encourage the pony from behind, standing safely to one side. This may be sufficient, but the helper should carry a stick, as a quick tap can encourage the pony to keep moving forward.
- Fit a long rope or lungeing reins to the back of the box or trailer and have a helper on each side of the pony to hold them taut. This helps to keep a pony straight and often encourages him to go in. The helpers should change sides as the pony moves forward, keeping the ropes taut but standing safely from his heels. If necessary, apply pressure with both ropes above the hocks and around the lower part of the quarters.

Care while travelling

The journey

Before driving away, recheck the trailer-coupling, ramps, side doors, legs and lights. As a pony cannot see out, he cannot anticipate the vehicle's movements and may lose his balance. Generally, drive steadily, not more than 48 to 64kph (30 to 40mph); less at roundabouts and on winding or bumpy roads and move slowly across fields and when reversing or turning. Proceed as smoothly as possible, avoiding jerks, violent braking and fast cornering.

Long journeys

Lengthy road journeys should be broken every 4 or 5 hours. The pony should be checked and offered water, and unless it is very cold, the ramp or a door should be opened to bring in some fresh air.

Poor travellers

Once a pony has been frightened, he seldom regains his full confidence when travelling. Loss of confidence is usually the result of being loaded in a space that is too narrow, being driven too fast, or sudden braking by the driver. Careful driving promotes easy loading and confident travellers.

Unloading

Walking forward down a ramp:

Once again, with an adult, and if you are unloading from a trailer, untie the pony or ponies before lifting the front bars in case they try to rush out. If more than one pony is travelling, first unload the one nearest to the ramp, keeping him nearby while you move the front of the partition across to prevent the second pony from scraping himself against it or getting stuck.

When unloading backwards down a trailer ramp, ensure the pony will stand safely while any doors and partitions, which might otherwise swing and hit him, are secured. You will need help.

Untie the pony before the ramp is lowered and bars/straps are undone. A responsible person can then gently back the pony out.

Note: If a pony rushes back, on no account, hang on to his head. All being well, a helper will be able to catch hold of the headcollar rope, but if not, it is far better for him to go loose than to damage himself by rearing and hitting his head or going over backwards.

A single pony in a double compartment (with no partition) should be tied to both sides (cross-tied) to stop him from trying to turn around during the journey. He may try to turn when he has been untied before unloading. Though there may be room for a pony to turn, there is seldom room for a horse, and you should try to prevent him from attempting it. Remove the rope from one side of the headcollar. Untie the other rope, leaving it through the ring. Lower the ramp and slowly but calmly move up beside the pony before he turns around. You can then back him out as described above.

After a journey

- Always muck out the box/trailer and ensure that the drain holes are cleared.
- Push dry bedding up to the front to allow the floorboards to dry.
- Close the ramps and doors once the vehicle is clean and dry.

Chapter 7

The Foot, Trimming and Shoeing

The Foot, Trimming and Shoeing

Conformation and structure: points of foot and limb

Every horseman should understand the care of a horse's feet, shoes, and shoeing. 'No foot, no horse' is an old saying that is still relevant today. If your pony is lame and there is no apparent cause, the problem is usually found in the foot. Your farrier should be employed regularly approximately every five to seven weeks. They will maintain the principles of good farriery, encouraging the correct growth and balance of the feet, and deal with short-term problems as well as ponies who may need long-term remedial treatment.

For signs of lameness – *see Chapter 8: Health, Condition and Fitness*

The structure of the foot

The exterior of the foot

This consists of three main structures: the wall, the sole and the frog. All three are horny structures and are insensitive, with neither nerve nor blood supply. This explains why shoeing nails can be driven through the wall, and the frog and sole can be cut with a knife without causing pain or bleeding.

The wall

This part of the hoof is visible when the foot is on the ground. It grows downwards from the coronet band, just like a fingernail. The wall encircles the foot, and at the heels is inclined inwards to form the bars. The toe, the quarters and the heel all form part of the wall of the foot.

The sole

This protects the foot from injury from underneath. It is rather thin for this purpose, and liberties cannot be taken with it. In its healthy state, it is slightly concave, like a saucer turned upside down, which helps to provide a better foothold.

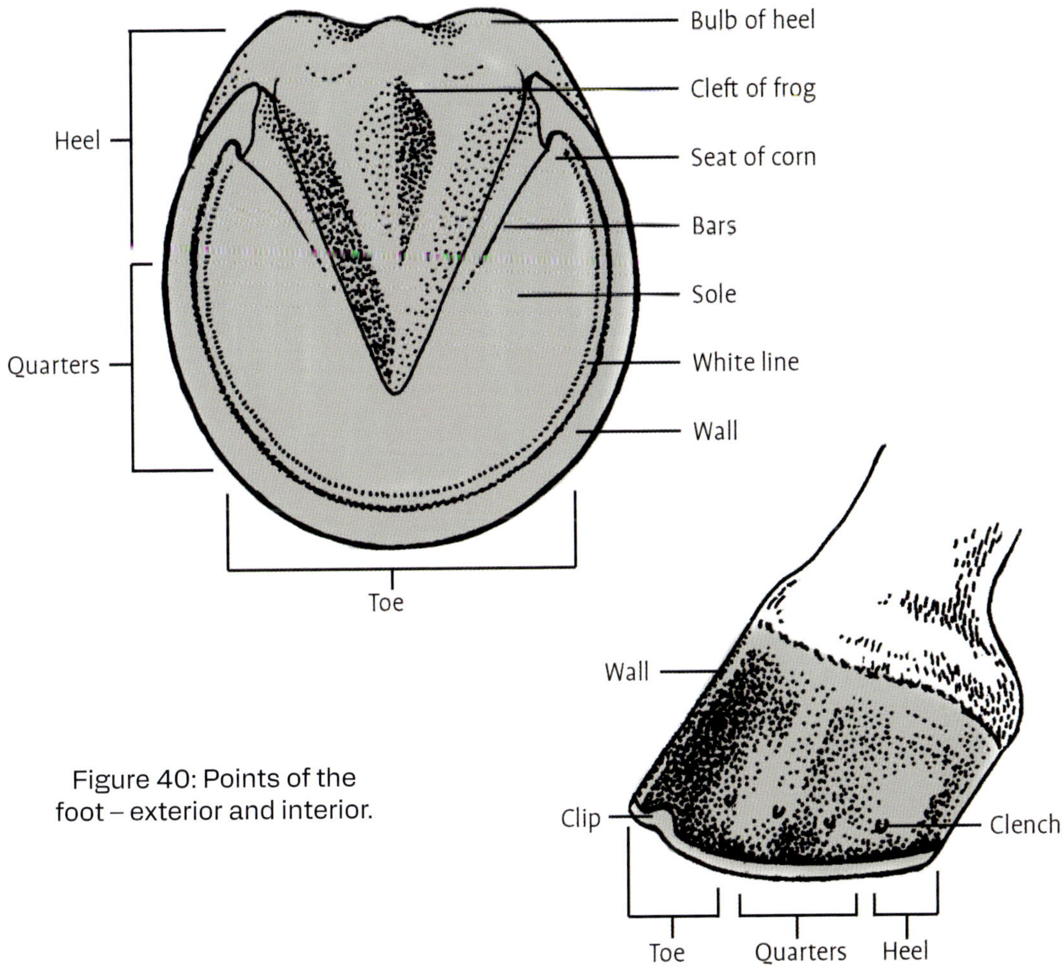

Figure 40: Points of the foot – exterior and interior.

The frog

The frog is nature's anti-slipping and anti-concussion device, which ensures a good foothold. Its peculiar wedge shape, irregular surface, and central cleft help it function as an anti-slipping mechanism. It is effective as a shock absorber because it is spongy and provides a cushion for the feet. A healthy frog helps the foot to function more efficiently.

The interior of the hoof

The inside of the hoof is a complicated and fragile arrangement of bones, ligaments, tendons, nerves and many blood vessels – structures which all need to work together and can be easily damaged.

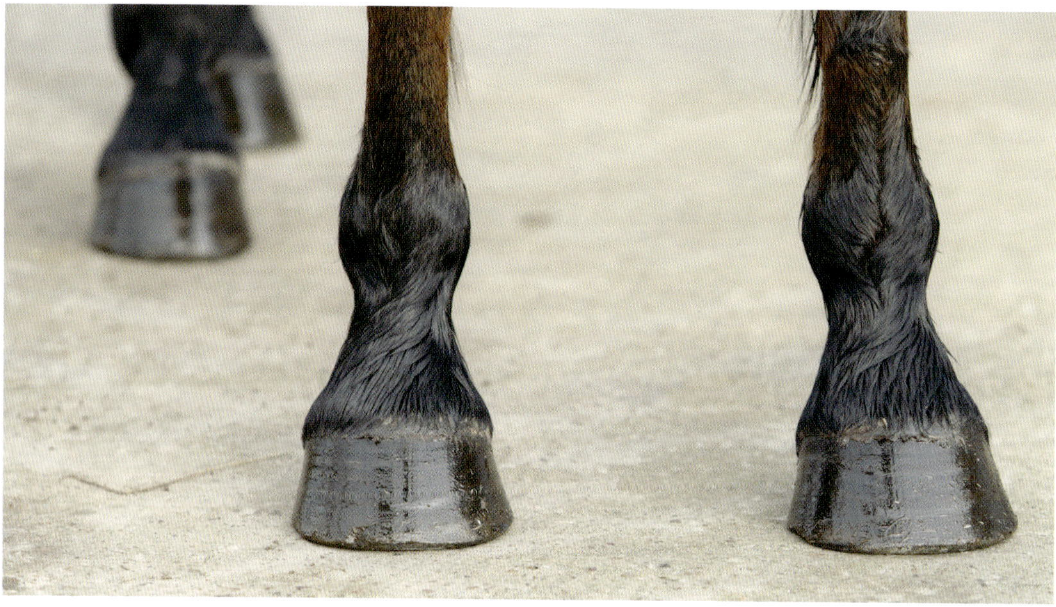

Figure 41: An example of good feet.

Shoeing procedure

Trimming

Ponies' hooves (feet) continue to grow just like your fingernails. You might think that walking around on them would keep them trimmed, but that's not always the case. Normal wear and tear can lead to cracks and chips in the hoof. Regular trimming approximately every five to seven weeks by a farrier is essential, ensuring that the feet remain in good condition.

A pony can be worked either barefoot or shod. The activities that he does will influence your decision as to which is best for your pony. Some ponies may be shod in front and be barefoot behind.

Benefits of going barefoot

- More cost-effective: trimming alone is usually less expensive than getting shoes, as you don't have to pay for them.
- Some riders believe that their ponies tend to be healthier and perform better when unshod, especially when working on a soft surface.

- More natural: wild horses don't wear shoes, as a result some people believe that keeping a pony as close to its natural state as possible is healthier and more comfortable. However, this is not necessarily the case for all ponies.

Factors to consider when going barefoot

- Increased risk of injury: while proper hoof maintenance and good nutrition can help build strength and resilience in the hoof and sole, there is always a chance that the pony may suffer a stone bruise or other injury while working. This risk also applies to shod ponies: neither option guarantees protection against injury.
- A barefoot pony may need more trimming and maintenance than one that is shod. Owners of unshod ponies must check and care for their feet and hooves, which can be time-consuming and needs to be overseen by someone with knowledge and experience.
- Extra protection may still be necessary: even for ponies accustomed to being barefoot, additional protection or traction in specific situations may sometimes be essential. For instance, ponies might benefit from wearing boots while competing or hacking in extremely wet, muddy conditions or on particularly hard or icy ground. This is why it is important to always check your rule books for each activity.

Shoeing

The need for shoeing ponies is a direct consequence of their domestication. Working a pony on hard roads or stony paths causes the wall of the foot to wear away faster than the rate at which it grows. The shod foot, therefore, calls for just as much attention as the unshod foot.

Generally, a shod pony will need the farrier's attention every five to seven weeks. Even when shoes are not badly worn, the horn will have grown enough to need trimming. This is particularly true of the toe region; a pony with an over-long toe is likely to stumble, and a foot that has been neglected could make the pony lame and sore.

Help your farrier to work efficiently and in pleasant conditions:

- The pony should be ready for him, with clean, dry legs and feet.
- A suitable sheltered place – with a flat, clean, non-slippery surface where the pony will stand in a settled manner, and both he and the farrier are protected from extreme weather.
- If the pony is to be shod hot, the farrier will need a bucket of water to cool the shoes before putting them on the pony.
- Refreshments for the farrier are always appreciated as this is hard work.

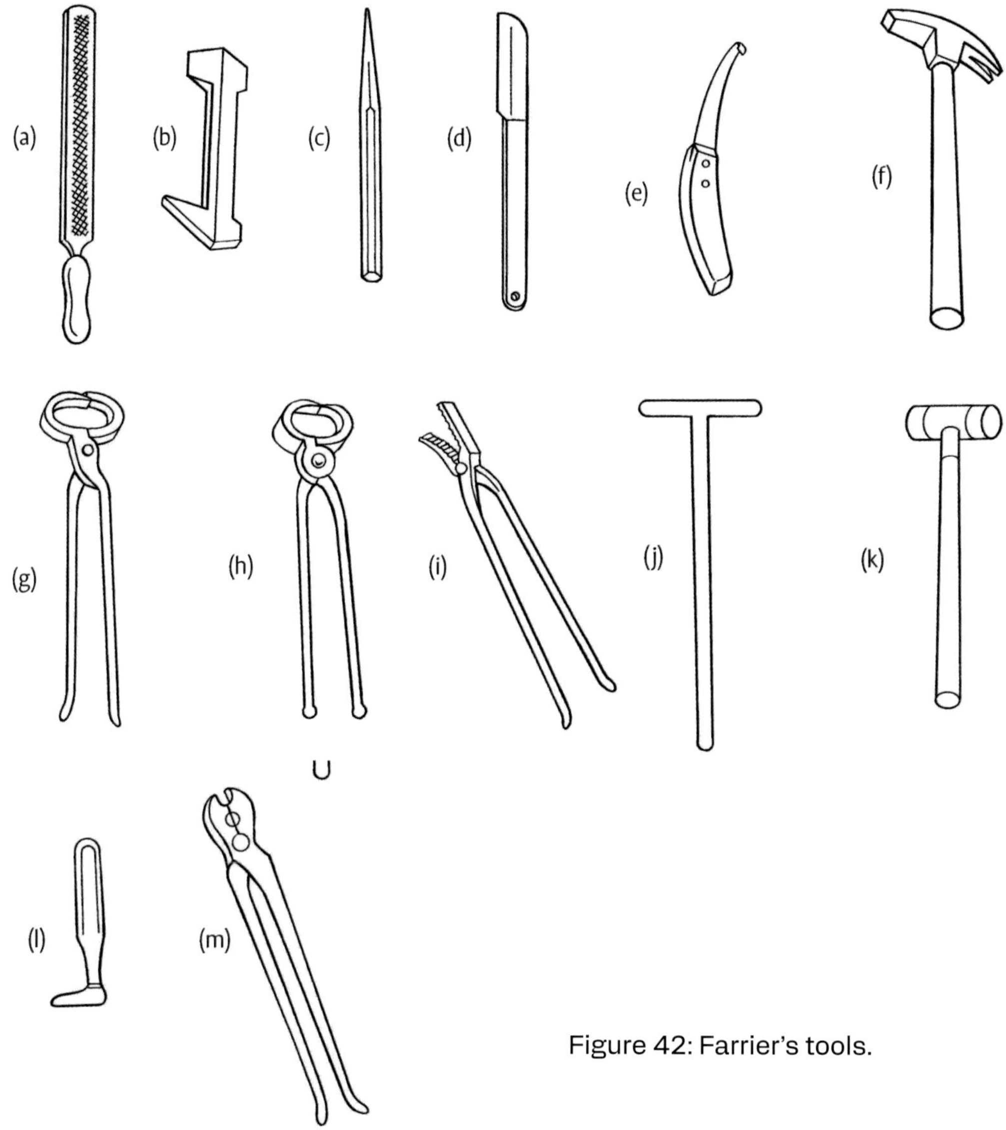

Figure 42: Farrier's tools.

a) rasp
b) buffer
c) pritchel
d) toe knife
e) drawing knife
f) hammer
g) hoof cutter
h) pincers (shoe-pullers)
i) nail clencher
j) T square
k) plastic mallet
l) clench groover
m) nail pullers

Note: Hoof cutters and pincers (shoe pullers) are similar, but hoof cutters have one or two sharp edges, whereas pincers have blunt edges.

Systems of shoeing

There are two systems: hot shoeing and cold shoeing. In hot shoeing, the shoe is specially made to fit the foot. It is tried on hot, and adjustments are made before it is nailed on. In cold shoeing, a shoe that has already been made is fitted. Minor adjustments to the shape are possible, in which case a forge is not required. Traditionally, hot shoeing is preferred.

Hot shoeing: The procedure for re-shoeing a pony using this method has six stages: removal, preparation, forging, fitting, nailing on, and finishing.

Removal: The farrier first cuts all the clenches (this is a term that describes the nail heads that you can see along the side of the pony's hoof). The farrier uses a buffer and driving hammer to remove an old shoe. He then levers the shoe off with pincers. If the clenches have been cleanly cut, there should be no breaking or tearing away of the wall as the shoe is released.

Preparation: The farrier needs to see the pony walk to assess limb flight and footfall to prepare the foot for the pony's requirements. He will clean the sole and frog, remove any excess, trim the hoof wall to the appropriate length, and then balance and rasp it level.

Forging: This is the process of making a new shoe. The weight and type of iron selected depend on the pony's work. After the iron has been shaped on the anvil, the nail holes are stamped, and the clips are drawn.

Fitting: Most farriers use manufactured shoes of fullered metal with nail holes already stamped. They come in various sizes and weights and generally require some shape adjustments to provide a good fit.

Nailing on: Horseshoe nails are designed with a particular type of head, which, correctly fitted, fills the nail hole however much the shoe wears away. Nails are made in various sizes, and it is important to use the correct size. The head of a nail that is too large will project and wear away too soon, while a head that is too small will not fill the nail hole. Both are equally bad faults that result in early shoe loosening. The end of the nail, where it penetrates the wall, should be turned over and twisted off, leaving a small piece called a clench. Clips help to keep the shoe in position and ensure greater security.

Finishing: The clenches are tidied up with the rasp, and a small indentation or bed is made for them in the wall beneath. After that, they are embedded with the driving hammer. Finally, to reduce the risk of cracking, the rasp is run around the wall's outer edge where the horn and shoe meet.

Re-shoeing: The procedure by which a slightly worn shoe is taken off, the foot reduced in length, and the same shoe replaced is traditionally known as a remove, but is sometimes described as a refit. A pony subjected to heavy work on hard roads may wear his shoes in less than a month and need new ones. The indications that he needs re-shoeing are:

- The clenches have risen and stand out from the wall.
- The foot is over-long and out of shape.
- Some parts of the shoe have worn thin.
- The shoe is loose, and its heel may be pressing on the seat of corn.
- A shoe has been cast (has come off).

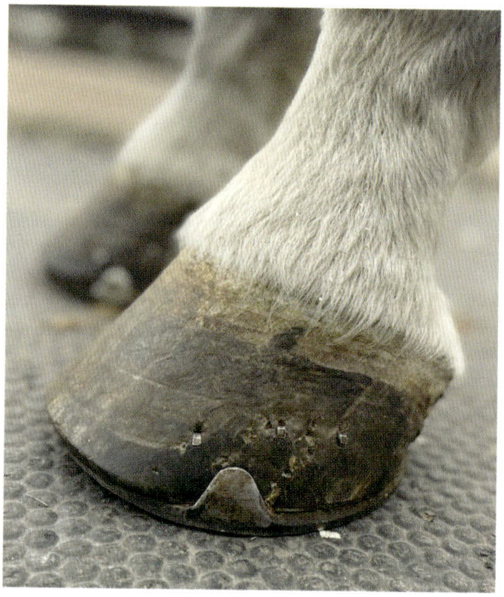

Figure 43: A foot that needs re-shoeing.

The newly shod foot

When a well-shaped and balanced foot is newly shod, check the following points:

- The shoe should give the pony a good platform for support.
- The type of shoe should be suitable for the work required of the pony.
- The weight of the iron chosen should be in correct relation to the pony's size.
- The foot should have been suitably reduced in length at both toe and heel and on each side to have a level-bearing surface.
- The sole and frog should have been cleaned and trimmed as necessary.
- The size of the nails should be correct. They should fit and fill the nail holes.
- The nail heads should not protrude more than 1mm above the shoe.
- The clenches (these are the end tips of the nail that are visible around the edge of the hoof, once the farrier has driven the nail though the hole on the shoe to secure it), should be well-formed and well-seated. They should be in line and the right distance (approximately one-third of the way) up the hoof wall.
- No daylight should show between the shoe and the foot – particularly at the heel region.
- The heels of the shoe should not be too short.
- The clips should fit smoothly to the hoof wall.
- A farrier is a highly trained craftsman, so be tactful if you request adjustments.

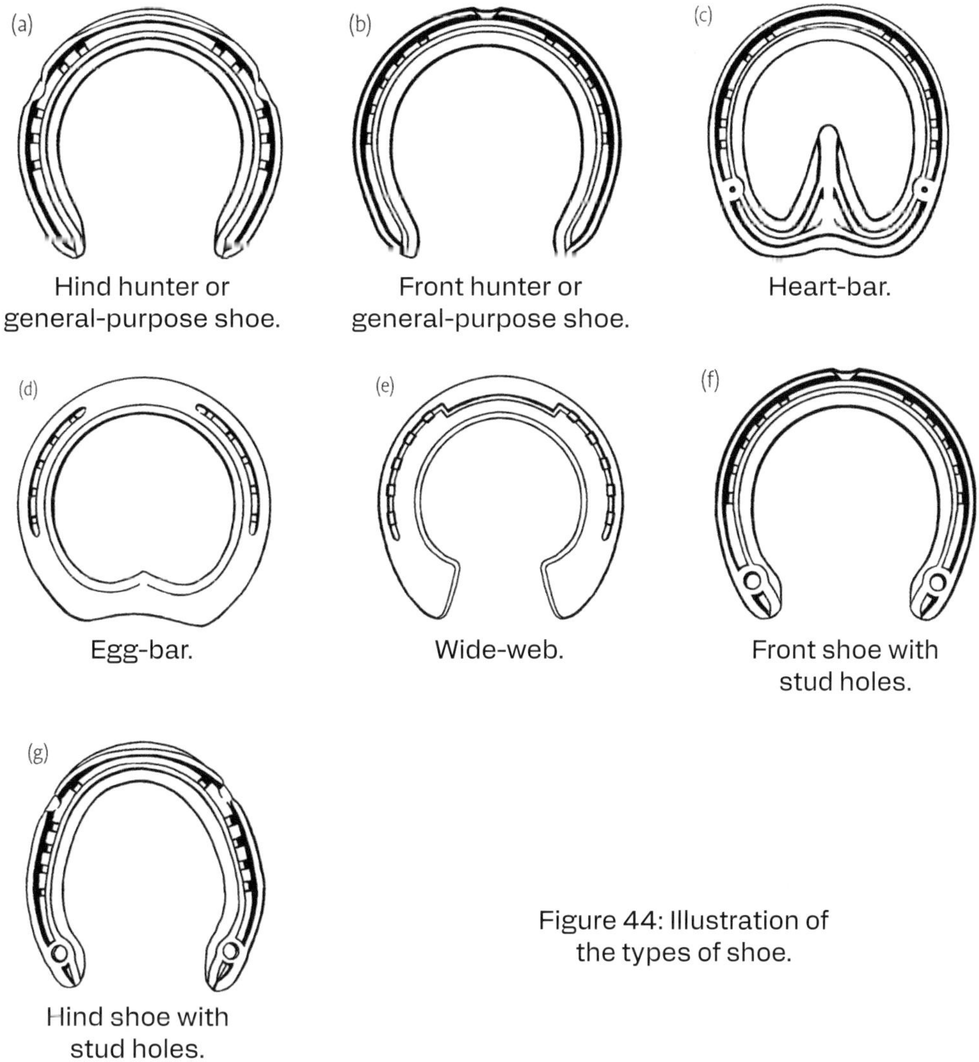

Figure 44: Illustration of the types of shoe.

Types of shoe

Many types of shoes are available, and they can be split into two main categories.

Shoes for fast-moving disciplines: These are fullered (have a groove in them), giving a better grip on all surfaces.

Remedial shoeing: Remedial shoeing is a very specialised area that can allow ponies with conformational weaknesses to achieve a much higher athletic level and enjoy lengthened working lives.

Remedial shoes either improve support or stabilise the hoof capsule, but it must be remembered that conformation and gait must be assessed by a vet or farrier before remedial shoeing takes place. Many types of remedial shoes are available, covering a wide range of requirements, and shoes can often be designed for specific treatments. For example:

- **Wide-web shoes** are mainly used for ponies whose legs suffer from concussion, or they have flat or brittle feet, or laminitis. Wider than a standard hunter shoe, they distribute the weight over a broader area and protect more of the foot's surface.
- **Bar shoes** – e.g. straight-bar, egg-bar, half-bar, combination egg/heart-bar, and heart-bar. All have an extra bar, which joins both heels of the shoe or supports the frog to apply or relieve pressure where necessary. The straight-bar prevents the heels from moving against each other once the foot is balanced.
- **Pads** – these go under the shoe and can do many things, such as help to protect the sole when the ground is very hard, and/or protect the hoof if damaged.

Studs

Metal studs are regularly used for competition horses and ponies, but opinion is divided over whether one or two studs per shoe is best. Two studs give maximum grip and do not upset the balance too much, whereas a single stud allows the horse's foot to rotate and turn.

Depending on the type of ground, different shapes of stud should be used. Pointed studs are designed for firm ground, whereas square, blocky studs are for soft ground.

Studs can be fitted into the heel of a shoe to lessen the risk of slipping. Ideally, they should be worn on the inside and outside of the hind shoes, thereby maintaining the balance of the foot. However, ponies who wear studs on the inside run some danger of causing injury by treading on themselves.

Studs worn on front shoes can cause concussion and are not recommended, but small studs or plugs are available if recommended by experts.

Road studs

These have a hardened metal core which, being slower wearing than the shoe itself, presents a rough surface to the ground. They are usually fitted when the pony is shod and remain permanently in the shoe. They do not protrude too much from the shoe, and the balance of the foot is hardly affected.

Competition studs

These can be obtained in various shapes and sizes to suit different conditions and needs. The farrier prepares a threaded hole, and the studs can be fitted or removed with a spanner. They are

Pointed, for medium/hard ground.

Rounded, for softer ground.

Small pointed.

Road stud.

Figure 45: Selection of studs.

not designed for use on the roads and should be removed after use, as they distort the balance of the feet; they can also cause damage to the floors of horseboxes and other surfaces, such as tarmac.

When the studs are out, oiled cotton wool inserted in the stud holes helps prevent them from clogging up; the cotton wool can easily be removed with a horseshoe nail. The nail can also clean out the holes if they become caked with mud. A metal tap is used if the holes need clearing or rethreading. After use, the studs should be cleaned and stored carefully to prevent them from rusting.

Care of the unshod foot

Working unshod

This is feasible, especially for native ponies, but work on hard, gritty roads or flinty tracks should be avoided. It does save on shoeing costs, and an unshod pony has a more secure grip on every type of surface. Also, injury from a kick by an unshod pony is likely to be considerably less severe. The feet of a pony working unshod must be checked regularly by the farrier, who will ensure that they present an even surface to the ground and that any splitting and cracking of the walls receive attention.

Unshod when at grass

It is beneficial to remove the shoes from ponies who are not in work if the rest period is to last for over a month. The hooves will grow without interference from nails. The farrier will still be needed every five to seven weeks to control the natural growth of the hooves and to encourage the correct shape. Keeping the pony unshod will not be beneficial if the ground is hard or if the pony has flat soles. Hard ground may cause the hoof walls to break, and ponies with flat soles tend to become footsore.

Youngstock

The feet of young ponies must also receive regular attention from a farrier because their feet may not grow evenly. Any defects in the feet must receive immediate remedial action to ensure they are correctly shaped and balanced.

Chapter 8

Health, Condition and Fitness

Health, Condition and Fitness

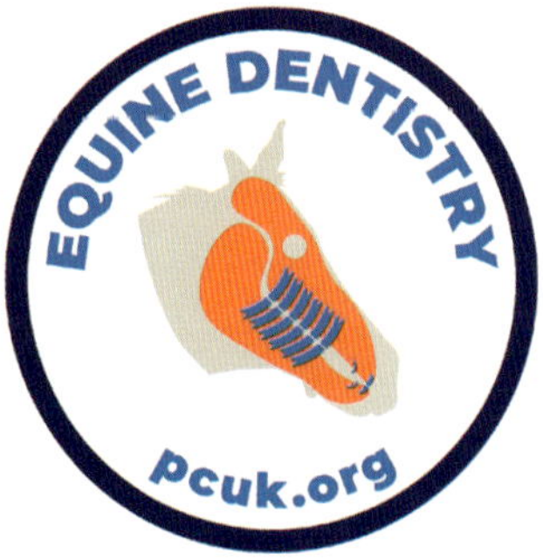

Health

When you spend a lot of time with a pony, you'll get to know him well. You'll notice whether he's feeling well or when he's sick or lame, and your observations will help keep him healthy. If you are concerned about a pony and he's not behaving normally, it may be necessary to call out a vet. Your vet should have checked out your new pony before he arrived on the yard (*see* Chapter 1).

The signs of a healthy pony

It is essential to recognise the signs of good health and to watch for any deviation from them. You will soon learn the characteristics of your pony or ponies in your care and know if everything is normal and well with them. The following are indications of good health:

- Standing and behaving normally, with a confident and alert look.
- The coat is sleek and lying flat.
- Skin is loose, supple to the touch, and easily moved over the underlying bones.
- At rest, there are no visible signs of sweating except in very hot weather.

- Eyes wide open and bright. When examined, the membranes under the eyelids and linings of the nostrils should be salmon pink.
- Eating up well and chewing normally.
- The body is well-filled out (bone structure is well covered) but not gross.
- Standing evenly on all four feet. Resting a hind leg (but not a foreleg) is quite normal.
- Sound in action, taking strides of equal length.
- Urine is colourless or pale yellow and passed several times daily.
- Droppings, which will vary in colour with the diet, are passed approximately eight times daily in the form of damp balls that break when they hit the ground.
- Their smell should be inoffensive. When the pony is at grass, the droppings may be looser but should not be as sloppy as a cow's.

Temperature: A pony's temperature is usually between 37.5 and 38.5°C (99.5 and 101.3°F). It is taken with a rectal thermometer.

Respiration (breathing rate): At rest, 8 to 16 inhalations per minute. This is taken when a pony is at rest (quiet and relaxed) by watching how often his rib cage rises and falls for a minute. In the winter, you can see the breath taken as he breathes out through his nostrils.

Pulse: This is the pony's heartbeat, which should be 35 to 45 beats per minute.

Maintaining good health

Your perception and assessment of a pony's health and condition are vital to his welfare. Any daily changes from the 'signs of good health' above, should be quickly noted, and appropriate advice sought and action taken.

- The pony should be checked in the stable first thing in the morning so that any overnight problems (such as injuries) can be dealt with promptly.
- The pony's grass should be checked at least once daily, even if he lives out on a large acreage in summer.
- The pony must be watered and fed correctly.
- Diet should be balanced and appropriate for the work and age of the pony.
- Be aware of the pony's condition and how much work or exercise he can perform.
- 'No foot, no horse.' Pick out his feet daily, even if he is out at grass.
- Check the condition of his feet and shoes. Look for any signs of thrush. Pre-book the farrier in good time to maintain a regular shoeing schedule.
- Assess the need for worming. Your vet or a suitably qualified person (SQP) will advise you.

- The pony should be inoculated against tetanus and influenza. Your vet will advise you.
- Teeth should be checked twice a year by your vet or a qualified equine dentist.
- If your pony is not thriving, seek expert advice after first satisfying yourself that he is well rested.
- Check that his respiration, temperature, and pulse are normal.

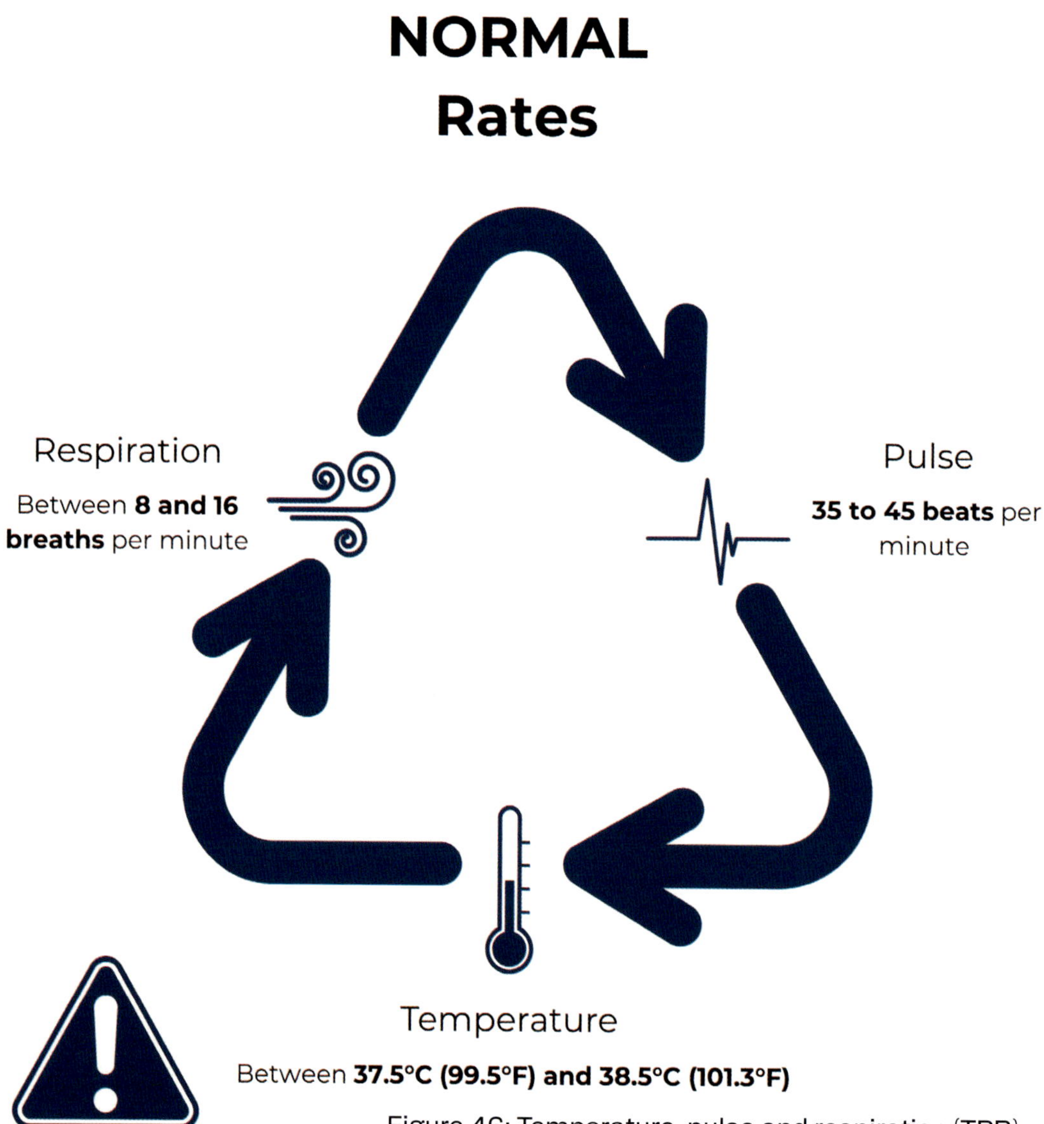

Figure 46: Temperature, pulse and respiration (TPR).

Condition

Good condition

A pony is said to be in good condition when he is carrying the appropriate amount of weight for his stage of training or the type of work required of him and is also thriving, having an appearance of well-being, with bright eyes and a healthy coat and skin.

Condition scoring also known as fat scoring

A pony's condition is the amount of weight he carries over his body, which is assessed as a 'condition score' using a range from 0 to 5. You can assess your pony's condition by 'fat scoring' (body condition scoring), how much fat your pony has in certain parts of his body. This way, the same system can be applied to everything from a non-ridden pony to a three-day-event horse. The ideal is between 2 and 3, with the optimum score for most leisure ponies being about 3. Ponies are designed to lose weight over the winter months so they can safely gain weight from the spring flush of grass, so don't worry if your pony's weight fluctuates a little.

Condition scoring/fat scoring 0–5

The scale in Figure 47 was taken from the World Horse Welfare guidelines and is used by British Equestrian and The Pony Club.

Types of condition

Soft condition: The pony is well but not fit. His muscles are slack. He is fat but not necessarily unhealthy. He is incapable of sustained effort without sweating and distress. Unexercised ponies on grass in summer are in soft condition.

Hard condition: The pony is fit and well. He is free of superfluous fat, both internally and externally. The muscles are hard and well-developed and ripple under the skin as the pony moves. The limbs are toned to withstand sustained effort without injury or distress. A hunter who regularly works in winter or a pony properly prepared for pony trials are in hard condition.

Poor condition: A pony is said to be in bad condition when he is not carrying the correct amount of weight for whatever he is expected to do and not thriving.

Body scoring

Six point scale 0 to 5

0 = Emaciated

- No fatty tissue can be felt – skin tight over bones
- Shape of individual bones visible
- Marked ewe-neck
- Very prominent backbone and pelvis
- Very sunken rump
- Deep cavity under tail
- Large gap between thighs

1 = Very thin

- Barely any fatty tissue – shape of bones visible
- Narrow ewe-neck
- Ribs easily visible
- Prominent backbone, croup and tail head
- Sunken rump
- Cavity under tail
- Gap between thighs

2 = Very lean

- Very thin layer of fat under the skin
- Narrow neck – muscles sharply defined
- Backbone covered but still protruding
- Withers, shoulders and neck accentuated
- Ribs just visible
- Hip bones easily visible but rounded
- Rump sloping from backbone to point of hips, only rounded if very fit

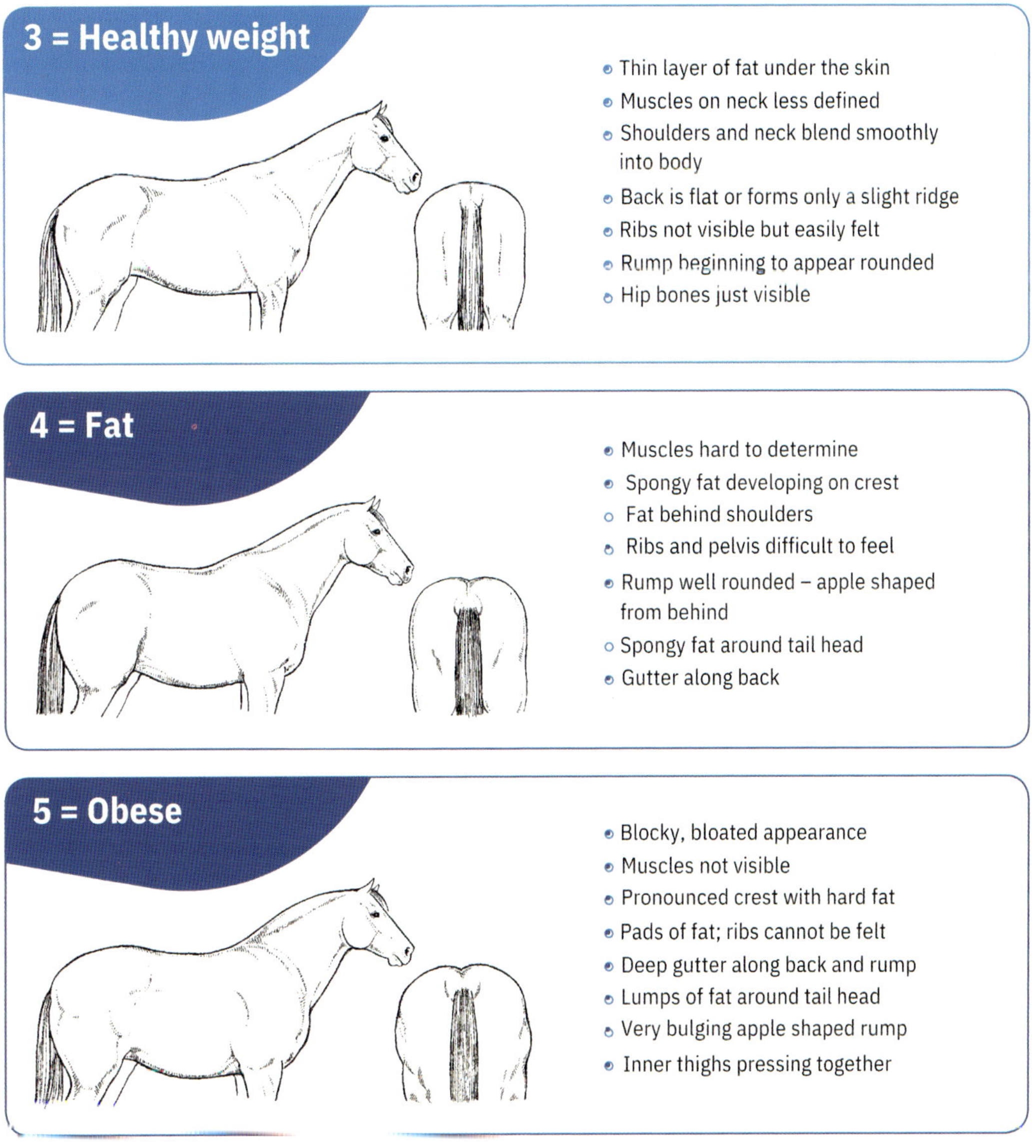

Figure 47: Condition scoring/fat scoring.

Causes of poor condition

Poor watering arrangements

A constant supply of fresh, clean water is essential to maintain the condition.

Insufficient feed intake

An ample supply of good-quality hay or grass is an essential basis to the diet.

Nutritional deficiencies in the diet

The pony may lack certain nutrients that are essential for their health and well-being.

Nutritional deficiencies in the diet

The pony may lack certain minerals, vitamins or fibre, most of which are in old pastures or good-quality meadow hay.

Indications of a craving for minerals are:

- Licking earth.
- Gnawing wood or bark.
- Eating dung (droppings).

Treatment: Check that your pony has access to a salt lick. It is best to feed plenty of fibre, such as meadow hay. Feed a proprietary brand of cubes or mix that contains a broad spectrum of vitamins and minerals.

Age: Unless they are fed carefully and are stabled overnight during the winter, old ponies may deteriorate to poor condition. From about fifteen years of age, they should be checked annually by a vet, both in their own interests and for the safety of their riders. Many ponies continue to work happily into their twenties.

Teeth: Defects in a pony's teeth can result in loss of condition and pain. Among the causes of discomfort in the mouth are sharp edges, teething and, occasionally, wolf teeth.

Teething: During teething, the mouth may be sore, so any work requiring the wearing of a bit should be curtailed. The problem usually resolves itself by age five, when teething is completed.

Wolf teeth: Small, underdeveloped teeth in front of the upper molars may or may not be present. If the tooth is immediately in front of the first molar and is firmly embedded, and if the bit is correctly fitted, there is no reason it should cause a problem. Wolf teeth are often blamed for an unsteady head carriage or reluctance to accept the bit, but this is rarely true. If the tooth is mobile (or, in other words, if it is not firmly embedded) or is sited further forward, it may be necessary to remove it.

Sharp edges: Ponies' teeth continue to grow after maturity. This balances the hard wear incurred when food, particularly hay and coarse grass, is masticated. Sometimes, the wear is uneven. The grinding process carried out by the molar (back) teeth often causes sharp edges to develop. These occur on the outside edges of the teeth of the upper jaw and the inside edges of those on the lower jaw. The inside of the cheeks and the tongue can become sore, and even ulcerated, chewing becomes painful and ineffective, and indigestion, reluctance to eat and loss of condition may result.

Eating problems

- Your pony drops food while chewing (called 'quidding').
- Takes much longer to finish meals.
- Leaves food in the feed bucket.
- Tilts head to one side while eating.
- Makes strange chewing motions or chews very slowly.

Behaviour changes

- Doesn't want to take the bit in their mouth.
- Tosses head up and down when or tacking up or while riding.
- Pulls to one side when you're leading or riding.
- Acts grumpy or uncomfortable during grooming around the face.
- He does not want you to touch their face or mouth area.

Physical signs

- Bad breath (worse than normal 'horse breath').
- Drooling more than usual.
- Swelling around the jaw or face.
- Cuts or sores you can see on their lips or gums.
- White or yellow discharge from the mouth.

Daily checks

- **Eating**: Watch how your pony eats. Are they eating normally?
- **Water**: Is your pony drinking enough water? Sore mouths can make ponies drink less.
- **Behaviour**: Is your pony acting like their normal self?

Worms

Worms are one of the most common causes of poor condition in ponies. They are often exposed to several types of internal parasites (worms). If the worm burden becomes too heavy, It can damage your pony's intestines, heart and lungs, making them sick and unhealthy. To reduce the likelihood of a pony getting worms, we can regularly pick up droppings from our fields, mainly if they are in small daily turnout paddocks.

To manage this, we should have a pony tested for worms regularly.

Take advice from your vet or suitably qualified person (SQP) on how you might do this.

Poo samples can be taken to assess how many worms are in your pony's system, and the wormer can be provided if needed to reduce this.

It is no longer recommended to routinely worm ponies as resistance to dewormers is a significant issue. Monitoring your pony's worm or worm egg counts and only worming when absolutely necessary is key.

Condition related to work

Fatness vs fitness

The fat, round, sleek appearance of a pony in soft condition at grass, though indicative of good health, is no indication of his physical fitness to undertake work. He will have excess weight to carry, which will cause strain on his limbs and organs.

The fit pony, in hard condition, can physically exert himself without damaging his health. Such exertion may be in the form of concentrated bursts of energy, such as in racing, pony trials and polo; or in prolonged, sustained effort, such as, long-distance competitions and driving; or in steady exertion over long periods, such as trekking.

A pony has progressive stages of fitness, similar to that of a human. The pony in light or medium work, such as hacking, or short periods of flat work and jumping, will not require the same degree of heart and lung fitness as a cross-country pony or hunter. It is true to say, however, that the fitter the pony, the better he can perform.

Getting your pony ready for harder work

- Start slowly so that your pony only works hard when they are already a bit fit from regular, gentle exercise.
- Monitor what you are feeding your pony, as this may need adapting if he loses weight, as he may need more energy and muscle-building food when working harder.
- Give your pony a day or two off each week as rest days.

First month plan:
The key is being patient and building up fitness gradually, just like athletes do.

- Week 1–2: Short, easy walks.
- Week 3–4: Work up to 1½ hours of walking with some trotting uphill.
- Make sure your pony walks with energy and keeps a steady pace.

The main idea is that ponies need to get fit gradually, just like people do when they start exercising. You wouldn't run a marathon without training first, and ponies need the same careful preparation.

A programme for getting a pony fit

A fittening programme would be expected to take between three to four months, assuming that the pony has been rested for a considerable time and is in soft but good condition. Remember that no two animals are the same. If in doubt, take expert advice. Adjusting the feed and increasing the exercise and work to bring the pony into hard condition must be gradual. Any pony that has had more than three months off will need longer than the twelve to fourteen weeks to bring into full work.

To start

- Check that your worming programme and your injections against influenza and tetanus are up to date.
- Have the teeth inspected and rasped if necessary.
- Check the fit of the tack, particularly the saddle.
- Make sure your pony's feet are in good condition (trimmed or shod).
- Trim and tidy up the mane, tail and heels as necessary.

Stage 1: Walking only

- Carry out daily walking work for at least three weeks.
- Start with roughly 30 minutes and build up to 1 to 1½ hours.
- If the pony has been rested for more than three months or due to an injury, the walking stage should be extended to six weeks and built up to 2 hours per day.
- After exercise, ensure that the pony is sponged clean of sweat marks and that there is no sign of galling under the saddle or girth.
- The saddle, numnah and girth must be kept clean and dry.
- Applying salt water or surgical spirit helps to harden the pony's skin.

Stage 2: Muscling-up

- Combine walking with slow trotting for the same periods and extend the exercise for up to 2 hours.

- Active walking, particularly uphill, is a tremendous muscle builder and does not cause undue strain or jarring to the legs.
- Some steady trotting on a hard road helps to harden the legs, but if overdone, particularly with older ponies, it can cause jarring to the feet and legs.
- Schooling on the flat, some slow cantering, and some simple jumping can be included towards the end of the stage.

Stage 3: Further muscling-up and developing the cardiovascular system

- After six weeks, your pony should be ready to canter in a more open area. This will continue the muscling-up process and help clear his wind.
- A good hill to work on at a slower pace is helpful.
- Choose good going and only canter slowly to develop the heart and lungs' efficiency. Start with by cantering for 1 to 2 minutes for two or three sets, which should be mixed with rests or walk or slow trotting.
- Increase the distance gradually.
- Towards the end of the period, the pony should cover about a mile in a strong canter, but not a gallop, once or twice a week.
- On other days of the week, he should be schooled, jumped, or hacked out for exercise.

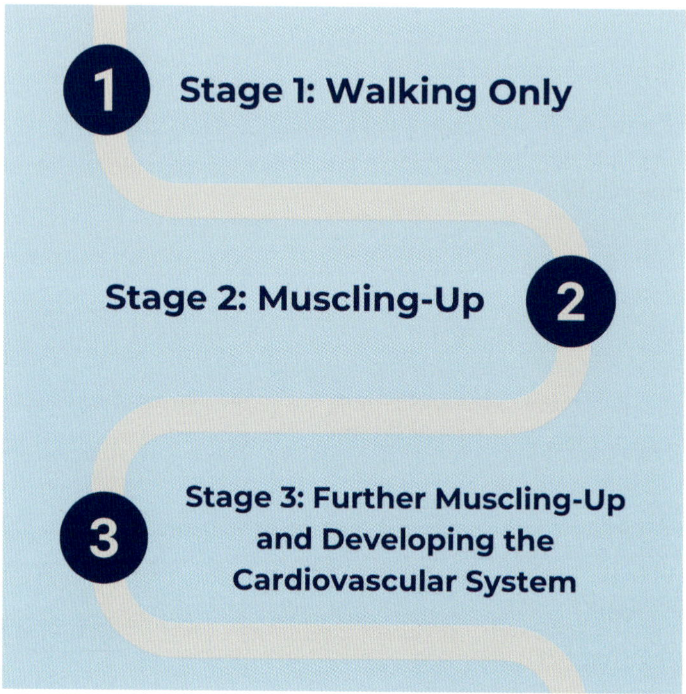

Figure 48: Fittening programme.

Lungeing

Lungeing is a means of exercising a pony when he is not being ridden. The pony moves in a circle around the person lungeing him and is controlled by a long lungeing rein attached to a lungeing cavesson on the pony's head.

Lungeing is also particularly useful in the following cases:

- When an exuberant pony needs to be settled before being ridden.
- When a pony has a sore or injured back and cannot tolerate a saddle.
- When a rider is, for some reason, unable to ride a particular pony, if you are sufficiently skilled, you may exercise the pony on the lunge.
- For the pony who has been rested for a long time, it will re-accustom him to the feel of being worked.

Note: Lungeing is hard work, especially for the unfit pony. Do not continue for longer than about 20–25 minutes.

Keeping your pony fit

Once the pony has reached a degree of fitness and competes regularly, he will not need as much exercise and work as in the interim periods. However, if he is stabled, he should still be ridden or led out every day.

Ponies at grass

They are very adaptable and will maintain a good degree of fitness if they are ridden at weekends and possibly once during the week; if they are kept at an appropriate weight.

The pony will need some conditioning to prepare him for the holidays when you will be riding more than usual. If no one is light enough to ride him, he should be led from another pony or lunged as an occasional alternative.

Roughing off

- This is the process whereby a fit pony is prepared for a rest on grass, day and night, for a prolonged period – for example, rest periods for competition ponies. The process must be gradual and should take ten days to a fortnight.
- Gradually reduce the hard feed and the work. Increase the hay and/or periods of grazing, thus ensuring that the pony has enough to eat.
- Stop grooming to allow the coat to form a natural oily protection.
- Remove rugs gradually. Having reduced the clothing to a single light rug, remove it during the day and replace it at night if the weather is cold.

Figure 49: How to keep your pony fit.

- Remove shoes and trim feet.
- Either gradually increase the time spent out at grass until his diet is based on grazing and his coat gives him sufficient protection to stay out all the time.

First aid

When to call the vet

If you think there is a problem but don't know what to do, the vet is the best person to call. A vet will be able to give you good advice on vaccinations, worming programmes, feeding, regular check-ups by the dentist and other ways to keep your pony healthy.

Call the vet immediately if your pony is distressed and you think it's an emergency – he's been hurt badly, looks sick, or won't eat.

If you can't speak to the vet or livery yard owner, contact your Pony Club coach or trainer rather than wait to see if the problem worsens.

Routine visits

You and the veterinary surgeon form an important partnership that helps ensure a pony's health. A vet can help in several situations.

- Prevent diseases before they occur by regular flu and tetanus vaccinations, as well as worming and teeth rasping.
- Diagnosis and treatment. If a pony is ill, has developed swelling, or is lame, you must make an appointment with your vet.
- Assessment of the pony before purchase; either by yourself or through a riding school. Your vet will examine the pony and, if appropriate, will issue a certificate that at the time of the examination, he found no clinical signs of disease, injury or physical abnormality likely to affect the pony's usefulness for your purpose.

Wounds which need immediate veterinary attention

There are many types of wounds. Some are easily managed, some need veterinary attention, and a few are emergencies. Blood spurting in a jet from a wound is from a damaged artery, and the bleeding must be stopped.

Action: Push a clean wad of cotton wool, Gamgee, or disposable nappy firmly into the wound. Hold or bandage it in place to slow the bleeding. Contact the vet.

Emergency visits

Make sure you have the number of your local equine vet stored in your phone, and displayed clearly and in plain sight on the yard in case someone finds a pony in distress.

Before calling an equine vet in an emergency, you should know whether the pony is covered by insurance as well as the excess level. You must be prepared to provide your name, postcode, directions to find the pony and mobile phone number. Try to remain calm and describe exactly what is wrong. Prompt action can be the difference between life and death or between a permanently lame pony and one that can return to full work.

Common signs of illness include dullness or depression, separation from other ponies with whom he is turned out, not eating or not finishing his food, weight loss, sweating, abnormal breathing, a runny nose, and an increase in temperature.

Signs of colic or stomach pain include sweating, not eating, box walking, with the pony looking at his sides, a tendency to lie down and get up repeatedly, and rolling. Reluctance to move may indicate laminitis.

Swelling or heat in a leg may indicate infection in the foot, cellulitis, cracked heels or tendon or ligament injury. Nodding of the head at the trot indicates forelimb lameness. Dragging a hind toe may also indicate lameness.

What is an emergency?

The following conditions all require veterinary attention as soon as possible:

- Severe lameness.
- Severe wounds.
- Colic.
- Difficulty in breathing.
- Choking for more than 20 minutes unless caused by dry sugar beet.
- Tetanus.

Symptoms which might indicate the presence of these conditions include

- Sweating; lying down and getting up a lot; rolling.
- Reluctance to move.
- Severe stiffness.
- Lameness at the walk.
- Very swollen leg.
- Difficulty breathing.
- Food material or thick discharge from the nostrils.
- Severe blinking or discharge from the eye.

Symptoms requiring veterinary attention within the day

The following symptoms do require veterinary attention but are generally not emergencies:

- Nasal discharge (running nose).
- Discharge from an eye.
- Cough.
- Abnormal breathing pattern.
- Abnormal breathing noise during exercise.
- Depressed appetite.
- Difficulty in eating.
- Weight loss.
- Drinking a lot and urinating a lot.
- Soft faeces or diarrhoea.
- Rubbing the mane or tail.
- Patchy hair loss.

- Abnormally long hair coat.
- Skin lumps.
- Lameness.
- Poor exercise tolerance.
- Poor performance.
- Abnormal behaviour.

General wound management

First aid kit

It is useful to have around a box of basic veterinary equipment. It should include:

- A clean bucket and a small container.
- Blunt-ended scissors to trim the hair from around a wound.
- A thermometer (digital or mercury).
- At least one roll of clean cotton wool is needed to clean wounds.
- A commercial antiseptic solution for cleaning wounds. The best contains chlorhexidine and should be available from your vet, such as Hibiscrub. An alternative is povidone iodine (Pevidine scrub).
- Non-adherent dressings (e.g. Melolin or Jelonet gauze) to apply to wounds.
- Disposable nappy to use as an absorbent pad for wounds and poultices.
- Gamgee, to wrap around a leg before bandaging, or clean Fibregee, or other soft conforming bandage, e.g. Soffban.
- Clean, non-stick bandages, e.g. crêpe bandages or stable bandages.
- Sticky bandage, e.g. Vetwrap, Elastoplast.
- Roll of adhesive tape.
- Animalintex poultice.
- Epsom salts, for 'tubbing' a foot.

Wound powders, creams, hydrogen peroxide, and salves are unnecessary and potentially harmful in the wrong hands.

Treating an injury

The size of the cut does not necessarily reflect its severity. A small superficial graze can be managed by clipping and cleaning the surrounding hair thoroughly. Any larger wound, a wound with severe bleeding, a deep puncture wound or any wound close to a joint, a tendon sheath or a tendon, or a wound on the back of the fetlock or pastern should be examined by a vet, who will assess whether vital structures may have been damaged and whether the wound needs stitching (suturing). If you have any questions, call the vet.

Cleaning the wound

Clip or trim the hair surrounding the wound with scissors so that hairs do not lie in it. Wash the wound with clean water from a clean container, preferably using an appropriate antiseptic solution such as chlorhexidine (Hibiscrub) or povidine iodine (Pevidine). Soak small wads of cotton wool in warm water. Squeeze the water out; water dripping down the pony's leg may frighten him. Pour some antiseptic solution onto the cotton wool and rub the wound. Repeat with multiple clean pieces of cotton wool for at least 5 minutes or longer if the wound is not clean. If the wound is dirty, wash it from above with a hose first. Careful and thorough cleaning will help to prevent infection.

Do not apply wound ointments/powders. They may make dirt stick and attract infection. Superficial minor cuts will heal quickly if the wound edges are close together. If possible, apply a non-stick dressing and then bandage the wound.

Keep the pony in a stable if you can. Wounds heal more quickly if the edges are not moving continuously and if it is easier to keep the wound clean. If the pony is out on grass and it is impossible to keep the wound covered, a fly repellent may be necessary around (but not in) the wound.

Check vaccination status

Further treatment is not required if the pony is fully vaccinated against tetanus. Still, if it is more than a year since the pony was vaccinated or the vaccination status is unknown, it is essential to call the vet, who will treat the pony with tetanus antitoxin and booster vaccination. Tetanus is a potentially life-threatening complication of any wound.

Puncture wounds

These can be dangerous because the surface cut may be small, but it is difficult to assess their depth, and bacteria are often pushed deep into the tissues. These wounds are, therefore, difficult to clean thoroughly. If there is any chance that the wound is near a tendon or a joint or on the back of the pastern, you must call a vet as an emergency. If the wound is not near any of these structures, a poultice is generally advisable and may help to clean it, but your vet may need to give antibiotics to control deep infection.

Large cuts

If the wound edges are brought together using stitches or staples, they will heal quickly. The final cosmetic result will also be much better: the amount of scarring will be reduced.

Bruised areas

These may benefit from cold poulticing for 24 hours to help reduce painful swelling. After this period, increasing circulation to the area is necessary to help remove the inflammation. This is best achieved by gentle movement. The exception may be if a wound has been sutured (stitched) since movement may disrupt wound healing. Your vet will be able to advise you about this.

Self-inflicted wounds

These are grazes, cuts or bruising inflicted by the pony knocking himself when he moves. Self-inflicted wounds sometimes happen purely by accident, but some chronic occurrences may result from weakness caused by immaturity or poor condition, faulty action, poor conformation, and inappropriate shoeing. Treat self-inflicted wounds according to their severity. Ask your farrier how trimming and shoeing might help.

- **Brushing** is when one foreleg or hind leg strikes the opposite foreleg or hind leg.
- **Overreaching** is when a back foot overreaches and treads on the bulb of the heel of a front foot. An overreach can result in a skin wound and bruising. The bruising may cause lameness for 24 to 48 hours, especially on hard ground. Some skin flaps will not heal and need to be cut off. Clean the wound thoroughly. If there is a big skin deficit, consider bandaging the heel; the bandage needs to extend beneath the branches of the shoe. If the laceration is deep and the edges are not jagged, it may heal best if your vet stitches it.
- **Strikes** happen in a similar way to overreaches but higher up the leg. Sometimes, the cut may even penetrate the tendon.
- **Forging/pulling shoes off**: forging is the term applied when a pony hits the toe of a front shoe with the toe of a hind shoe. It may occur because the pony is unbalanced, or his feet are inappropriately trimmed and shod. Some ponies may tend to pull front shoes off by treading on the heel of a shoe with a hind foot. Chunks of the hoof wall may thus be pulled away, which can cause problems in replacing the shoe. It can abruptly halt the stride, possibly resulting in a tendon or ligament injury. If the shoe is pulled off a long way from home, the foot may become bruised on the return journey. Seek advice from your vet and your farrier on resolving the problem.
- **Treads** are wounds to the coronet region caused by the pony being trodden on or treading on himself, usually while travelling.

If your pony tends to brush, overreach, or strike into themselves, brushing boots, overreach boots, or tendon boots used appropriately will help to protect their legs. However, note that rubber overreach boots tend to rub if they are worn for hours at a time. When travelling, the pony can be protected from treads with padding over the coronet band secured by stable bandages.

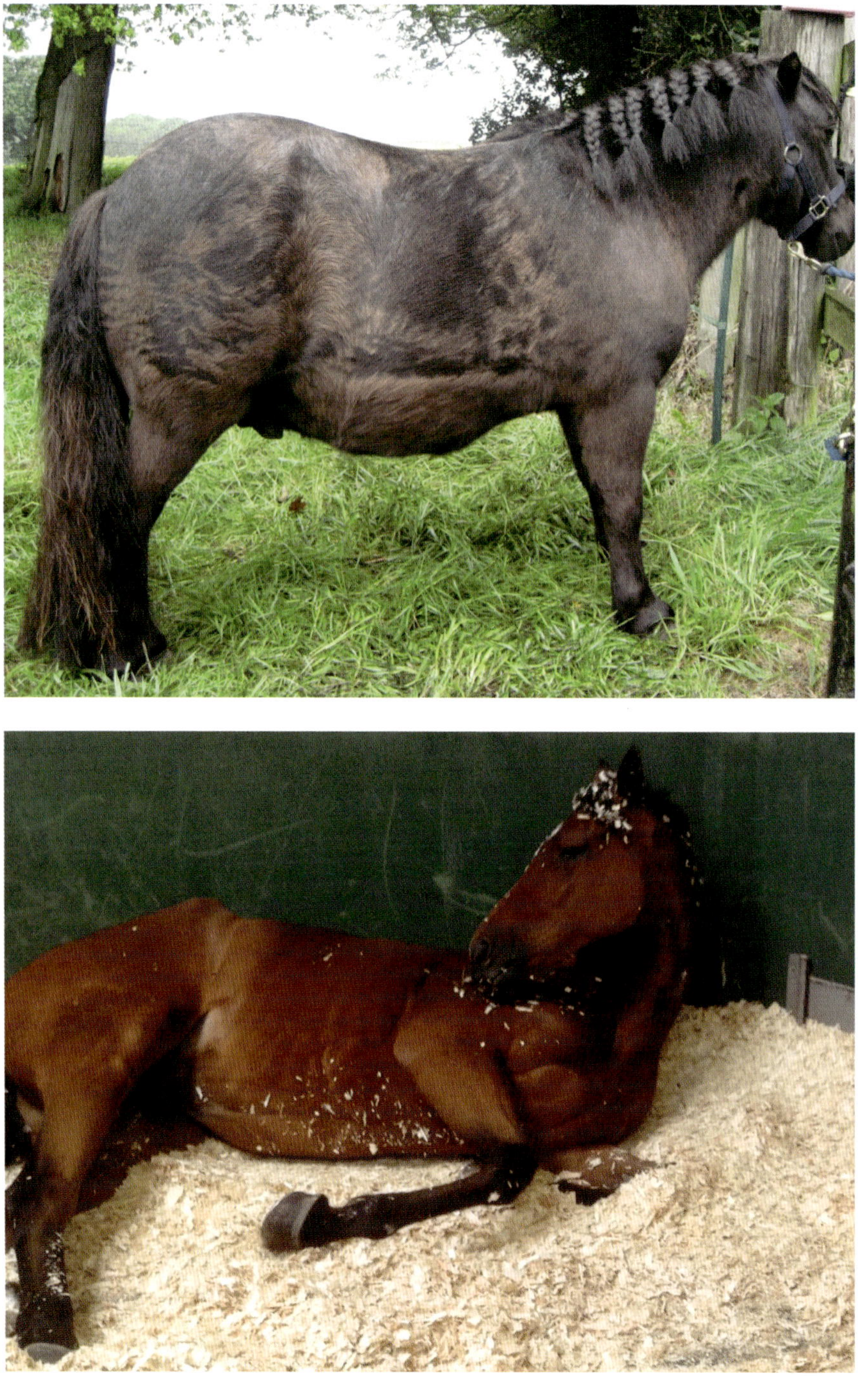

Figure 50: Images of laminitis and colic.

There are several key behaviours that your pony might show you, indicating that he is not very well or poorly.

Colic (upset stomach). Your pony may have stopped eating, maybe sweating, and turning their head to look towards their belly as they become uncomfortable. They may paw the ground and try to urinate. This may be followed by trying to roll. The vet should be called immediately, as this can be a very serious issue.

Fever: A fever is when your pony's temperature becomes 1° above normal. It may indicate that he is getting a cold or a virus such as the flu. His vital signs (TPR) should be monitored, and the vet should be called immediately.

Coughing (more than a normal cough when your pony might clear their throat when you begin to ride them). It is important to note if it's a wet cough with mucus in their throat, and they may have runny eyes and nose. You should note whether the mucus is white, yellow, or green.

Diarrhoea (loose, running manure) or dry, hard manure balls can lead to dehydration and should be monitored.

Unusual eating habits: If the pony refuses to eat, he drools or drops food.

Losing weight, having a dull coat, or a behaviour change.

Injuries: Any cut, swelling, heat or tenderness in a leg or on his body; a closed or swollen eye; bleeding or lameness.

Important information to give the vet

If the vet must be called, you should first write down all the pony's symptoms, if possible, and get an experienced horse person to take his vital signs (temperature, pulse and respiration). You should record how long he has had symptoms and if you have done anything before calling the vet; giving the vet as much information as possible will help them decide how to look after him.

Recognising lameness

Lameness is when a pony cannot walk or trot normally, and he 'favours' – or limps on – his sore leg. He may be standing with his weight on the good leg and resting the sore one. He may try not to take his weight onto the sore leg when he moves.

If it is the **front leg** he will try to lift his head up as the sore leg comes to the ground.

If it is his **hind leg**, he will lift his hip higher than the opposite one and drop his head down as the sore foot comes to the ground.

To find out if he is lame

- Lead him in walk, jog or trot in hand, with someone watching to see how he moves.
- Keep your lead rein loose so he can freely move his head up and down.
- Walk a straight line on hard, level ground.
- Sometimes, you can hear him take a heavier beat as his lame (sore) leg is placed on the ground, such as 'clip, CLOP'.
- The sore leg usually takes a shorter step.

If a pony goes lame:

- First, check his feet by cleaning them out and looking for a twisted shoe or something stuck in his foot, such as a stone or nail.
- Feel his legs to see if anything is sore or tender, or if he moves his leg away from you.
- When you touch him, a leg may feel hot or puffy.
- It would help if you compared the lame leg with the other leg.
- Call your vet or ask a knowledgeable person for advice, and don't ride him until you have determined the problem and treated it.
- Some lameness can get worse if you ride or work your pony.
- If your pony has a minor cut on his leg, it should be safe to clean it and put antibiotic ointment on, while waiting for someone to check for you.

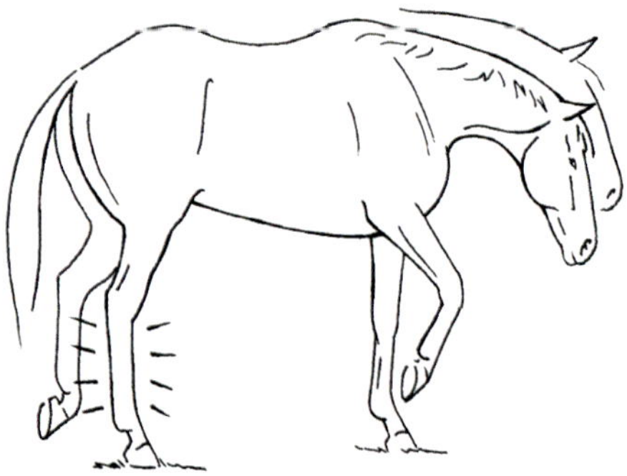

Figure 51: How to assess lameness in the front limbs and back limbs.

Chapter 9

Tack and Equipment

Tack and Equipment

Choosing a saddle

Saddlery, often called tack, is a necessary and frequently expensive investment. The basic requirement is a saddle with its fittings, girth, stirrup leathers and stirrup irons, plus usually a numnah or saddlecloth and a bridle with its bit.

An enormous variety of saddlery and additional items is available to suit different ponies and types of riding. In this book we will deal mainly with what you need for general-purpose riding and schooling. Always check with an expert, or The Pony Club rule books if you are unsure whether an item is permitted.

Good saddlery

A well-fitted and clean saddle contributes greatly to both the pony's and rider's comfort and appearance.

Well-fitted saddlery will:

- Fit both the pony and rider.
- Be of the correct type for its purpose.
- Be well cared for, clean, and supple.

Badly fitting saddlery will:

- Be dangerous for both ponies and riders.
- Cause pain and injury to the pony.
- Devalue an expensive investment.

Buying saddlery

Seek expert advice when buying saddlery. A good place to start is with someone who is registered with the Society of Master Saddlers and/or holds its saddle-fitting qualification. It is not recommended that you make important purchases via the internet; it does not always work out cheaper, and you cannot put a price on being able to examine tack and benefit from knowledgeable advice. Checking the fit and suitability, particularly of the saddle and the bit, requires knowledge and experience.

Leatherwork

Leather is the best material for long life and comfort. Good saddlery is made of the best leather and is, therefore, expensive. You can buy it second-hand, but if you do, check that the stitching and leather are in good condition and ensure the saddle tree is not broken. Many kinds of inferior saddlery are on the market, and some may even be dangerous. Some synthetic saddlery has improved enormously in quality, design and appearance but is unlikely to last as long as well-cared-for leather tack. Brightly coloured tack is not recommended for general use.

Metalwork

- Bits and stirrup irons should be made of the highest-quality materials.
- Stainless steel is the safest and most satisfactory. Plated metal chips and flakes off.
- Bits are measured in centimetres. As a rough guide, find a bit which fits the pony and measure the width of the mouthpiece for the type and size of bit that your pony needs.

Bridles

Bridles and their parts are made in many styles and sizes, often labelled as 'pony', 'cob', and 'full', but the size of the pony does not always relate to the size of his head. Sometimes you may need to mix and match parts to achieve a good fit; for instance, you may need to use a full-size headpiece with cob-size cheekpieces. When a bridle is fitted correctly on a pony, the buckles should be on or near the centre holes – so that, if necessary, minor adjustments can be made up or down. For the parts of the bridle and how to assemble them, *see* Figure 60.

The saddle

A good saddle is an investment to be proud of, and if treated with care, it will last a lifetime. Before making this important choice, it is helpful to understand the saddle's functions and have a basic knowledge of how it is constructed. The saddle should be comfortable for both the pony and rider. Its purpose is to distribute the rider's weight and help them maintain a correct position as evenly as possible over the pony's back.

Not every design is suitable for all ponies, all saddles must be fitted by a professional saddle fitter to fit both pony and rider. Saddles should be checked twice yearly to ensure the pony stays comfortable while he muscles up and changes shape.

The structure of the saddle

The tree

Most saddles are built on a tree, a framework that can be made from and incorporate various materials, including laminated wood, flexible steel, carbon, and plastics. The tree's size, width and profile together determine the saddle's size and width, and whether it will suit the shape of the pony's back. Most trees have some flexibility. Buying from a knowledgeable, reputable saddler will help ensure that you buy a saddle built on a tree that meets relevant specifications, is undamaged, and is suitable for you and your pony. You may also see saddles which are built on partial trees or are treeless.

The seat

The seat is built on a base of webbing strips stretched along and across the tree. These strips must be of exactly the correct tension if the saddle's seat is to have the right dip, with its deepest part in the centre. The seat is padded over the webbing and covered by leather.

Girth straps

Girth straps are attached to the webbing strips stretched crosswise over the tree. There will be two, three, or four straps; most designs are attached by separate webbing over the tree. For safety, the girth should always be buckled to the first strap and either the second or the third.

Stirrup bars

These are attached to the tree and are traditionally open-ended to allow the stirrup leathers (looped over them) to slip off, thus preventing a rider from being dragged after a fall if a foot is caught in the stirrup iron. On most stirrup bars, a hinge allows the point to be turned up so that the leather will not slip off when a saddled pony is being led without a rider. The points should never be up when the pony is being ridden. Bars which are not open-ended or are in the form of a D are unsafe unless safety stirrups are used.

The panel

The panel is the underside of the saddle, acting as a cushion for the pony. It is padded and shaped to ensure that the rider's weight is evenly distributed over the back muscles and that the pony's spine is completely protected, untouched by the saddle. Therefore, panels should be soft, wide and flat, with a wide gullet running between them. Various panel designs incorporate knee rolls at the front, which help the rider maintain a correct leg position. Some also have thigh rolls behind the rider's legs.

Figure 52: Structure of the saddle.

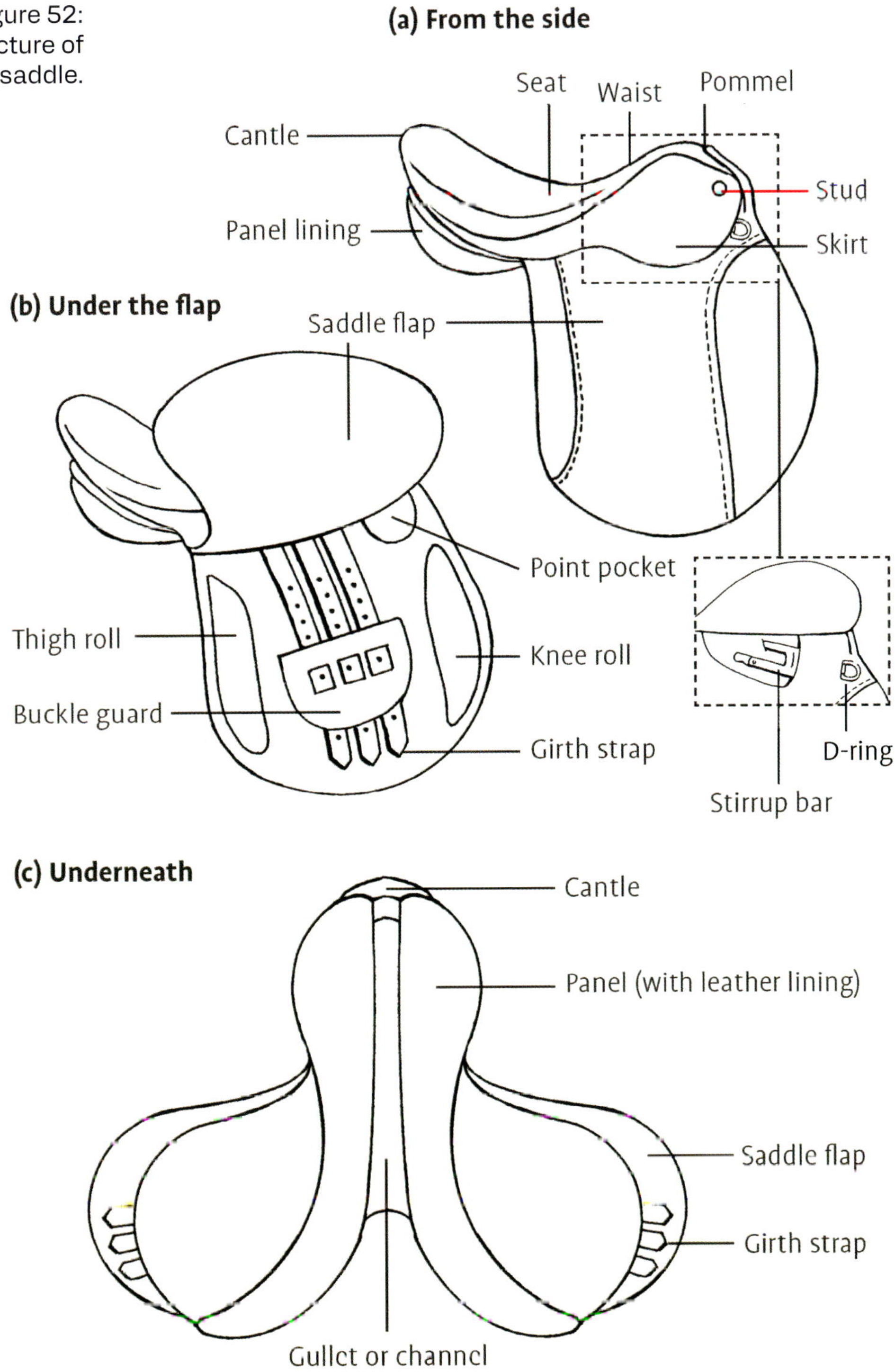

Full and half-panels

A full panel is sometimes quilted almost to the bottom of the saddle flap. A half-panel only cushions the rider's weight for the pony. It reaches halfway down the saddle flap and has a large sweat flap on which the girth buckles lie.

Single (or mono) flap and double (standard) flap saddles

The two designs are made slightly differently, but the only variation for the rider is that the single flap has a single thickness of leather under the rider's thigh. In contrast, the double flap design has a double thickness.

Stuffings

All panels are stuffed, either with wool or a wool mix (pure wool is superior), synthetic foam, felt, or they are air-filled. The panel must never feel lumpy, especially in weight-bearing areas. A new saddle should have symmetrically stuffed panels, but there may be occasions when a saddler will alter the stuffing distribution to accommodate a pony's asymmetry. However, a saddler may prefer to suggest the use of a numnah incorporating removable pads to achieve the same effect. The reason for a pony's asymmetry should be investigated, which inevitably demands input from a vet.

Linings

Leather linings are easy to clean and last long if they are well looked after and the saddle is used frequently. Clean other materials according to the manufacturer's instructions.

Buckle guards

All saddles should have buckle guards to prevent the girth buckles from damaging the saddle flap. Some guards are detachable, and others are attached under the saddle flap.

Types, sizes and widths of saddles

Types

A saddle must fit the pony and rider. It must also be suitable for purpose. You do not need a specialist saddle; a well-designed general purpose saddle will allow you to take part in all Pony Club activities.

The most common types of saddle in use by English-style riders are:

General-purpose saddle

As its name implies, this saddle is designed for general riding and is suitable for most Pony Club activities. The saddle flaps' cut, and the seat's length are midway between dressage and show-jumping saddles.

Dressage saddle

This has a straight-cut flap and is designed to accommodate a longer, straighter leg position than that used for hacking or jumping. It is fitted with long straps and a short girth to prevent the girth buckles from lying under the rider's thigh. Most, but not all, dressage saddles have a deeper rather than a flatter seat, but, as always, they must be built on a tree that suits the profile of the pony's back

General purpose

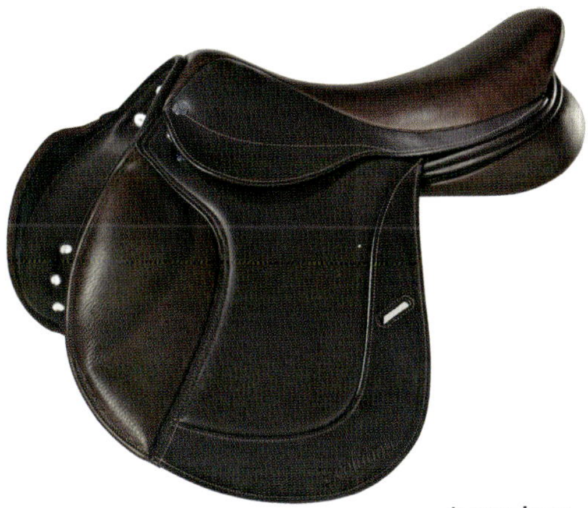

Jumping

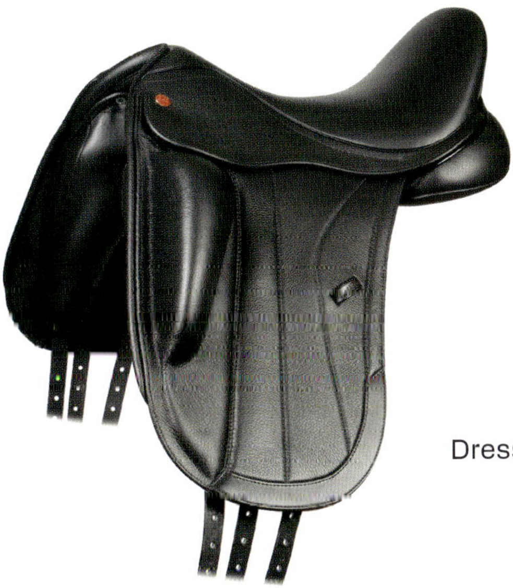

Dressage

Racing

Figure 53: Different types of saddles.

Show-jumping saddle

This type of saddle usually has a flatter seat than the dressage type. It is designed for riding with shorter stirrup leathers and has a forward-cut saddle flap. Some saddles are designed specifically for cross-country. They have flat seats to allow maximum adjustment of the rider's position and will accommodate a shorter stirrup length than that used for show jumping.

Synthetic saddles

These types of saddles are being produced in ever-increasing quantities and of ever-increasing quality. In some cases, they may be a cheaper but more satisfactory substitute for leather.

Showing saddle

Modern designs have a straighter flap than general-purpose saddles, but they are not as straight cut as dressage models and have flat seats. Care must be taken that the saddle does not make it difficult for the rider, especially a child, to maintain balance and stability. A working hunter saddle usually falls halfway between a general purpose and a dressage model.

Designs for small children

Pad saddles made from felt were traditionally used for very small children. They have either no tree, or just a tree forepart. These are still available and if used, should have a tree forepart or front arch to help the child sit correctly. Some pad saddles are fitted with D-rings instead of standard stirrup bars. In these cases, the stirrup leathers are attached firmly to the saddle, so safety stirrups must be used to prevent a rider being dragged after a fall. Get expert advice on whether the girth straps, attachments and the girth itself are safe before using a traditional pad. Some modern, synthetic designs are more comfortable and give greater support. When

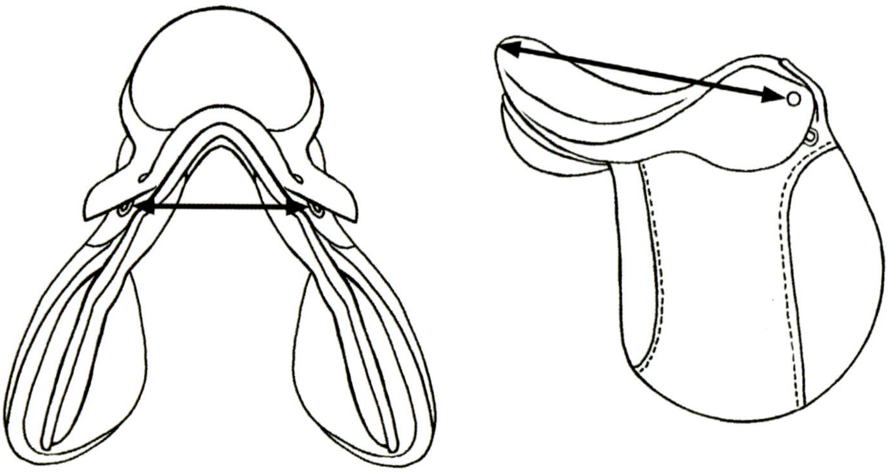

Figure 54: How to measure a saddle.

small children are learning to ride, a saddle must give enough security to help them find balance and confidence.

Measuring the width of a pony for a saddle

Size

Saddle seat sizes are measured from the metal stud at the side of the pommel to the cantle. Standard sizes are from 38 to 45.7cm (15 to 18in). The saddle should be the correct size for the shape and size of the rider.

Widths

Many types and sizes of saddle are made in three widths, narrow, medium and wide. Some saddles are also produced in extra-wide versions. The width of the saddle must be correct for the width of the pony. When choosing a new saddle, decide with your saddler's help, on one which fits your pony and suits the length and profile of his back and is of the type and size appropriate to your own needs.

If you are buying a new saddle or having an old one re-stuffed, the saddler needs to know the width and shape (profile) of your pony's back. The saddler should measure the pony and fit the saddle for you. The usual method of taking a wither profile, which will help decide on the correct width, is to use a flexible ruler, usually called a Flexi-Curve or something similar. This is moulded over the withers, about 5cm (2in) back from the point of the shoulder (scapula) where the front arch of the saddle should rest. Lift it off and pencil the shape (inside) on a piece of stiff paper or cardboard.

Fitting the saddle to the pony

Fitting saddles is a specialist job, but riders need to be aware of fitting criteria, so they know when to call in a saddler to check and adjust a saddle if necessary. The guidelines below apply whether you are buying a new or second-hand saddle.

A pony will change shape with the seasons and with the amount of work he's doing. Also, if your pony has any exaggerated conformation points, such as very prominent withers, or if the balance of the saddle needs to be adjusted so it sits correctly on the pony's back without tipping you forward or back, your saddler must fit the saddle to the pony and make any necessary adjustments.

Note: When a pony is fat, perhaps after a summer's rest, the saddle that fits him when he is in hard condition may perch too high on his back. In this case, it is better to begin riding him in a wider saddle than to risk spreading the tree of your best saddle, which he will use later. Both saddles should be fitted with equal care.

The saddle will be fitted without a numnah, but the saddler will, if necessary, make any adjustments to consider any numnahs or pads which need to go underneath it.

The tree of the saddle must be the correct width for the pony. If it is too wide the arch will be too low over the withers and press down on them. If it is too narrow, the panel on each side of the channel will pinch the spine, and there will be too much pressure underneath the points of the tree. Saddles may have a broken tree (see later on how to recognise this) and cannot be used.

You should be able to see a clear passage all the way through the channel over the pony's spine, although the saddle should not perch too high on the pony's back. Ponies with high withers will sometimes suit a saddle with a cut-back head, or pommel, which may be a more comfortable fit than a saddle with a high arch.

There must be no weight on the loins. This may happen if the saddle is too long.

The saddle should lie flat on the pony's back and the centre of the seat should be the lowest point.

The saddle must not hamper the movement of the pony's shoulders. This may happen if the panel is too forward-cut, or if the saddle is fitted too close to the back of the scapula/shoulder.

The panel must be correctly stuffed so that the rider is able to maintain contact with the pony. It should also provide some support to the knee. There should be sufficient stuffing at the back so that the seat does not slope, causing the rider to slide backwards.

The saddle must not slip forward. If it does so on a fat pony or on one with flat withers, ask your saddler to advise you on ways to prevent this movement while allowing freedom of the shoulders. For some ponies it may be necessary to fit a crupper (see Additional fittings later).

The effect of the saddle on the rider

The saddle must be the correct size for the rider too. One that is too small will not be comfortable, and the rider's knees will overlap the saddle flap. One that's too large may affect the rider's security and balance.

The saddle must allow the rider to sit in the centre of balance without tension. The seat must not slope down towards the back. If it does, the rider will sit on the back of the saddle with the lower leg stuck forward. If the saddle slopes up too much at the back, it will pitch the rider forward. If the saddle slopes to one side (which can be due to unlevel stuffing OR because the rider puts more weight on one stirrup than the other), it will sit crookedly. A saddle which puts the rider out of balance may do so because:

- The design is faulty.
- It does not fit the pony.
- It does not fit the rider.

If any of the above points happen, it is time to call the saddler as the saddle will need re-stuffing to put it into balance. If you buy a new saddle, your saddler should check it after it has had time to settle. He or she will tell you when this needs to be done.

Testing for a broken tree

Knowing how to do this is useful, especially when buying a second-hand saddle; however, if in any doubt, always seek expert advice, as a saddle with a broken tree should not be used. The saddle should be checked before it is placed on the pony.

The front arch

If the front arch is broken, the saddle will tend to fit too low and will probably touch the top of the withers.

To check for a break, apply strong hand pressure to the points (on each side of the saddle), pressing them towards, and then away from, each other. There should be no movement or noise (click or squeak).

Do not confuse the movement of the flexible ends of the points with that of a broken tree. If the tree is broken, the movement will come either from underneath the arch, which is the most usual place, or from the area of the metal stirrup bars upwards to the arch of the saddle.

The cantle

Check that the cantle is rigid. If you can twist it, the tree has broken. A rider who mounts from the ground and pulls on the cantle not only causes discomfort to the pony but may damage the tree. This is one very good reason to always use a mounting block when getting on a pony.

The waist

Hold the saddle in front of you with one hand under the cantle and the other under the pommel. Lift one of your knees above the saddle, press down on the waist, and carefully try to bend it in the middle. Or press the cantle in towards your ribs and try to bend the waist by pulling the pommel in towards you.

A spring tree saddle when tested in this way should flex across the centre of the waist and seat. It should feel as if it is about to spring back firmly into place. If the spring tree is weakened or broken, you will feel a softness and lack of spring. A spring tree is liable to break on one side, so you may well feel more give on that side only.

Be careful not to confuse a broken tree with a well-used spring tree, which although it may have become very soft, still retains its springiness. A broken spring tree is almost impossible to repair, as reinforcement would eliminate the spring effect of the tree. Wrinkled leather across the seat is often a sign of a broken tree.

A twisted tree

This would injure a pony's back, so it must be recognised. From the cantle, look towards the pommel to check that the cantle and pommel are symmetrical in relation to each other. A rider pulling on the cantle while mounting from the ground can cause the tree to twist. Again, whenever possible, use a mounting block.

Saddle fittings: girths and stirrups

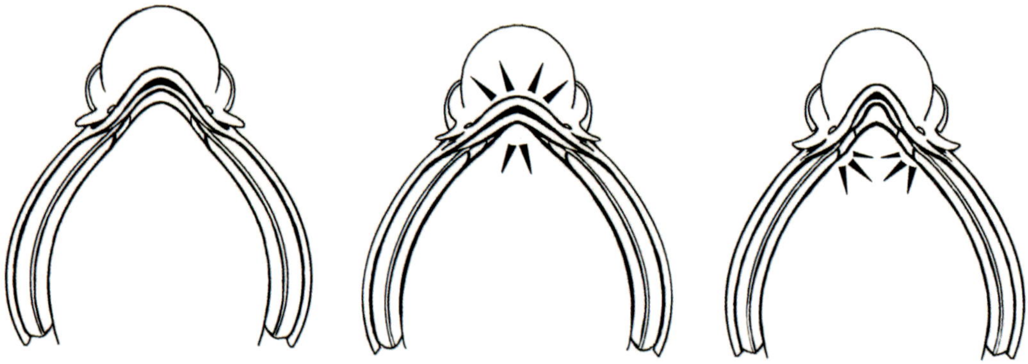

Figure 55: Saddle width fittings (left to right): correct, too wide causes pressure on withers, too narrow pinches at withers.

Girths

A girth keeps the saddle secure on your pony's back, so it is vital for your safety and his comfort and efficiency. Any stitching should be checked regularly. Girth sizes, including the buckles, are determined by their measurement from end to end. Girths are most frequently made of leather or soft but strong synthetic material, sometimes incorporating cotton. A girth's design and the material from which it is made should help to ensure that it does not pinch the pony behind the elbow.

'Humane girths' are deemed to be unsafe, as many common designs will cause the girth to fail completely if a single strap breaks. These girths are not permitted in training or competition. In some activities such as polo, they can be worn, as an additional surcingle is worn. This is why it is important to always check the individual rule books before choosing to use a humane girth.

Leather girths

These are very satisfactory and wear well, but you should pay particular attention to the stitching for your own safety and to the softness and cleanliness for the comfort of the pony.

The traditional Atherstone girth is shaped for the comfort of the pony. You will also see curved leather girths, said to add to saddle security and increase the comfort and even the stride length of the pony. These are often referred to in general as anatomical girths (fit the individual body shape of the pony).

Elasticated girths

Leather or synthetic girths may have an elastic insert at one or both ends, between the main girth and the buckles or at the centre. This allows greater freedom of movement and eases the pony's breathing, especially across country.

Synthetic, string.

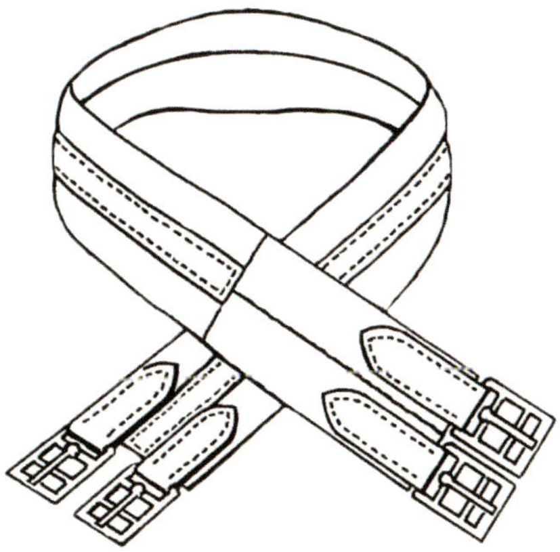

Elasticated.

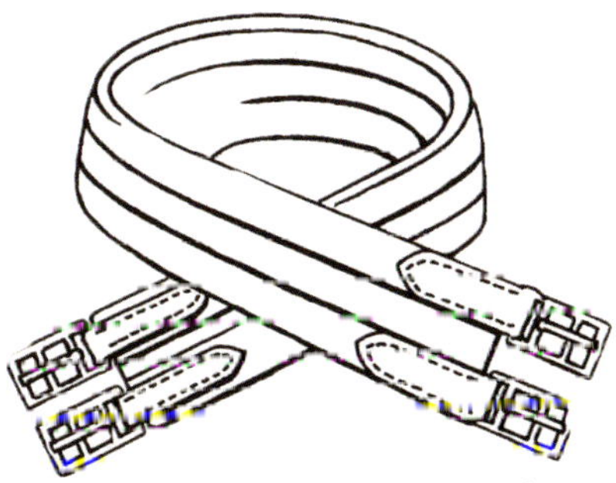

Leather non-elasticated.

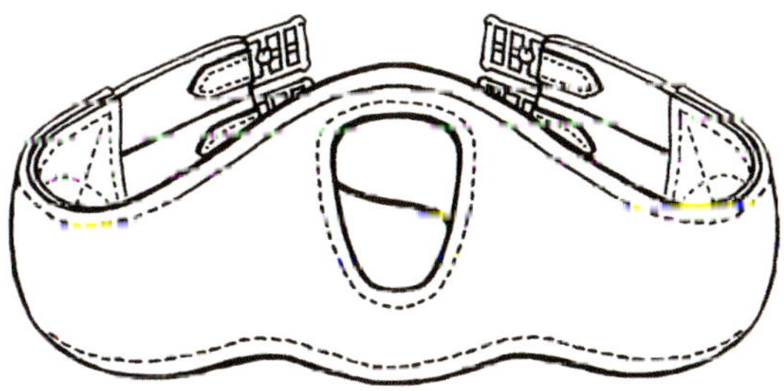

Anatomical.

Figure 56: Selection of girths.

Girths with elastic inserts at both ends or in the centre are preferable, as those with elastic at one end only are more likely to distribute pressure unevenly. If you use a girth with elastic at one end, the elasticated end should be fitted on the offside (right side) to avoid inadvertent over-tightening.

Note: A girth which has been done up too tight will cause extreme discomfort for the pony, and haematoma (swelling).

Tubular synthetic fabric

These have a soft filling and are comfortable and strong (but check after cleaning). Some are shaped like the Atherstone and have similar advantages.

String girths

This is a traditional design that has come back into use. It consists of tubular nylon strands joined at intervals with woven string and two buckles at each end. These good general-purpose girths let the air through between the strands and offer security, particularly on an unclipped pony.

Stirrup irons

Traditionally stirrup irons were made from stainless steel. Many modern stirrups are made from a mixture of strong, synthetic materials. Stirrups must be large enough to allow about 7mm (¼in) at each side of the rider's foot. The measurement should be taken at the widest part of the boot or shoe, with a well-defined square cut heel to avoid the risk of the rider's foot slipping through and becoming jammed. It is particularly dangerous for small children to use stirrup irons designed for adults which allow their whole foot to slip through. Check on the current rules and regulations on the type of stirrup that can be used (specific disciplines or disabilities). Rubber treads are often fitted to the irons to help prevent the rider's foot from slipping, and to add comfort. Some jockeys and event riders use specialist designs, including lightweight carbon irons. Some riders, particularly those involved in endurance riding, prefer irons with extra broad treads for support.

Safety stirrups

These are designed to prevent the rider's foot from becoming wedged in the stirrup. They are recommended for all riders, but particularly for children. Popular designs include the Peacock, Bent-leg (Australian or Swan-neck) irons, as well as synthetic designs.

Peacock

Peacock safety irons have a thick, rolled ring of rubber replacing the metal on one side. This ring should be on the outside. This design's disadvantages are:

- They do not hang straight, as they are weighted more on one side than the other.
- When a rubber ring comes off or breaks, it can be inconvenient. However, the chances of losing the ring are lessened if it is attached to the stirrup at one end by a small, tight-fitting loop, which will retain it if the other end comes off.
- They have been known to bend or break under heavy pressure and are unsuitable for riders other than lightweight children.

Bent-leg or swan-neck

The bent leg of the stirrup should protrude forwards and be on the outside as it hangs. These irons hang straighter than the peacock type and are usually satisfactory once you are familiar with their feel. Until then, they will feel strange, and your feet may tend to slip out too easily.

Safety irons are always recommended and are essential if the saddle is not fitted with safety stirrup bars. Depending on the construction quality and condition of the saddle, a stirrup leather may not release quickly even when safety stirrup bars are fitted, and the end is left down. This is something that needs to be checked regularly.

Stirrup leathers

Many stirrup leathers stretch over time, so it is also a good idea to check that, after stretching, the holes are still level with each other. It is a good idea to switch over the left- and right-hand leathers on your saddle occasionally; the one on the left tends to stretch more due to the rider mounting on that side. Some stirrup leathers are made with a central synthetic core to prevent stretching.

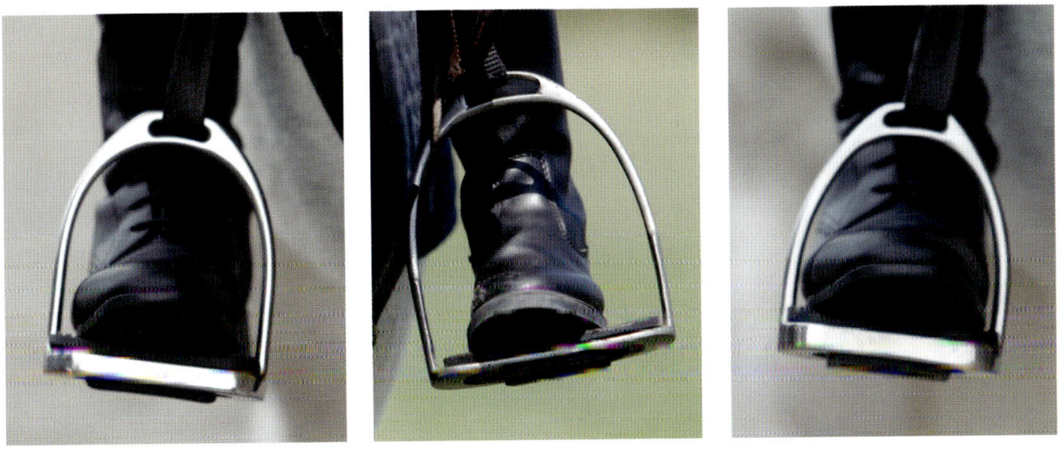

Correct. Too big. Too small.

Figure 57: The correct fit of stirrups against foot.

Choose stirrup leathers of an appropriate type and length for the rider and the use to which they are put – a knowledgeable saddler will advise you. Dressage riders often prefer leathers that adjust near the top of the stirrup irons rather than at the stirrup bars, as this minimises bulk under the rider's thigh. However, these are not recommended for jumping, as the adjustment fittings may not be as safe.

Stirrup leathers are traditionally made from three different types of leather:

- Ordinary leather (stirrup butt leather): can break under extreme pressure, but top-quality leather is the smartest and most comfortable for normal riding.
- Bonded stirrup leathers have leather over a nylon core, which is very strong and unlikely to change in length.
- Rawhide: virtually unbreakable and a traditional favourite for cross-country riding. Some types are rather thick and clumsy. Those made for racing are finer.
- Buffalo hide: also virtually unbreakable, but being reddish in colour, the least attractive, especially as it will never tone down to match the saddle. It often stretches more than other types.

Additional fittings

Cruppers

A crupper stops a saddle from slipping forward. It consists of an adjustable leather strap with a loop on one end, which fits under the tail. The other end of the strap passes through a metal D attached to the back of the saddle's cantle. The tail loop must be made and maintained to avoid rubbing the pony's dock. These are used for ponies when securing the stability of the saddle is difficult and not because the saddle does not fit.

Grass reins and balanced support reins

Grass reins and balanced support reins are fitted to prevent a pony from placing its head too low, such as trying to eat grass when ridden. They can be used for activities and using small jumps up to 30cm.

Numnahs and saddlecloths

A numnah is a pad cut in a saddle shape; a saddlecloth is square-shaped. Worn under the saddle, they have the following purposes:

- To protect a sensitive back.
- When fitted with additional, removable pads, saddles can be used by a saddler or a rider who understands saddle fitting to help adjust the saddle's balance. Although it is

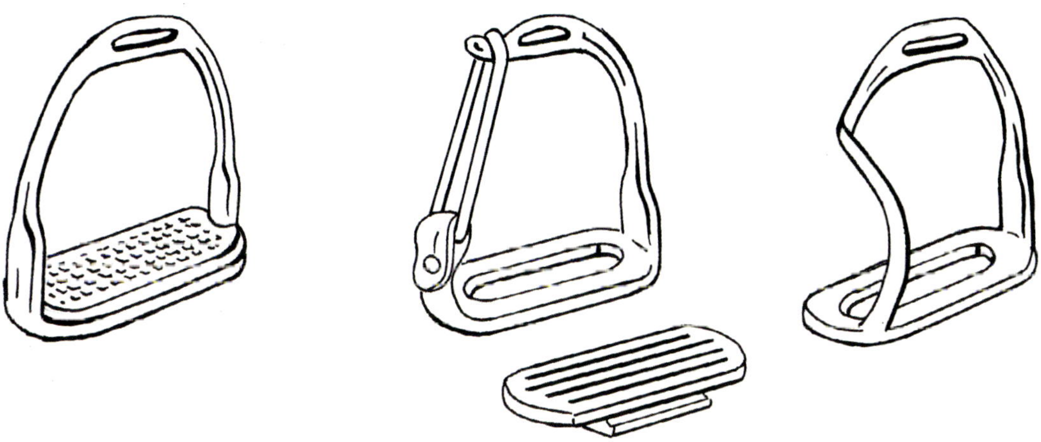

Figure 58: Standard stirrup, peacock and bent-leg stirrups.

recommended that every pony has its own saddle, these pads may mean that a saddle can be used on more than one pony if the profile and width are correct for both.

- Cushioning between rider and pony can be advantageous if the saddle is wide enough to accommodate it. Many numnahs and saddlecloths absorb sweat.
- This, of course, means that they must be kept clean.

Materials and design

Numnahs and saddlecloths should be designed to fit into the saddle gullet, not slip down and cause pressure on the withers or back. Check that straps which attach to the girth straps, or through which the girth passes, are correctly placed. They are usually made from:

- **Cotton**: inexpensive, warmer to a pony's back than leather, and helps to keep the saddle clean.
- **Sheepskin (sometimes sheared)**: a natural fibre that absorbs sweat.
- **Synthetic sheepskin**: varies in price and quality. The type that absorbs sweat is satisfactory.
- **Cotton-covered foam**: semi-absorbent.
- **Others**, made of top-quality materials, are expensive but absorbent, easy to wash, and minimise pressure and concussion for the pony.

Before buying numnahs made from synthetic materials, seek expert advice.

Fitting a numnah or saddlecloth

A numnah and saddlecloth should be slightly larger than the saddle to be visible for at least 7.8cm (3in) all round when in place. A loop is usually attached to the front on each side of the numnah, and another is sewn across the bottom edge.

The top strap can be fitted to the D-ring of the saddle or one of the girth straps is threaded through it (this will depend on the make and size of the numnah). The girths strap (one or both) is passed through the bottom part of the numnah to prevent the numnah from slipping backwards and hold the numnah in place.

- Before saddling the pony, fit the numnah to the saddle.
- Push it well up into the front arch and along the length of the channel.
- Check this again when saddling the pony and see that the numnah is lying flat on both sides.
- It must not lie wrinkled or folded up under the saddle.

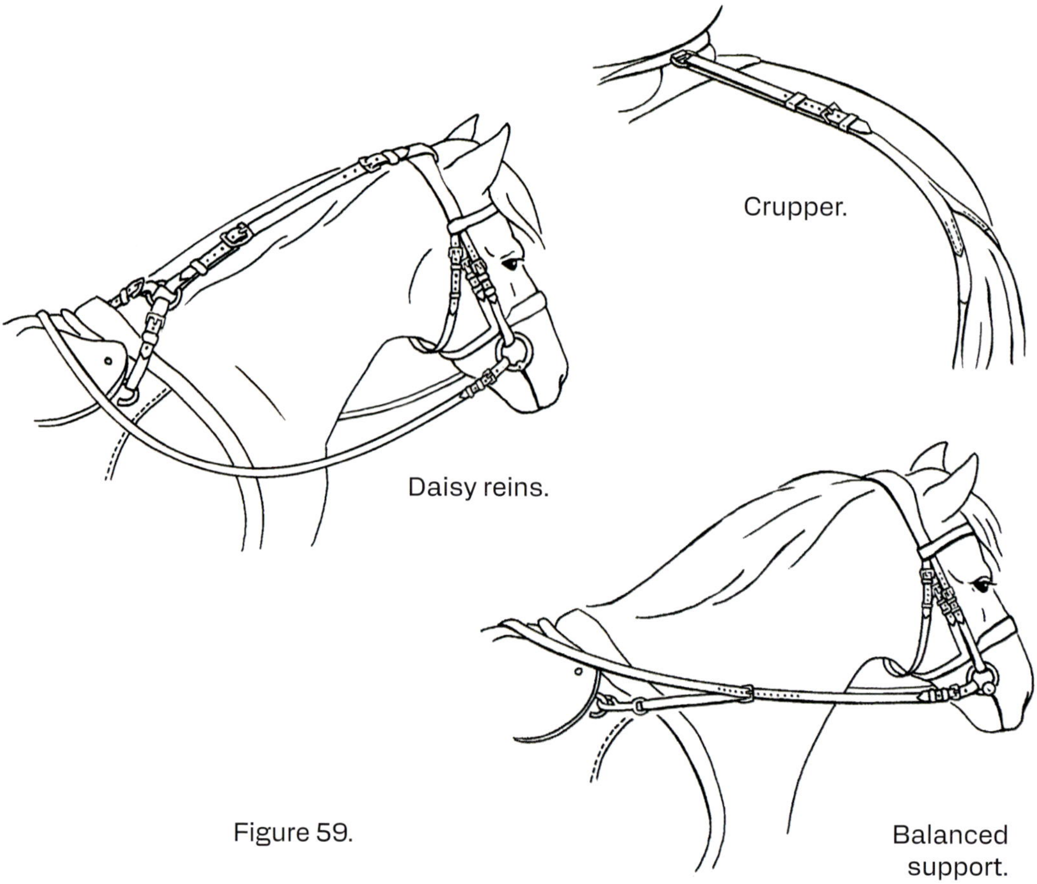

Figure 59.

Bridles: types (snaffles/other), mouth conformation, bitting, fit, action, care of

The bridle

A snaffle bridle is a bridle that takes one bit, although that bit does not have to be a snaffle bit but can be from one of the other families of bits. A double bridle can hold two bits, the bradoon and curb, with an additional headpiece called a sliphead.

The parts of the snaffle bridle

Headpiece

In conjunction with the cheekpieces, the headpiece supports the bit in the pony's mouth and is made from the same piece of leather as the throatlash.

Throatlash

The throatlash is designed to help keep the bridle in place. Still, when correctly fitted (not too tightly), it will not prevent the bridle from being pushed forward over the pony's ears (particularly if the rider falls off over the pony's head). It is made from the same piece of leather as the headpiece.

Browband

The browband stops the headpiece from slipping backwards.

Cheekpieces

The cheekpieces are attached at one end to the bit and at the other to the headpiece.

Nosebands

The following types of nosebands have been designed to help overcome specific resistances in the pony's mouth. Get expert advice before using a particular type of noseband on a pony who habitually puts his tongue over the bit or gets his tongue out of his mouth.

Cavesson noseband

This is the standard type of noseband. It fits around the nose, above the bit. It is the only noseband that should be used with a double bridle and a pelham.

Flash noseband

This is a cavesson noseband, fitted as such but with an additional lower strap attached to the front. This strap should pass well above the nostrils at the front of the nose and be fastened below the bit like a drop noseband. Ideally, the cavesson should be padded for extra comfort.

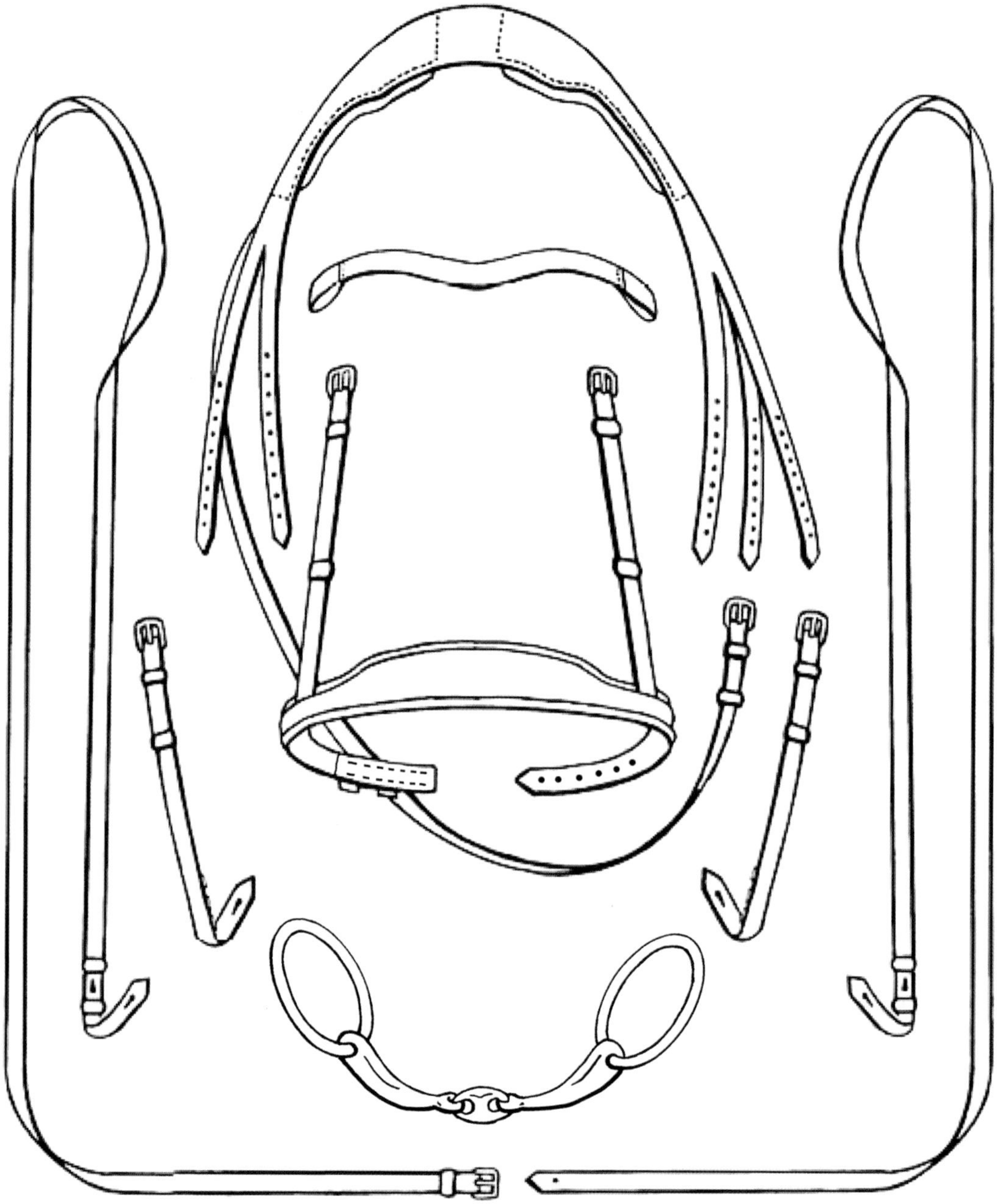

Figure 60: Parts of a snaffle bridle.

Drop noseband

This noseband must be carefully fitted to avoid interfering with the pony's breathing. It is fastened below the bit, which must be some form of snaffle. The front should be four fingers' width above the nostrils, and the back should rest in the chin groove. The front strap must be short enough to allow the cheekpieces to be well in front of the line of the pony's lips; so that the noseband does not pinch or rub the corners of the mouth. The noseband should be fitted loosely enough for the pony to relax his jaw but snugly enough to feel the pressure on his nose when he tries to open his mouth too wide, cross his jaw, or draw his tongue back.

Grackle (or crossed) noseband

This is used for the same purpose as the drop but has an additional strap above the bit. It acts over a wider area and is thus more effective in preventing the pony from crossing his jaw. It comprises two leather straps that cross over the bridge of the nose with a pad beneath the join. The straps pass around the pony's face and are buckled above and below the bit.

The grackle is fitted higher up on the nose than a drop noseband and acts over a wider area. The principle of fitting is the same as that for the drop-noseband. There are two types of grackles, the high-ring or Mexican grackle fastens higher on the pony's face than the traditional grackle, avoiding pressure on the cheek teeth.

Anatomical nosebands

There are many nosebands that are anatomically designed to fit the pony's head. Anatomically cut cavesson nosebands eliminate pressure on the tip of the nose bone and encourage chewing and movement of the jaw. Many of the nosebands are made of treated soft leather, making them very soft and supple.

Reins

Reins come in pairs, attached to the bit at one end and with a central buckle joining them together at the other end. They are made in various styles, lengths and widths and should suit the size of the rider's hand: if they are too wide they will be uncomfortable to hold, but if they are too narrow they will be difficult to hold and slip through the fingers too easily. Bright colours should be avoided except in endurance riding or using a high-visibility bridle on the roads; black or brown is the most used.

Reins are made of the following materials:

- **Plain leather** feels good but can become slippery in the rain or on a sweaty pony. Wearing suitable gloves can overcome this problem.
- **Laced or plaited leather** is less slippery but more difficult to clean. They are often used on the bradoon bit of a double bridle or as the top rein of a pelham when two reins are used.

Cavesson.

Flash.

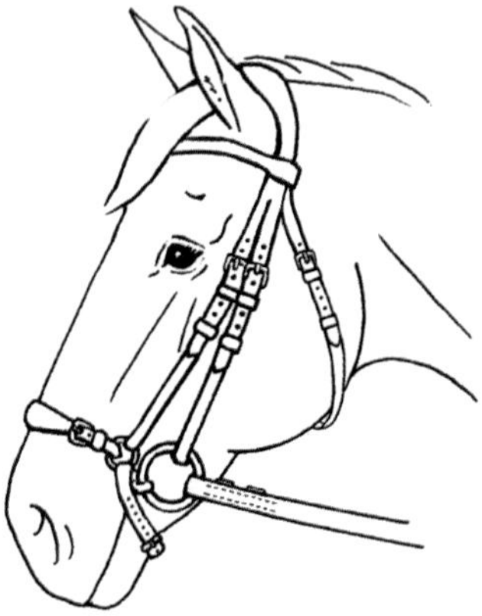

Drop.

Comfort.

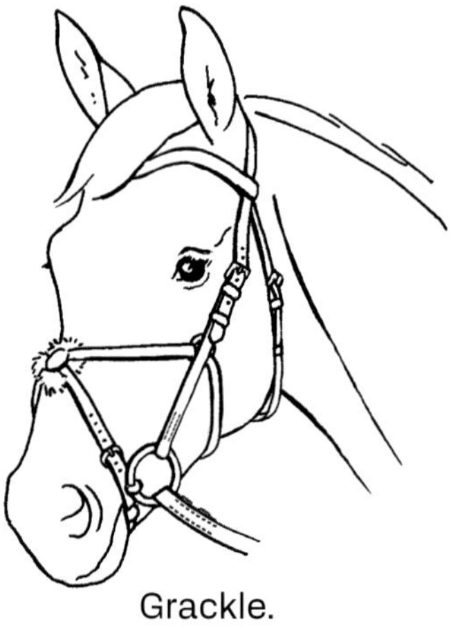

Grackle.

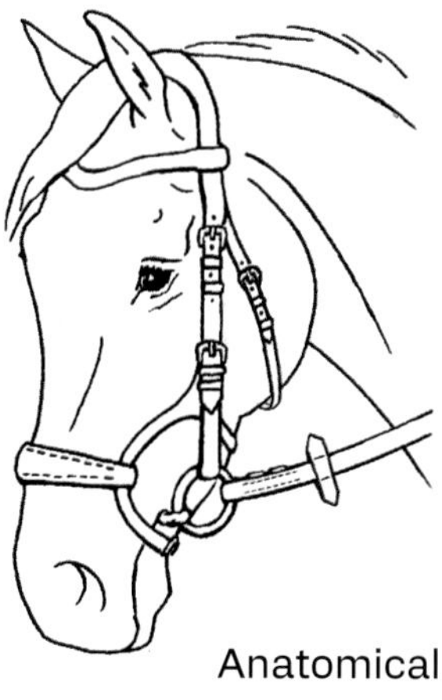

Anatomical.

Figure 61: Types of nosebands.

- **Rubber grip** over leather gives the best grip if the pony is strong, or in rain or if the pony is sweaty. Strong but soft rubber grip reins, sometimes nicknamed 'jelly rubber' reins, are less bulky and more comfortable to hold.
- **Web**, with leather bars (Continental reins). Give a good grip, and the bars prevent the reins from slipping through the fingers.

Attaching the bits

Various bits may be used with a snaffle bridle. The cheekpieces and the reins are attached to the bit by one of the following methods:

- Hooked billets are practical because the reins and cheekpieces can be easily detached for cleaning or for changing the bit. Billets can wear loose and should be checked regularly for safety.
- Buckles are also used, and compulsory for pony racing, because they are considered to be safer.

Bits and bitting

Care of the pony's mouth

Regular professional examinations of the pony's mouth and teeth (at least every twelve months) will help avoid problems and stop any existing problems from developing into bigger ones. No pony will be happy if his bit makes him feel uncomfortable.

Considerations when bitting

Bits and bridles are communication tools; ponies often wear bits to help control their speed and direction and to aid performance. The pony should be bitted in a way that ensures maximum comfort and performance, allowing it to work in harmony/union with the rider without experiencing pain or fear. As with all good communication, success will rely on the rider listening and asking. Riders may want to change a bit when they are stepping up to a new activity, changing a bit is not a short cut to correct training.

Keeping bitting simple

Bitting is a huge subject with many opinions, so it is usually best to first learn the basics and build on that knowledge. Riders must understand not only the individual action of a bit on the pony but also the pony's consequent reaction to it. Thus, bits can be selected logically. It is also important to consider the conformation (shape) of the pony's mouth because the more comfortably a pony is bitted, the more likely he is to accept the bit and work happily in it.

Above all, riders must remember that regardless of the bit's design, any bit will only be as mild or strong, successful or ineffective, as the rider using the reins. Your balance, skill and understanding as a rider, will create the desired results. Correct bitting, training and riding are demonstrated by the pony's acceptance of the bit. You should think of the bit as being placed in your hands rather than the mouth of the pony.

What are bitting points?

When we put a bit in a pony's mouth, it touches different spots on the pony's head and mouth. These spots are called 'bitting points' – they're like the places where we can gently 'talk' to our pony through the reins.

The six important spots: Think of these six spots like buttons on a remote control – each one helps us communicate with our pony in a gentle way. We need to be very gentle with all these spots on our pony. The bit should never hurt – it should feel like a gentle tap on the shoulder to get attention. Remember: a happy, comfortable pony is a safe pony to ride. When we understand these six spots, we can:

- Make sure our pony is comfortable.
- Communicate clearly without being harsh.
- Keep our pony happy and willing to work with us.

Inside the pony's mouth (three spots)

- **The lips** – where the bit touches the corners of the pony's mouth.
- **The tongue** – the soft part inside the mouth that the bit rests on.
- **The bars** – the smooth gum area between the front teeth and back teeth (where there are no teeth).

Outside on the pony's head (three spots)

- **The poll** – the top of the head behind the ears (through the headpiece strap).
- **The nose** – across the bridge of the nose (through the noseband).
- **The chin groove** – the soft area under the chin (through the curb chain if using one).

Not all bits act on all six bitting points. Every type of bit places pressure on the lips, corners of the mouth, the tongue and the bars, but the degree varies according to its design. The rider needs to understand and be aware of the action of each bit as well as the pony's possible reaction to it.

- Gentle pressure on the nose encourages lowering of the head.
- Any bit with a central arch (port), will act on the roof of the mouth as the bit tilts forward with rein contact. Some bits have a very shallow arch to allow more room for the pony's tongue, which is more comfortable.
- Pressure on the poll encourages a pony to lower his head.

- When the curb chain or back strap (on a lever bit) comes into contact with the chin groove the pony is encouraged to bring his head down and inwards.

Before selecting a bit, think about the following:
It is important that the pony is as comfortable as possible when the bit is in his mouth. Every pony will have a different shaped mouth. Ask an experienced person to help you understand the type of bit that would be suitable for the pony. Look at as many ponies as possible to compare the different mouth shapes; to grow your knowledge and understanding of bitting.

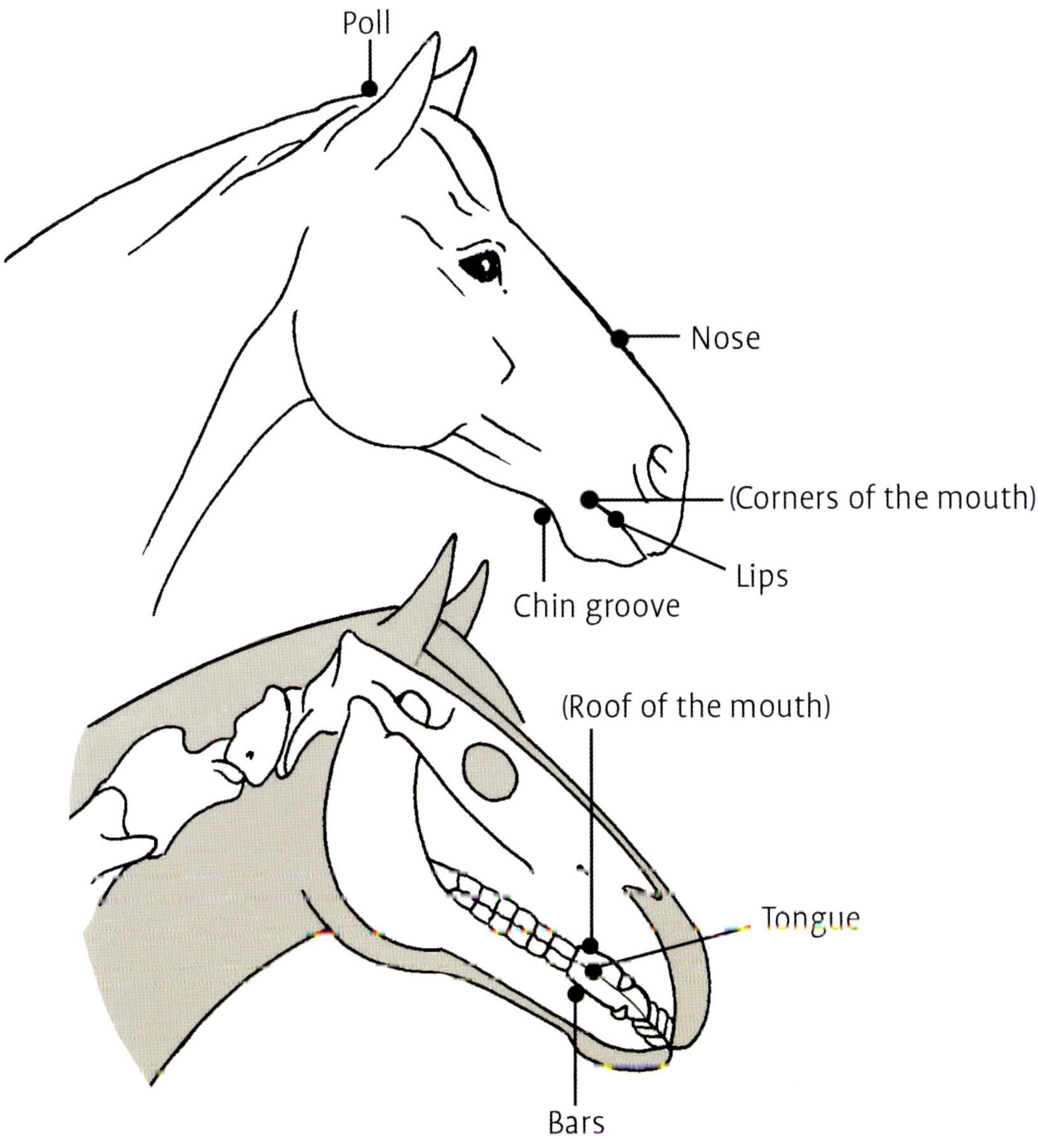

- For instance, if he has very fleshy lips, they will wrinkle at the corners when the bit is in place, but if he has fine lips, a correctly adjusted bit will fit snugly into the corners without obvious wrinkles.
- The mouthpiece should be the correct thickness for the size of the mouth. If it is too thin, it may be too severe, as all the pressure will be exerted on only a small area of the bars of the mouth. A thick mouthpiece has a greater bearing surface, but if it is too thick, the pony will have difficulty accommodating it in his mouth. Does he have a long, fine mouth and jaw or a short 'full' mouth with thick lips and a full (big) tongue? Will he be happier in a thick (fat) or fine (thin) bit?
- Where is his chin groove in relation to the corner of his lips? Will a curb chain fit on him so that it acts in the correct position?
- Is the roof of his mouth high or low?
- Does he have tushes, the canine teeth found behind the incisors (front teeth), normally absent in mares? Make sure that the bit will not interfere with these.
- Does he have wolf teeth? These are small, underdeveloped teeth just before the upper molars. Seek professional advice.

Select a bit that will best suit this.

Fitting the bit

All ponies' mouths and their tongues vary in size and shape. The bit must be the correct size and type for the pony. Before fitting the bit, you must put on the bridle but leave the noseband unfastened and you should always be seeking professional help and guidance.

The mouthpiece needs to be the correct thickness for your pony's mouth. A thin bit can be severe, as all the pressure will be in a smaller area. However, it may work well for a pony with a 'full' mouth. A thicker mouthpiece has a greater bearing surface, but it will not fit comfortably in your pony's mouth if it is too thick.

A bit that is too narrow for the pony will pinch the corners of his mouth, while one that protrudes too much can move excessively from side to side and cause soreness.

In the case of a jointed snaffle, a mouthpiece that is too wide will lie with the joint too low in the mouth, which often encourages the pony to put his tongue over the bit. This leads to discomfort and problems, as the cushioning effect of the tongue is lost.

A traditional single-jointed snaffle has a stronger squeezing action than one with a central lozenge double link. A single joint applies concentrated pressure to the centre of the tongue.

Some bit designs promote comfort by using curved 'arms' and specially designed joints, which may or may not be covered with a sleeve or barrel. It is easier for the pony to accept the bit when there is not too much pressure on his tongue. A bit should be chosen which allows the tongue to lie comfortably below the mouthpiece.

Measuring the bit size

Having the correct type of bit is no advantage if it is the wrong size or wrongly fitted. Get experienced help to show you how to fit the correct size of bit.

The role of the rider

A rider's position and aids are the most important way to control their pony effectively. It is important to remember that harsh, unyielding hands and poor riding will cause damage to a pony's mouth and make him frightened and/or resistant.

Fitting the jointed or double-lozenge snaffle

Measure the width by holding the bit with a hand on either side so the joint is straight in the pony's mouth. The width is correct when the mouthpiece protrudes about 5mm (¼in) on each side (or sometimes a little more if the bit has cheekpieces).

- To check the bit's height in the mouth, lightly put your finger on each side and press down gently to ensure the pony is not holding the bit in place.

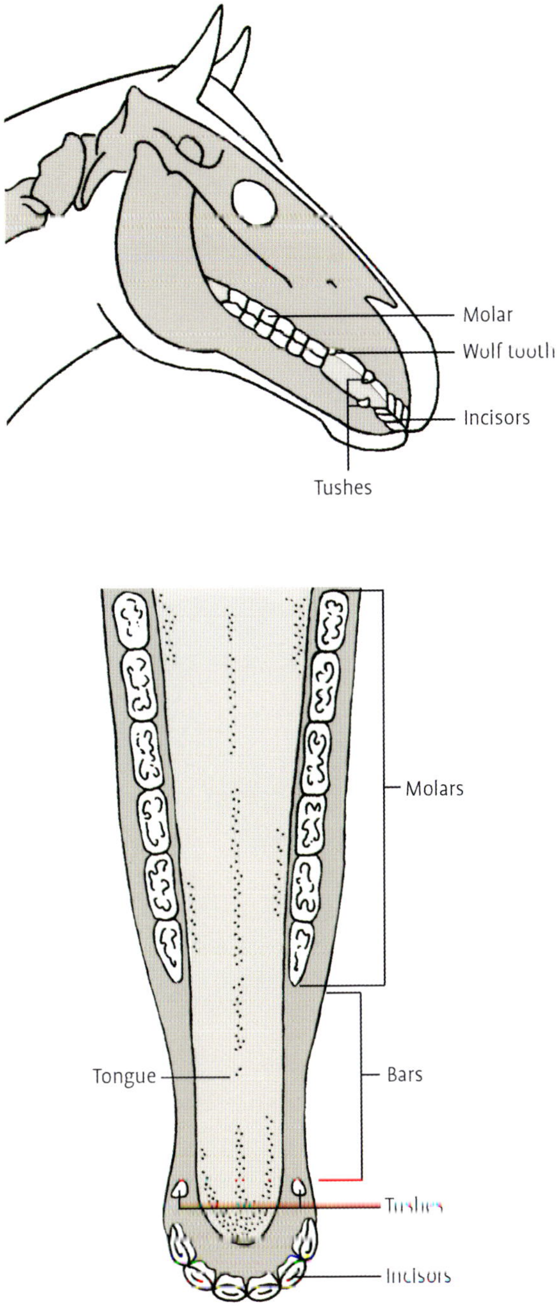

Figure 83. Shape of the jaw and mouth.

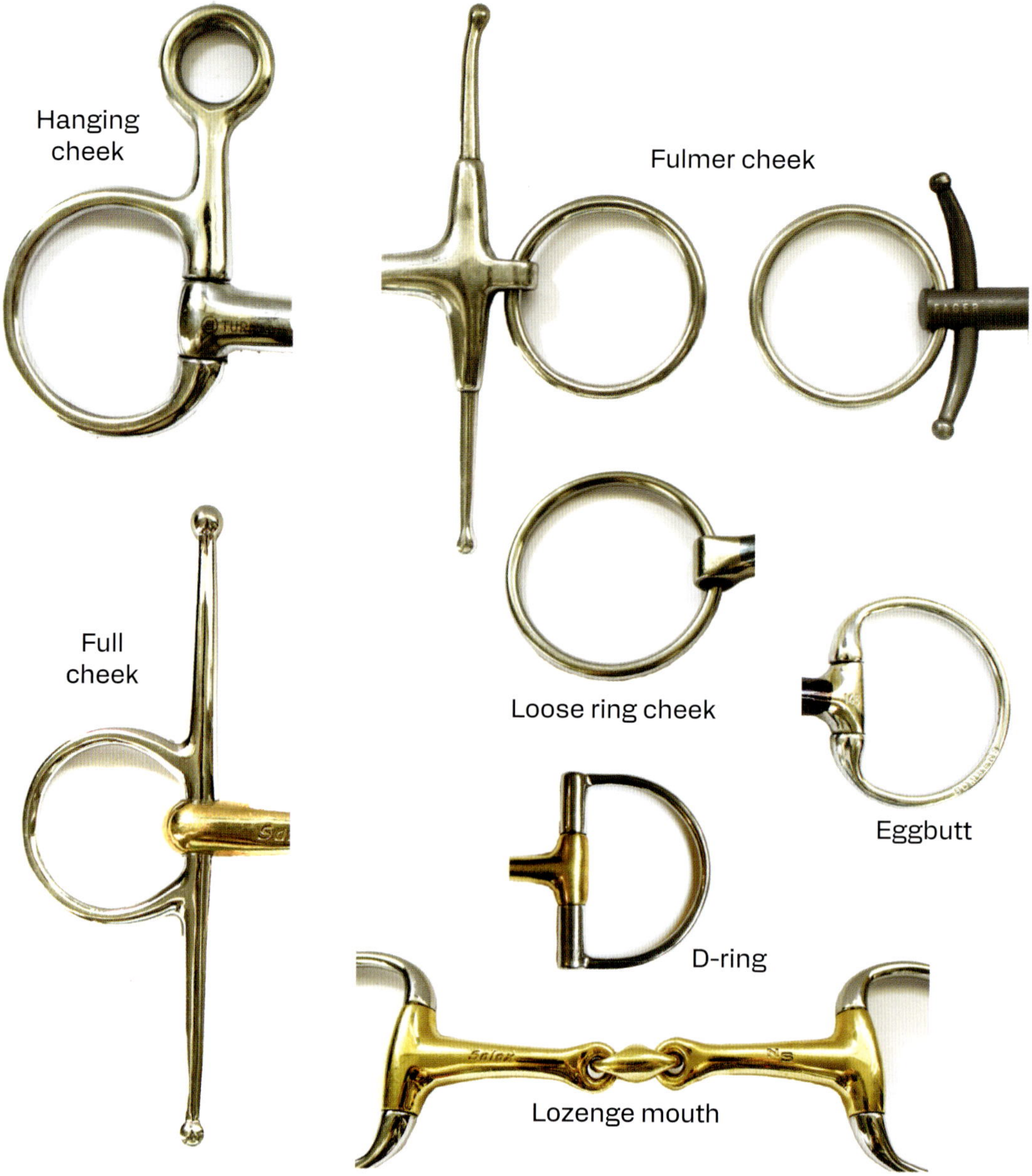

Figure 64: Different types of snaffle bits.

- Then, if necessary, adjust the bridle cheekpieces so the bit is at the correct height, using the guidelines below:
- Look in the pony's mouth to check that it lies on the bars of the mouth. It should not touch the teeth, or drag the corners of the mouth too high, or drop down too low on the tongue.
- When the rider is mounted and has touched the reins, the cheekpieces should not sag outward but lie against the pony's face.

Fitting the mullen mouth, straight-bar snaffle and pelham
The principles are the same as for the jointed snaffle. The mouthpiece should protrude about 0.5cm (¼in) on each side, and the height is correct when the mouthpiece lies against the corners of the mouth without causing wrinkles.

No matter how well the bit fits, the pony will not be comfortable with any soreness in his mouth. If in doubt, seek expert advice.

Basic families of bits

- **Snaffles** have no curb chain and do not apply any leverage.
- **Pelhams and kimblewicks** are fitted with a curb chain.
- **Lever snaffles** (sometimes called a gag) apply pressure on the poll.
- **Bitless bridles** do not have a bit in the pony's mouth.

The snaffle

A selection of snaffles

Jointed loose-ring snaffle: Made of metal, rubber, or synthetic material with a single joint in the middle, it acts principally on the lips and corners of the mouth, the bars of the mouth, and the tongue.

Eggbutt snaffle: This has the same action as the ring snaffle, but the smooth side joints prevent possible pinching. Other varieties of snaffles (described below) may also use the smooth eggbutt side rings.

Snaffle with cheeks: 'Cheeks' can help reinforce gentle steering. It will not pull through from side to side or pinch the pony's mouth. A D-ring or full-cheeked bit will help keep your pony straight. When keepers are used to attach the cheeks of the bit to the cheekpieces of the bridle, the bit moves minimally in the mouth.

Double-jointed snaffle: There are many different types, available with a variety of rings or cheekpieces:

A central lozenge: The lozenge allows the bit to follow the internal contours of the pony's mouth and does not have a concentrated pressure point on the centre of the tongue. It avoids the nutcracker action of the traditional single-jointed snaffle.

French link: The central plate is rounded and lies flat across the tongue. The bit's action is on the lips and corners of the mouth, the bars of the mouth, and the tongue; again, the action of the single-jointed snaffle is avoided. This sometimes makes it a satisfactory bit on a pony with a large tongue or a narrow lower jaw.

Figure 65: A selection of bits.

Mullen mouth (half-moon) and straight-bar snaffle: The action of these bits, made of metal, vulcanite, synthetic material or rubber, is primarily on the lips and corners of the mouth and the tongue. A mullen mouthpiece has a slight arch to allow room for the tongue, making it more comfortable for the pony. Straight-bar bits are used mainly when leading, such as when showing in hand or driving, though straight-bar bits made from flexible materials act more like a mullen mouth design. Some ponies go well in unjointed mouthpieces, but others learn to hold the mouthpiece away from the bars by pushing up with the tongue. This can also indicate a sore mouth, or an insensitive rider has ridden the pony.

Hanging cheek snaffle: Suspended, rather than resting, in the mouth, this snaffle is suitable for a pony who dislikes too much weight on his tongue. The action is on the lips and bars of the mouth and, to a lesser degree, on the tongue.

Other types of snaffles

Many other bits are on the market, but some are very severe. Before making any changes, discuss with your coach whether it is advisable and, if so, which type to use. These types must not be confused. Always check your rule book, as there is a wide range of snaffles, many of which are prohibited in The Pony Club.

The pelham

This bit is a combination of the curb and bradoon on one mouthpiece. The bradoon and curb reins are attached to separate rings, thus attempting to make the one bit perform the duties of two. In principle, this is not a sound policy, but experience has shown that some ponies will go better in a pelham than in anything else. The top (bradoon) rein causes the bit to act on the corners of the mouth (the lips) and on the tongue. The lower (curb) rein causes the bit to act on the bars, the chin groove and the poll.

The pelham can have a variety of mouthpieces, but the mullen mouthpiece is the most used and usually the most effective. The mouthpiece can be made from various materials.

Sometimes, a single rein is used with a pelham attached to a leather rounding, which is attached to the bradoon and curb rings on the cheeks of the bit. Ideally, a cavesson noseband should be used with a pelham to ensure that the curb chain's action is not compromised by a strap fastening below the bit. However, some riders use a flash or grackle because they feel this gives extra control when jumping. Get expert advice if you feel this is necessary.

The kimblewick

This looks like it acts similarly to the top part of a pelham, but it's milder than the pelham, it can have a variety of mouthpieces. Keen ponies sometimes respond well to its mild action.

Lever bits

There are many types such as a Dutch gag or three-ring lever bits. The action is on the lips and corners of the mouth, the tongue and the poll. It can be very severe. It may be used with one or two pairs of reins. For maximum effectiveness, it should be used with two pairs of reins, one direct to the snaffle ring and the other attached to the cheekpiece, which runs through the bit rings, to offer the choice of an ordinary or gag snaffle action. Some riders and trainers prefer to use a single gag rein when jumping, especially cross-country.

Bitless

These bridles have no mouthpiece but use leverage on the nose, poll and chin groove. Hackamores are a type of bitless bridle, but there are many others. Although the mouth area is not affected by a bitless bridle, it should be realised that the nose, poll and chin groove are all delicate, highly sensitive areas and are just as easily damaged. These types of bridles should be used with careful guidance as incorrect use can be harmful to the pony. If you need a hackamore or any bitless bridle, get expert advice on its use and fitting.

Resistance to the contact

A pony may resist the bit for any of the following reasons:

- Lack of balance and training.
- Condition of the teeth.
- Pain and fear of the bit.
- Insensitive (damaged) mouth.
- Conformation.
- Poorly fitting tack (bit, bridle or saddle).

Lack of balance and training

Before his muscles are developed and he has accustomed himself to the rider's weight, a pony will often – through lack of balance and no fault of his own – have trouble in answering the rider's aids. He will respond in a slow and often clumsy way. It should be realised that at this stage, the pony's mouth is still 'unmade', so unless the rider uses tact and sympathy, much harm will result. The mouth may seem insensitive because the pony is unable, and in any case has not yet learned, to respond quickly. If the rider uses force, the situation will worsen.

Condition of the teeth

A sore mouth, although sometimes caused by bad riding, may also be due to the condition of the pony's teeth or through a condition such as an ulcer or injury.

Pain and fear of the bit

Any bit which does not lie comfortably in the pony's mouth will cause resistance. A sore mouth or an ill-fitting bit will often cause a pony to pull to escape from the resulting pain. His instinct is to flee. A tongue over the bit, a dry mouth, or an excessively frothy mouth may all be evasions of pain caused by incorrect bitting and/or bad training. The mouth bars are easily injured, and the underpart of the tongue may also be damaged if the tongue is over the bit.

Insensitive (damaged) mouth

The bit lies across the tongue and on the bars of the mouth, which are extremely sensitive, as they are thinly covered with skin containing a mass of nerves. These nerves easily become numbed; then the feeling in the mouth is lost. Finally, the bars may develop splint-like bony lumps. When this happens, the pony may resist permanently. He may be referred to as hard-mouthed and veterinary advice, together with a careful choice of bit or the use of a bitless bridle, is needed.

Putting a more severe bit on a pulling pony is a mistake. The secret of a good mouth lies in the training or retraining of the pony in a suitable bit and in the pony's increased attentiveness and obedience to the rider.

Conformation

The conformation of a pony's head, neck and jaw is important in bitting. The pony may have difficulty flexing correctly if the head and neck are too closely coupled (thick through the jowl). If the jaw is too narrow or the tongue is too thick, the bit will have less room to lie comfortably in the mouth. If you think that these faults are why your pony is resisting, seek an expert's assistance to help you choose and fit a suitable bit.

Temperament

Ponies who are calm and cooperative by nature are easier to manage, but regardless of temperament, some ponies (particularly young ones) will often become strong when excited. Ideally, they should be ridden in a snaffle, and care should be taken not to damage their mouths. If a mouth becomes sore, it must be allowed to heal before the pony is ridden again. A spoiled pony who is unwilling, resentful or nappy will often display his characteristics by a refusal to accept the bit correctly.

The 12 Rules of Bitting	
1.	Have your horse's mouth and teeth routinely maintained by a vet or equine dental technician at least once a year. Check the horse's mouth and lips regularly for bruising.
2.	Choose the bit according to your pony's age, education and the rider's ability.
3.	Consider the individual shape of your pony's mouth and the size of the tongue when selecting his bit.
4.	The bit you choose must be the correct size and width, and it must be fitted correctly.
5.	Bits are split into different families of bits. Make sure you understand the actions of various bits and how your pony may react.
6.	Know the different materials used in bit manufacture and how they affect the horse differently.
7.	If the bit is uncomfortable, too severe, or your pony does not like the action of the bit, he may show unsettled behaviour, resist the contact or become even stronger.
8.	Be aware of the effect of additional tack upon the bit, as nosebands and martingales may affect the contact. Nosebands and martingales must never be too restricting.
9.	Wash the bit thoroughly after every ride to prevent any rubbing or sore areas.
10.	Remember that the bit is only as severe as the rider holding the reins.
11.	Never be rough with the contact; always ride with soft and forward kind hands.
12.	To use the reins sympathetically, you need to develop an independent position.

Figure 66: Table of 12 rules of good bitting.

Equipment: martingales, breastplates, boots, bandaging, rugs – fit and care of

Martingales

Standing martingale

This is fitted from the girth at one end to a cavesson noseband (or to the cavesson part of a flash noseband) at the other. It passes between the forelegs and through a loop on the neckstrap, which supports it. A thick rubber ring holds the two together. The purpose of the standing martingale is to prevent the pony from raising his head beyond the angle of control. It also helps to prevent him from hitting you in the face if he throws his head back. It should not be fitted any tighter than is necessary and should not be used to hold the pony's head down.

Fitting a standing martingale

Check the correct length after the martingale has been attached to the girth and noseband. When the pony stands with his head in the correct position, lift your hand under the martingale. As a rough guide, it should just reach as far as the throat. The neckstrap buckle should be on the left side of the pony's neck. It should fit to allow a hand's width at the withers. To keep the girth loop neat and safe, one keeper should be positioned immediately behind the buckle and the other next to the girth.

Running martingale

This is attached to the girth and passes between the forelegs. It then divides into two, each of the two ends fitted with a ring through which the reins are passed. Like the standing martingale, it is supported by a neckstrap. A running martingale provides a regulating influence on a pony that carries its head too high. It must be correctly fitted so it only takes effect when the pony raises his head beyond the control angle. If it is fitted too short, it will place constant pressure on the bars of the mouth, which may then become bruised.

Fitting a running martingale

As a rough guide, when the martingale is attached to the girth and both rings are taken to one side, the martingale should be long enough to reach the pony's withers. The reins should be threaded through the rings so that the rings can run freely up and down the reins, as shown in Figure 60. The reins should be fitted with stops between the rings and the bit to prevent the rings from getting caught over the hook billets of the rein or any part of the bit. The neckstrap should be fitted as for the standing martingale.

Irish martingale

This consists of two rings connected by a strap approximately 10cm (4in) long. Its purpose is to keep the reins in place and prevent them from going over the pony's head.

Fitting an Irish martingale

The snaffle reins should be passed through the rings underneath the pony's neck.

Breastplate and breast-girth

A breastplate is a leather neckstrap attached to the Ds at the front of the saddle by a strap at each side of the pony's neck and to the girth by a broader strap passing between the forelegs. Its purpose is to prevent the saddle from slipping back, but it cannot turn a poorly fitting saddle into one which fits correctly. This happens more often if the pony is fit, does not carry excess weight, or is naturally 'herring-gutted'. Still, a breastplate is a sensible addition to your security during cross-country work or when riding in a hilly country.

Specially made standing or running martingale attachments may be fitted to the breastplate if required. Fit the breastplate so that there is room to slide the width of your hand under the neckstrap (about 10cm). The straps to the D-rings should lie flat and quite loose when the pony is standing normally. Remember that his shoulders and neck need the freedom to extend when galloping.

A breast-girth is a strap of web or elastic fitted across the pony's breast and attached to the girth straps on both sides. A leather strap attached to it passes over the neck in front of the withers to hold it in position. Its purpose is the same as that of the breastplate, but as it is light and easily fitted, it is especially useful for a young pony, who may buck and move his saddle out of position. The breast-girth should be fitted loose enough to allow the full width of your hand

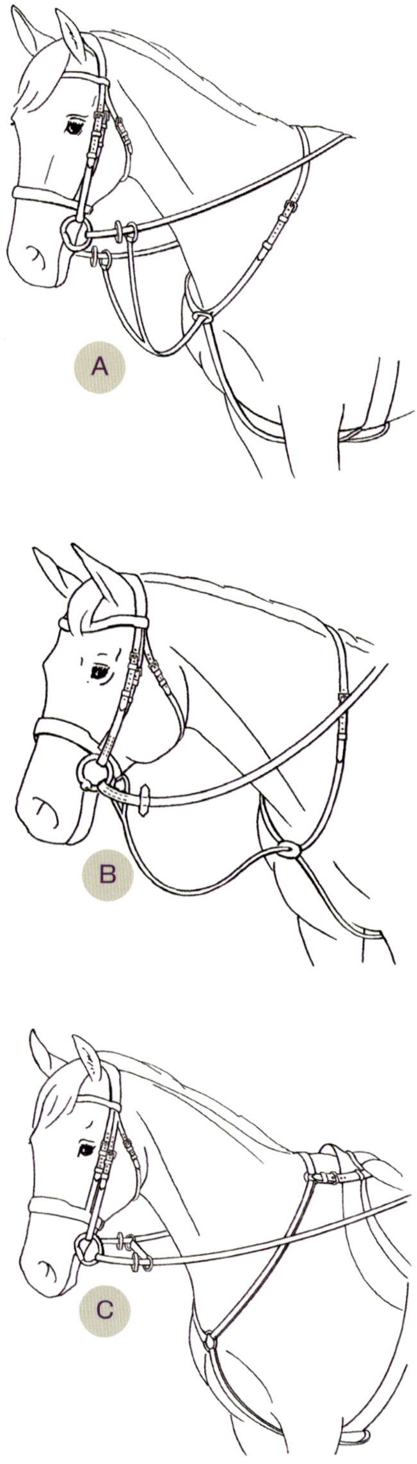

Figure 67: Types and fit for a) running martingale, b) standing martingale and c) Irish martingale.

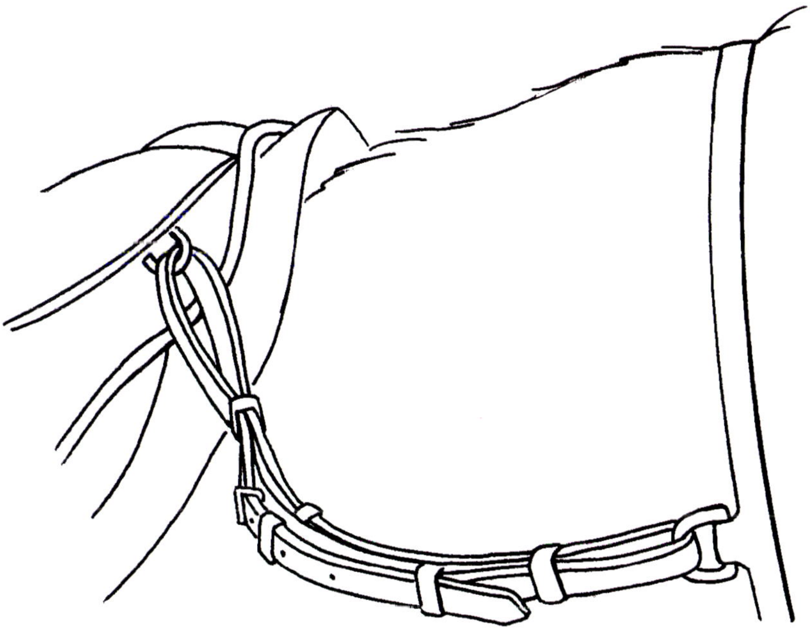

Figure 68: Securing a neckstrap.

between it and the pony's breast. It must not lie so high that it restricts the neck's movement or the windpipe's functioning.

It is important to note that neither a breastplate nor a breast-girth can turn a poorly fitting saddle into one which fits correctly.

Neckstrap

This is a simple leather strap that passes around the pony's neck. The neckstrap of a martingale or breastplate is the neatest, but a stirrup leather will do equally well.

In an emergency, its object is to provide the rider with something to hang on to other than the reins and thus to lessen the risk of pulling on the pony's mouth. It is a great help, especially to young riders in rough, hilly country, and particularly when riding a pony with a hogged mane. It is essential when riding a young pony or teaching a rider or pony to jump. Straps can attach it to the front Ds of the saddle to prevent it from slipping forward when the pony lowers his head. It should be fitted one-third of the way up the pony's neck for jumping.

Boots

There are many types of boots designed to prevent a pony from injuring himself or being injured:

Brushing boots

These are designed to give extra protection to the soft tissue on the inside and sometimes at the back of the leg.

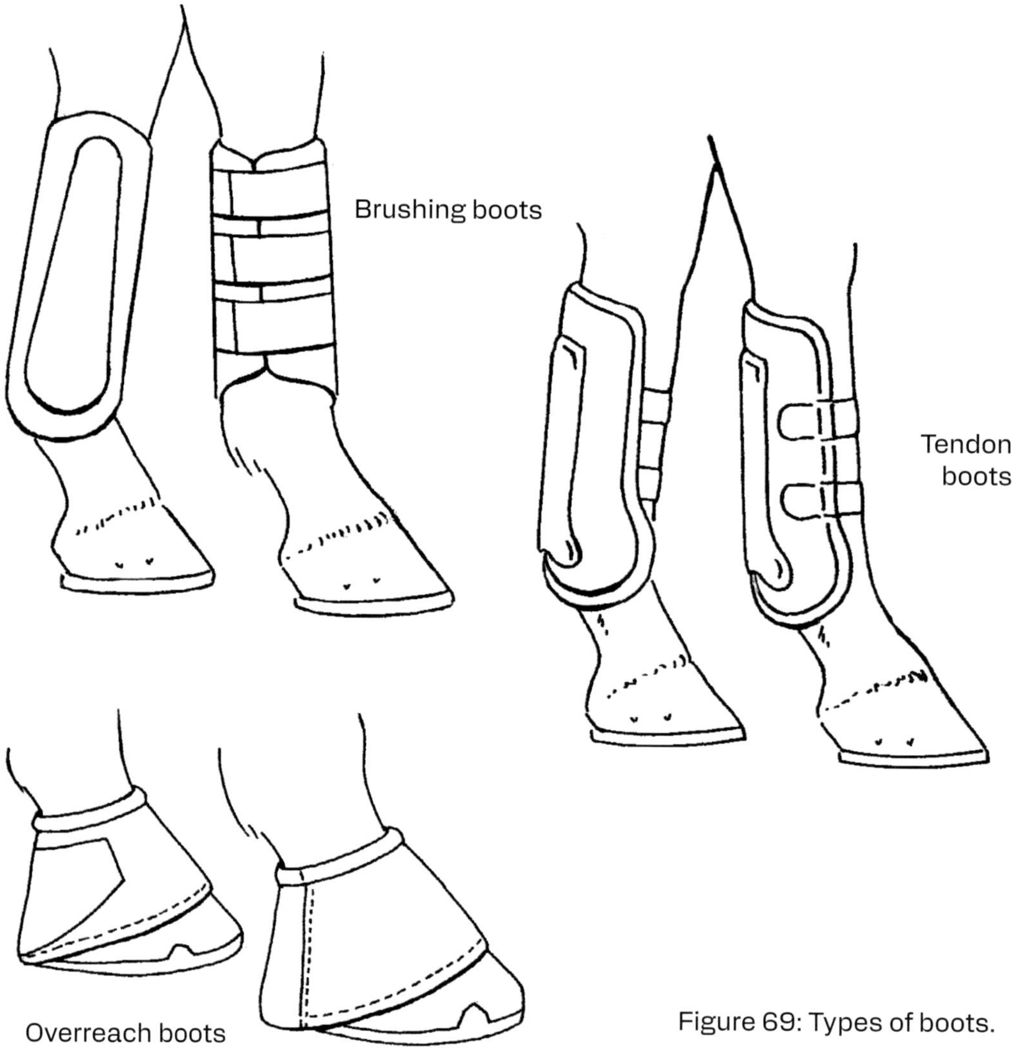

Figure 69: Types of boots.

Open-fronted tendon boots

These protect the tendons against a high overreach. They are like brushing boots, with a shaped pad protecting the tendon and fetlocks. They are open at the front of the cannon bone and are mainly used for show jumping.

Cross-country boots

These resemble a brushing boot in shape. The difference is usually in the type of material used and where the boot is reinforced to protect the legs, should your pony knock a solid fence. This protection is located on the front and back of the front boots, as well as on the front and sides of the hind boots.

Overreach boots

Bell-shaped and made of rubber, these fit around the lower pastern, encompassing the hoof. They protect the heels and the coronet. Some are fitted with straps. If they are not, they are put on by turning them inside out and pulling them on over the hoof.

The use and fitting of brushing and tendon boots

All working boots are designed for protection over a short period. If worn for a long period, they are likely to cause soreness, especially in muddy or wet conditions. Well-made boots are shaped to fit the contours of the leg. Poorly shaped or badly fitting boots may cause discomfort, soreness and even pressure on the tendons, which could result in permanent damage. Keep boots in pairs or sets. Sometimes, the front and hind-leg boots of a set are different in shape.

- In a set of four, the front boots generally have one less strap than the hind boots. When fitted, the fastenings should be on the outside of the leg, with the strap ends pointing to the rear.
- Select the correct boot from your set or pair and put it around the leg. Fasten the middle strap first. Work upwards and then downwards, making sure that the pressure is even all the way and no tighter than is necessary to prevent the boot slipping.
- Boots fastened by metal clips can come undone if knocked.
- When removing a boot, unfasten the middle strap last to prevent the boot from falling off if the pony moves.

Care of boots

Boots must be thoroughly cleaned after use, as any mud and muck left on them will harden and may cause sores later. Depending on the material, clean them as described for saddlery.

Try to keep straps and keepers as soft as possible. If stiff and hard, they will be difficult to fasten and unfasten, and they may crack and break. Velcro fastenings must also be kept free from dirt, etc., which clogs them up and makes them less secure.

Procedure for tacking up

Collect the tack you will use, together with your hat, gloves, etc.

The saddle

- Check that the stirrup irons and leathers are neatly run up on the saddle.
- Check that the buckle guards are on.
- Attach the girth on the right side, leaving at least four holes above the buckles.
- Fold the girth back over the seat of the saddle.
- If you are using a numnah (or saddlecloth), place it on top of the saddle.

The bridle

Checks and adjustments are best carried away from the pony, preferably in the tack room.

Unfasten the throatlash and the noseband. If a double bridle or pelham is used, unfasten the curb chain and lip strap from the left side.

If a martingale is used, release the reins from the rings and place the centre rein buckle on top of the headpiece.

If it is not the pony's usual bridle, leave the cheekpieces buckled, not in their keepers or runners. You will need to measure the bridle against the pony's head and adjust it so that it will be a generous size for him when you put it on. You can then readjust it to fit correctly.

Additional saddlery

Collect the breastplate or martingale and any leg coverings, such as brushing boots if you use them. When you get to the pony, hang up the bridle nearby. Put the saddle over a fence or door or on the ground; do not leave it where the pony can reach it with his feet or teeth.

Tacking up and untacking

First, tie up the pony – whether in or out of the stable – and keep him tied up until you are ready to mount. This will help to keep him under control. It will prevent him from damaging his saddlery by rolling or treading on the reins. Before you ride or do any work with your pony, you need to give him a quick clean-up.

- Brush off any dry mud or sweat, especially where the saddle and girth will go.
- This helps keep your pony comfy and stops the tack from rubbing or causing sore spots.

If your pony is wearing a rug

- Undo the straps under his belly (they're called surcingles).
- Tie the straps up in a knot so they don't dangle and hit his legs.
- Fold the back of the rug up over his quarters so you can groom the front of him.
- Give his shoulders and front a good groom.
- Then fold the front part of the rug back over his shoulders and pull the back part forward.
- Now you can groom his hindquarters.
- This method is called quartering – it just means grooming one part of the pony at a time while moving the rug around.

Figure 70: How to carry your saddle and bridle.

After grooming

- Leave his rug on but don't do up the chest straps yet.
- This way, if the rug slips, it will just fall off instead of hanging around his neck – which could scare him or damage the rug.

Add protection (if needed)

If your pony usually wears brushing boots or other leg protectors for work, now's the time to put them on.

Putting on the saddle

Talk to your pony as you approach. If he is strange to you, saddle up from the left side; otherwise, make a habit of saddling up from either side. Proceed as follows:

- If you use a neckstrap, breastplate or martingale, untie the pony's lead rope and put it on. The neckstrap buckle should be on the left side. Tie him up again.
- If the pony is rugged, fold the rug behind where the saddle will lie.
- Smooth down the hair with your hands where the saddle and girth will lie, ensuring no mud or old sweat can cause a sore or gall.
- Pick up the saddle with the front arch in your left hand and the cantle in your right.
- Place it lightly but firmly, well forward on the withers.
- Slide it back into position, checking that you will not be sitting too far forward or too far back either on the pony's shoulder or his loins.
- Never slide the saddle forward against the lie of the coat.
- Check that the sweat flap and buckle guards are lying flat and that everything is smooth under the saddle flap.
- If you are using a numnah or saddlecloth, make sure it is lying flat and pulled well into the saddle's front arch and gullet.
- Go quickly but quietly under the pony's neck to the right side, lift the girth and bring it down gently. See that everything is smooth and flat under the saddle and the flap. Go round the pony to do this, as you cannot check properly by leaning over the saddle.
- Return to the left side, keeping your shoulder close to the pony's shoulder, bend down, and take hold of the girth. Put it through the loop of the martingale or breastplate (if used) and buckle it up tightly enough to keep the saddle from slipping. You should then attach the straps of the breastplate.

The girth should be buckled at approximately the same height on both sides. From time to time, tighten the girth on alternate sides. You should always have a few holes to spare. Run your fingers down between the girth (where it meets the saddle panel) and the pony's skin to ensure that the skin is lying smoothly. If the pony is rugged, leave the rug over the saddle with the front buckle undone. Before you mount, ensure your girth is tight enough; then check it periodically while riding, especially if your pony is inclined to blow himself out before you mount.

Putting on a crupper

If used, a crupper should be put on after the saddle is girthed. Again, a crupper should not be used to compensate for a poorly fitting saddle.

- Standing close to the left hind leg, gather up the tail in the right hand and pass it through the loop of the crupper.

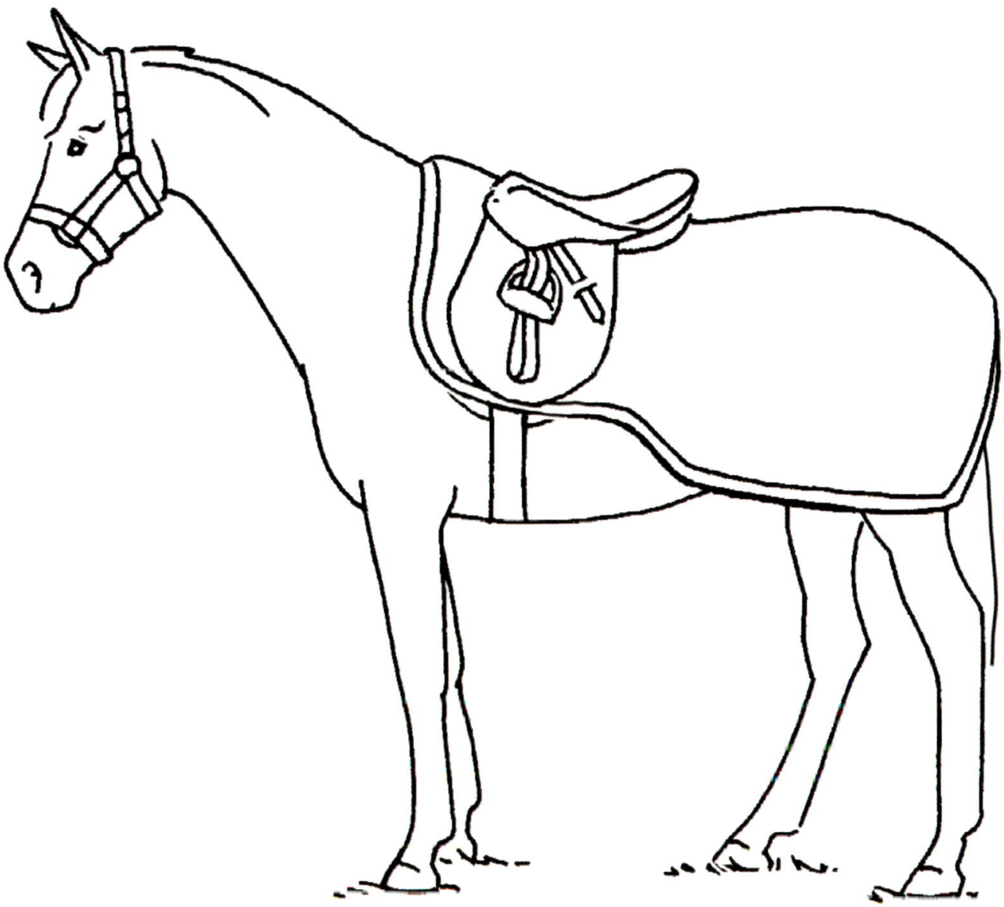

Figure 71: Exercise rug.

- Take care that the crupper lies well to the top of the dock and that all the tail hairs are through it and lying flat.
- Pass the strap through the D on the back of the saddle and adjust the length so that it steadies the saddle, but is not so short that it pulls up the tail.

Fitting an exercise rug under the saddle

An exercise rug is traditionally useful for clipped ponies in bad weather. A lightweight, waterproof design that will not cause overheating can be used when you need to keep a pony dry, perhaps because you are rugging and turning him out immediately afterwards. Some riders like to use a high-visibility exercise rug as part of their visibility equipment when riding on the road.

Specially designed exercise sheets that fit round rather than under the saddle are the most popular. However, you can also use one with a square front (a quarter sheet) or an ordinary day rug made from a lightweight wool mix, fleece or thermal fabric fitted under the saddle. Any rug must be securely fitted to prevent it slipping back while the pony is ridden. The rug should have a fillet string to prevent it from flapping or blowing up in a gust of wind.

With a rug which fits under the saddle:

- Place the rug on the pony and then put on the saddle.
- Push the rug well into the saddle gullet so there can be no pressure on the withers and backbone.
- Secure the rug by running the girth through the loop fittings on each side or folding the front corners back between the saddle panel and the girth straps before fastening the girth.
- If a day rug is used, the chest buckle and strap should not be beneath the saddle flap or the rider's legs.

Putting on a bridle

- Hang the bridle over your left arm, with the browband nearest your elbow and the rein buckles over the headpiece. This will free both your hands.
- Untie the pony's lead rope.
- Place the reins over the pony's head and neck. When removing the headcollar, you can hold him with the reins around his neck.
- Remove the headcollar and hang it up. Do not just drop it where you and the pony can tread on it.

- If the pony is in a box or stable, turn him to face the light. Put your right hand under the pony's jaw and round the other side to the centre of his face, just above the nostrils.
- Take both cheekpieces in this hand, keeping it close to the pony's face.
- With your left thumb, open his mouth and guide the bit into the mouth while your right hand eases the bridle up.
- Using both hands, place the headpiece gently and carefully over the pony's ears

Once the bridle is on:

- Arrange the mane and forelock so they are not caught under the leather.
- Check that the bit is level and that the browband and noseband are straight.
- Fasten the various buckles. Be sure to put the end of each strap neatly through its keeper and runner. The bridle should fit as described below:

Throatlash

This should be fastened first. It must never be fastened so tightly as to interfere with the pony's breathing or flexing. Allow the full width of your hand between it and the side of the jawbone.

Browband

The browband should not be so long as to sag in the centre of the forehead but long enough not to interfere with the hang of the bridle or to rub the pony's ears. It should lie just below but not touching the ears.

Noseband

This should be adjusted to allow two fingers' width between it and the front of the pony's face, thus allowing the pony to open his mouth slightly and relax his jaw. Adjust the height of the noseband so that it lies at the correct height for its design without rubbing on the facial bones. Straighten it by easing its headpiece below the browband on one side and manoeuvring it down on the other. Do not try to pull it through both loops of the browband simultaneously, as this will almost certainly pull the whole bridle crooked. Check that it is fitted so the side pieces will not touch the pony's eyes.

Breastplate

When fitting the breastplate, you should ensure that a hand can fit between your pony's chest and the strap. This allows for unrestricted movement and prevents excessive pressure on the saddle. There should be a hand clearance (10cm) over the wither and the strap. Some girths allow you to attach the breastplate strap (or martingale strap) to the girth using a buckle, whereas others require threading the girth through this strap. If the gap between the strap and your pony is too large, there is a risk of your pony catching a leg in the strap if he stumbles or jumps excessively high.

Martingale

When fitting a martingale (whether on its own or as an attachment to the breastplate), the running and standing martingale should share the same neckstrap. When fitted correctly, you should be able to place a hand between the top of your pony's neck and the strap (approximately 10cm). The rings of the running martingale ought to reach up to the withers. For a standing martingale, it should be adjusted so that when lifted to align along the neckline towards the gullet, a hand's width (10cm) can still fit between the strap and the pony's throatlash. If either is too short, it will generate downward pressure, which can restrict neck movement or exert downward pressure on the reins.

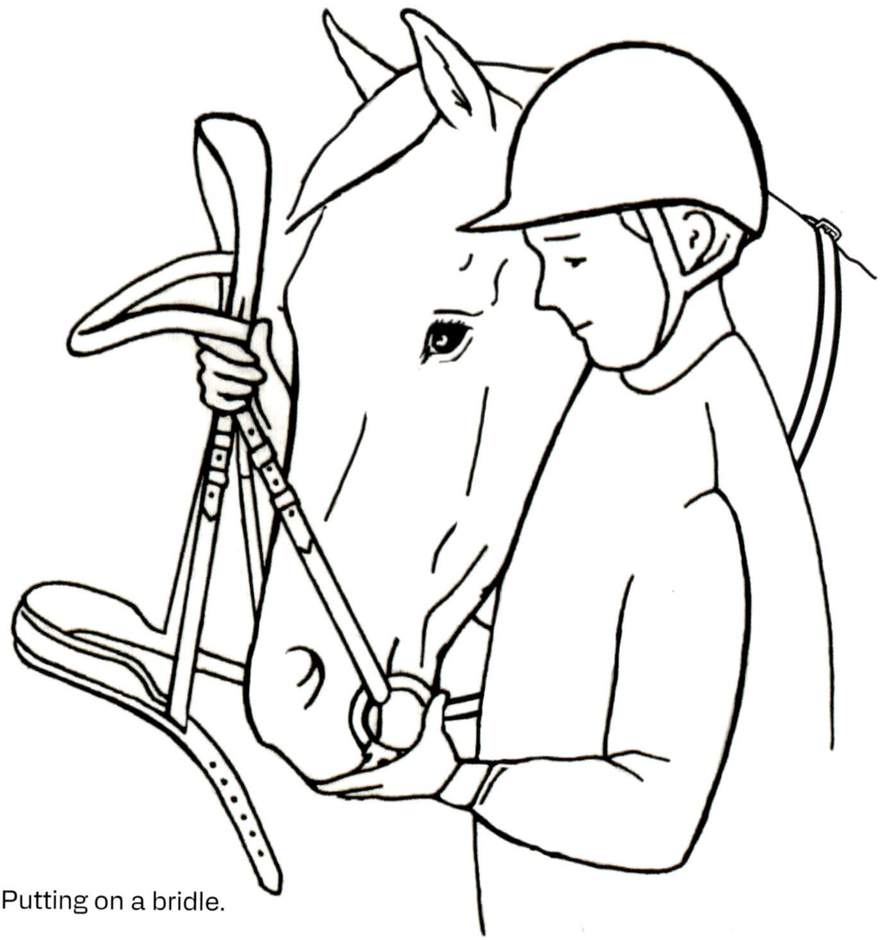

Figure 72: Putting on a bridle.

Bit

If necessary, the level of the bit should be adjusted through the buckles of the cheekpieces. Adjust the bit as explained earlier (refer to The 12 Rules of Bitting, Figure 66). Count the holes on each side of the headpiece to ensure they are as level as possible. Fine-tune the adjustment, if necessary, by adjusting the bridle a hole higher on one side than the other, then gently adjust the bit so it is level in the mouth.

Fitting the curb chain and lip strap

If a pelham or kimblewick is used, fit the curb chain so it lies in the chin groove and has the same number of rings on each side. The curb chain should come into action when the cheeks of the bit are drawn back to an angle of approximately 45° to the line of the mouth. Fit the spare end of the lip strap through the fly link and buckle up on the left side.

If you leave the pony saddled and bridled in the stable

If the reins are very long, loop them under the stirrups, or, as an added precaution, twist the reins round each other under the throat and pass the throatlash through one of them. Then put on the headcollar over the bridle and tie up your pony. Otherwise, he may roll and damage the saddle, or shake the reins over his head, and tread on them and break them.

If the pony is rugged, fasten the front buckle, lengthen the surcingle's and fasten it over the saddle and the rug. If the pony is to be left where there are two stout pillars or posts, for example, in the passageway of indoor stables, he may be cross tied.

Preparing to ride

When you are ready to leave the stable, pick out the pony's feet into a skip. Untie the pony and remove the headcollar. Hang it on a hook or somewhere handy for when you return. Take the reins over the pony's head and ensure that the stirrup irons are run up to avoid getting caught on any projections, particularly in the doorway.

Before mounting, look around again to ensure your saddlery is correctly fitted. Tighten your girth and adjust the buckle guards. Lifting each foreleg in turn and pulling it forward is a sensible precaution, but not essential, to smooth out any wrinkles in the skin under the girth. Pull both stirrup irons down. You are then ready to mount and move off.

Untacking

It is usual to untack from the nearside in this order: (1) saddle, (2) bridle, (3) martingale. The method varies, so the following is a guide:

To take off a saddle

Note: If there is a crupper, it must be removed first. Tie the pony up using a headcollar or ask a helper to hold him while you unfasten the crupper and slide it down the tail.

- After dismounting run up your irons. Take the reins over the pony's head and loop them over the arm nearest to head.
- Raise the saddle flap and unfasten the girth.
- If a martingale is worn, slip its loop off the girth.
- Release the girth carefully so it doesn't swing down and hit the pony on his legs.
- With one hand under the front arch and the other holding the cantle, slide the saddle off towards you and onto your forearm, with the front arch in the crook of your elbow.
- Take hold of the girth with the other hand as it comes over the back, placing its underside on the saddle seat.
- Put the saddle on the stable door or a fence or lay it carefully on the ground not too close to the pony's feet.

To take off a bridle

- Hold the headcollar over your arm or shoulder.
- Take the reins over the pony's neck.
- If you are using a curb bit, unhook the curb chain on the left side, leaving the lip strap fastened.
- Unfasten the noseband and slip off the loop of the standing martingale (if used). If a running martingale is used, unbuckle the reins, remove the martingale rings and re-buckle the reins.
- Unfasten the throatlash.
- You are now ready to remove the bridle.
- Put your left hand on the pony's face, well above his nostrils.
- With your right hand, slip the headpiece over the ears and lower it slowly, allowing the pony to ease the bit out of his mouth. If it is dropped out quickly, he may throw up his head and frighten himself by catching it on his teeth. For this reason, never remove a bridle with the curb chain or noseband fastened.
- Slip off the martingale neckstrap and place it with the headpiece on your left shoulder, leaving the reins around the pony's neck to give you control over him while you put on the headcollar.
- Take the reins over the pony's head onto your left shoulder and tie him up.

Keeping the bridle and martingale over your left shoulder, pick up the saddle and girth baton, and carry them correctly to a safe place. This way, you will leave nothing behind and avoid trailing the girth or reins on the ground.

- Put the saddle on a saddle stand and the bridle (and martingale) on the cleaning bracket or other hook. It is a good idea to wash the bit with a sponge and water soon after removing it and before any dirt hardens.
- Return to your pony and run your hands over his back and girth groove to feel for lumps or soreness. Pat the back briskly, but not heavily, to restore the circulation and help it to dry. Remember to deal with both sides.
- Groom as necessary.
- Rug up if appropriate.
- Check the corners and bars of the mouth and the chin groove for signs of rubbing. Treat any sore places with petroleum jelly and avoid whatever is causing the rubbing.
- Check that nothing lying about in the stable might get lost or damaged.

Care of your tack and equipment

Tack cleaning

- When cleaning tack, you should also check the stitching for safety and any signs of wear and tear that may be unsafe or uncomfortable for your pony.
- Clean tack breaks less often and is much less likely to rub a pony's skin. You can feel the difference if you wash a dirty bridle and touch and handle it before and after you use the saddle soap to clean it.
- You will need a bucket of warm water, two sponges, one for washing, one for soaping, some form of saddle soap or leather conditioner, and a small towel for drying bits and stirrups.

Figure 73: Cleaning tack.

- Bits must be washed in clean water after every use. The bit around the rings should be cleaned carefully, and the bit rings should be dried with a towel or cloth.
- Girths must be thoroughly inspected and cleaned after every ride. Mud, sweat and grease must be removed to keep the girth soft and comfortable.
- A saddlecloth or numnah should be washed frequently. Bio-detergents should not be used.

Frequency of cleaning the tack

Daily care: All bridles and saddles should be cleaned and conditioned after use.

Weekly care: Dismantle, clean, and condition thoroughly. Check all stitching and then reassemble. Wash numnahs/saddlecloths.

Monthly care: Check that the saddle still fits, including the tree, stuffing, and stitching.

Storing leather: If any leather work is not being used for a while it can be cleaned and stored to project it. To do this, treat with a leather dressing and wrap in cotton towelling.

Chapter 10

Training Horses and Ponies

Training Horses and Ponies

This chapter will introduce you to the basics of riding, including how to mount and dismount, sit and hold the reins, and start, stop and turn when riding. This will allow you to ride safely, control the walk and trot – both sitting and rising – and develop your work towards canter.

These are simple tasks to learn, but it's important that you start in the right way to ensure that you stay safe and are fair and kind to your pony; this way, you can have fun while learning to ride.

Safety checks: girth, stirrups

Safety first

Safety must always come first at every level, especially when learning to ride. When you learn to do things safely, these actions become the right habits to follow, resulting in fewer chances of accidents or injuries to yourself, your pony, or others. When we are all safe together, we can enjoy ourselves more while riding, whether alone or in a group.

It is important to consider safety rules for all riders, not just beginners.

- Dress safely for riding.
- Correct hat: Check Pony Club Rules, and an appropriate coloured tag is needed.
- Riding or jodhpur boots with a flat sole and clearly defined heel.
- Jodhpurs, or suitable trousers that do not wrinkle and become uncomfortable.
- No loose clothing that flaps, such as hoodies or scarves.
- Coats must be securely zipped.
- Hair, if long, is securely tied up.
- A responsible person should check your tack before you mount, checking both sides of

the saddle and bridle to ensure everything is safely and securely buckled.

- Ride a pony suitable for you, which you can handle and control safely, particularly when riding in a group.
- Ride, with supervision, in a secure, enclosed place and listen to any instructions your coach may give you.
- When riding in company, keep a safe distance (at least one pony's length) between your pony and any other pony.
- Pay attention to the pony you're riding, and how he is feeling and behaving. Always take good care of your pony after you ride him.
- Tell a responsible person if you think your pony doesn't feel well or behaves in a way you are not happy with.

Figure 74: A well-turned-out rider.

Checking your tack

Even if somebody else has tacked up the pony, you should always do a safety check before mounting. You should always check the girth to ensure it is sufficiently tight to prevent the saddle from slipping.

Follow the steps: once your pony has been tacked up, you should check all the tack.

- Start by keeping your hands on the reins so that you can always control the pony and stop him moving when you check the tack.
- Check the right side of the bridle. All the buckles should be fastened properly, and nothing should be twisted.
- Begin on the pony's right side(offside) and ensure the saddle is straight and the girth is securely fastened securely and threaded through the girth loop of the saddlecloth.
- Pull down the right stirrup, ready for mounting.
- Moving to the left side (nearside), check the fit of the bridle and that all the buckles are done up correctly and the ends are tucked in. Move to the saddle and check that the girth on this side has also been passed through the loop in the numnah and is tight enough for you to get on and that the saddle and numnah are straight.
- Check that the saddle flaps lie smoothly and that the girth guard is pulled down and over the buckle.
- Finally, pull down the left stirrup and be prepared to mount.

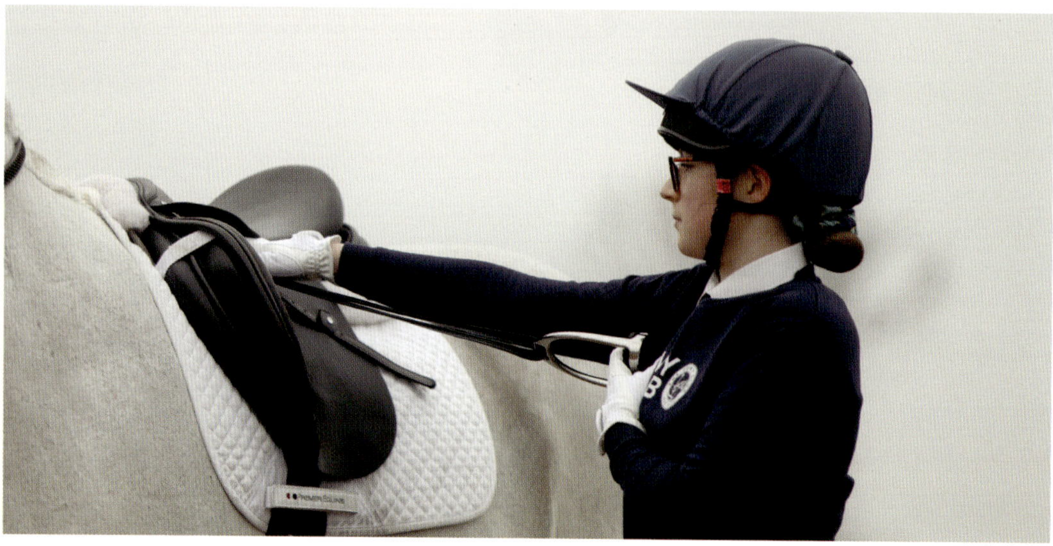

Figure 75: Checking stirrup length before mounting.

Mounting and dismounting: from the mounting block, ground, and leg up

Figure 76: Checking the stirrups are level (your pony should always be held when doing this).

When first learning to mount, you should have a responsible person to help you.

Before getting on, the stirrups should be pulled down on both sides. To ensure that the stirrup length is suitable before you mount, you can hold the stirrup to the inside of the armpit and measure with your fist to the saddle bar; this gives approximate guidance for the appropriate length for general riding. It doesn't matter if you are doing this from the left or right arm. Once you have adjusted the stirrup length, do the same to the other side and then stand in front of the pony, keeping hold of your reins, and visually assess that both stirrups are level.

Mounting from the mounting block

Mounting from a block rather than from the ground or with a leg up may be easier when learning to mount.

Mounting blocks are available in various heights and are often found both in and outside the arena. Portable blocks can be taken along if you travel to a rally or show. The benefit of mounting from a block is that it is kinder to the pony's back. There is also a reduced risk of your saddle twisting or slipping.

- You should lead your pony to the block and ask him to stand still so that his shoulder/saddle is level with the block.
- You should stand on the block facing towards him, putting the reins and baton (if you are carrying one) in the left hand and, with the right hand, take hold of the left stirrup and turn it clockwise.
- Place your foot into the stirrup, which will now be easier for you to put your foot in. As the block has a raised height, you can reach across the pommel of the saddle with your right hand.
- Push off from the block with your right leg and lightly and quickly take the right leg over the pony's quarters, making sure you don't brush the quarters with your right leg, landing quietly in the saddle and then placing the foot in the stirrup.

Mounting from the ground

When mounting from the ground, the same process is followed as when using a mounting block.

- To mount from the pony's left side (the nearside), stand with your left shoulder on the same side as the pony's left shoulder.
- Make sure you hold the reins and the baton (if you are carrying one) in your left hand to have sufficient control should the pony want to move. Check that the reins are separated so it is easy to adjust them into both hands when you get on. Having the right rein slightly shorter than the left is helpful, as this restricts the pony from moving away from you.
- Place your left hand in front of the wither, and with your right hand, turn the stirrup clockwise towards you, placing your left foot in the stirrup iron. It should still hang quite close to the pony.
- Then put your foot into the stirrup with the weight onto the ball of your foot. You can then take a step to swing up to the nearside, making sure your toe points down and does not dig into the pony's body.
- Turn around to face the saddle, and, with your right hand, ideally, hold the right-hand side of the pommel (or if you're not tall enough, on the right side of the seat).
- Springing quickly and lightly up, straighten your knees and swing your right leg over the pony's back, ensuring you miss the quarters with your right leg.
- As you do this, move your right hand to the front of the saddle.
- Sit quietly and gently, avoiding a bump or a bang, as this may upset the pony. Quickly place your right foot into the stirrup and then take the reins into both hands.
- As a best practice, it is helpful to be able to mount from both the near and the offside, as sometimes, when hacking, it is not easy to get on from the nearside.
- Once you are mounted and sitting correctly, recheck your girth and security. The pony may have taken a breath in (blown out), and it may be necessary to re-tighten.
- Lastly, check the lengths of both stirrups and ensure that they feel suitable and comfortable before moving off.

Receiving a leg-up

This is where someone helps you mount from the ground without a mounting block.

- Make sure your girth is sufficiently tight to prevent the saddle from slipping, and that both stirrups are down and at the correct length. Then prepare to mount as you would at a mounting block.

Figure 77: Mounting from a block.

- Take the reins into the left hand and place them on the pony's withers.
- If you are holding a baton, keep it in your left hand and make sure it sits on the right side of the pony's neck to avoid catching the person giving you a leg up in any way. Stand close to the pony and face the saddle.
- Bend your left leg backwards from the knee so it is at a 90° angle across the knee.
- The person giving the leg up will stand to the left of you and then place their left hand below your bent knee; their right hand is then placed around your left ankle or underneath your shin. (Exactly where the right hand is placed depends on your size and the efficiency of the person giving the leg-up).
- Keep your body parallel to the pony. On an agreed signal, (for example on the count of 1, 2, 3) you will jump upwards as the person legging up pushes your knee upwards, which allows you to jump higher and closer to the pony.
- At this point, you can lift and swing your right leg over the pony's quarters, landing quietly and lightly into the saddle.

You must keep your back straight and avoid leaning forward; if this happens, you may lose balance, making it challenging to receive a safe and efficient leg-up. As you are about to land in the saddle, the person helping you should stop pushing up and allow you to sit gently in the saddle.

Tightening the girth when mounted

- Before tightening the girth, you should check how tight it is.
- To tighten the girth on the left-hand side, take the reins (and baton if you are carrying one) into your right hand, always keeping your foot in the stirrup.
- Bring your left leg forward over the knee roll, then using your left hand, lift the saddle flap upwards and reach down for girth buckles.
- Slide the index finger along the tongue of the buckle, pulling the strap upwards with the rest of your hand. As you pull, you should be able to feel the higher hole (on the girth strap), and then you can guide the buckle tongue into the hole.
- Repeat the process on the other buckle, ensuring the girth is secured evenly on both straps.
- When you finish making any adjustments, pull down the girth guards to check that they are lying flat against the girth buckles.

Figure 78: Tightening the girth.

Dismounting

- First, to dismount from the left side (nearside), remove both feet from the stirrups. Place the reins and the baton in your left hand (if you are holding one), then place your left hand on the pony's neck.
- Swing your weight forward, placing your right hand on the front of the saddle.
- Quickly and calmly swing your right leg back, clearing the pony's quarters, allowing you to land with both feet on the ground simultaneously, making sure you bend your knees to land gently.
- Once standing, run up the stirrups and adjust your reins so you can lead or move the pony as needed.

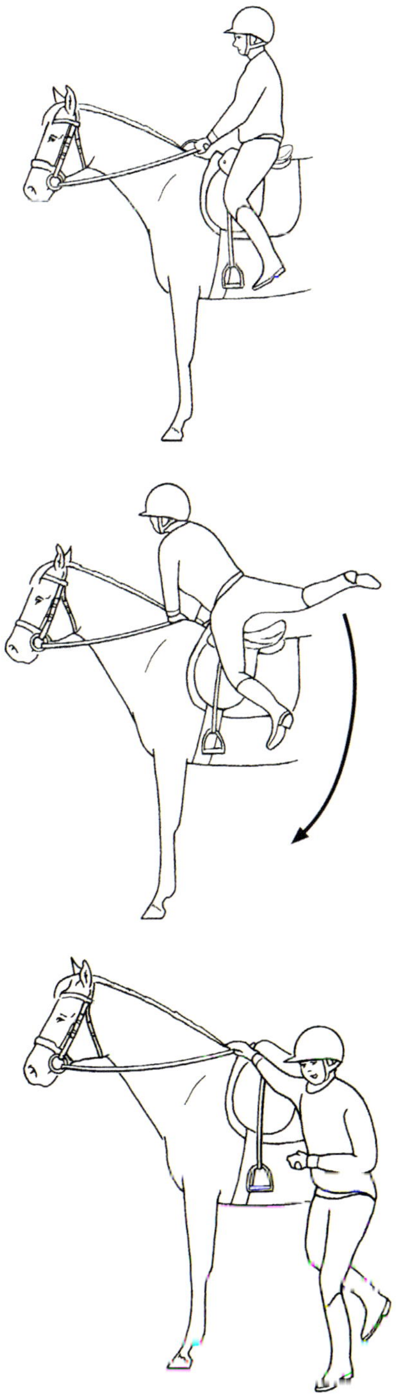

Figure 78: Dismounting

- Never dismount by swinging your leg forward and over the pony's neck. You must let go of your reins if you do this, and if your pony moves off, you could fall and hurt yourself.
- If you are not riding your pony for a while, you can loosen the girth by a hole or two.

Altering the length of the stirrup when mounted

Shortening stirrups

- When adjusting the stirrup length, your feet should always remain in the stirrups.
- As most people are right handed, it is easier to learn this process with the more dexterous hand.
- First place the reins into your left hand, starting with the right stirrup. With your right hand, take hold of the spare end of the stirrup leather and pull upwards to release the buckle from the stirrup bar.
- With your index finger, pull the stirrup leather up through the stirrup bar. You will be able to feel the holes remaining in the stirrup leather, and adjustments can then be made of a hole or two.
- As you pull the leather upwards, the tongue of the buckle should come free from the leather.
- You can then pull the stirrup leather through the stirrup head and feel the appropriate hole to allow the buckle to fit into the hole.
- Once adjusted, lean slightly forward and take hold of the inside part of the stirrup leather, pulling it down to bring the buckle to the top of the stirrup bar.
- Once completed, replace the spare end of the stirrup leather with the strap on the side of the saddle flap to stop the stirrup from interfering with the comfort of your leg when riding.

Lengthening

- The stirrup leather can be lengthened similarly to shortening.
- Your feet should always remain in the stirrups when adjusting the stirrup length.
- First, pull up the stirrup leather, releasing the buckle from the stirrup bar.
- As before, you should use your index finger against the tongue of the buckle; at the same time, press down with your right foot into the stirrup, and this will pull the stirrup leather through the stirrup bar; again with your index finger feel for the appropriate hole and allow the stirrup leather buckle to come into that hole.
- When doing this, the buckle will probably remain on the top of the stirrup bar, so there is no need to pull the stirrup leather through from the inside to ensure the stirrup buckle is on the bar again.
- Adjust the remaining excess stirrup leather to secure and tuck it into the saddle flap before riding.

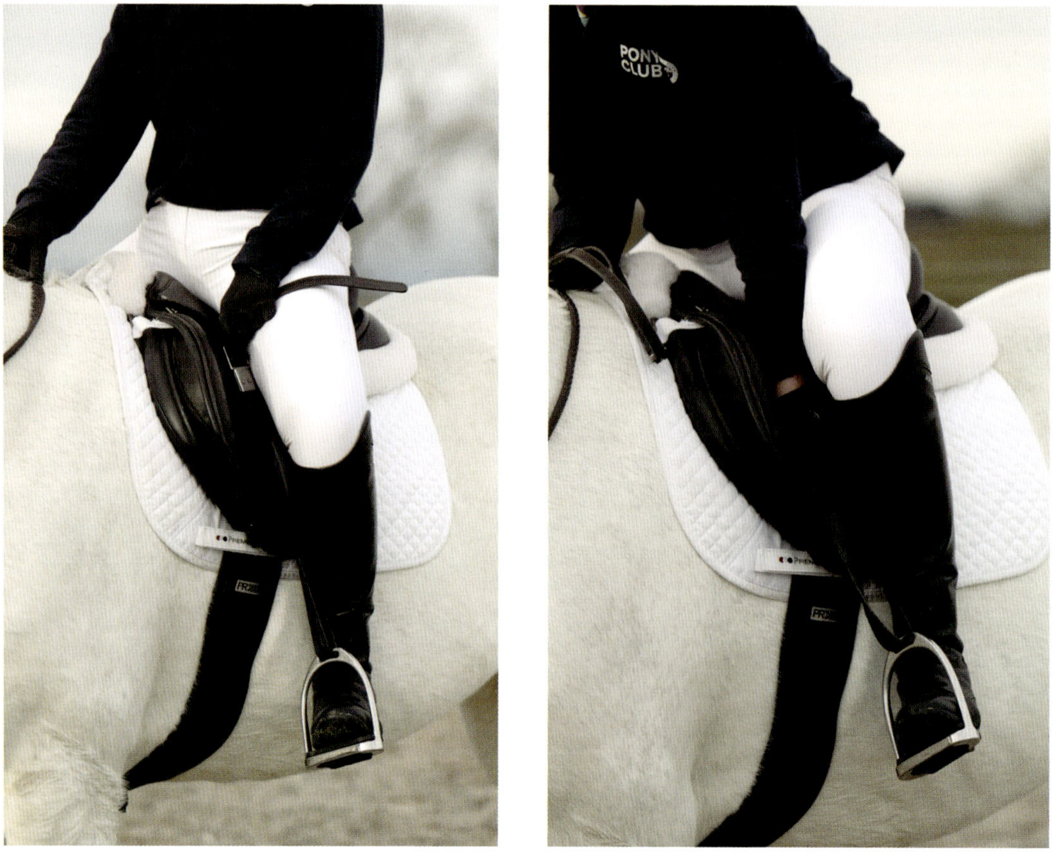

Figure 80: Adjusting stirrups.

Chapter 11

The Correct Riding Position

The Correct Riding Position

To become a good rider – both safe and skilled – it is important for you to sit in the saddle in the correct place keeping an independent position on the flat and over fences. You aim to keep your weight in a place where the pony can carry you easily and comfortably. This is just behind the wither, close to the pony's centre of balance or gravity.

Figure 81: Sitting correctly.

Standing still: seat, legs and hands

Sitting on your pony

- Sit in the lowest part of the saddle.
- Hips and shoulders square to the pony.
- Viewed from the side, there should be a straight line from your elbow continuing to your wrist to the hands and along the reins towards your pony's bit.
- There should also be a visual straight line from the shoulder, through the hips to the ankle.
- The weight of your body is carried equally on both seat bones.

Head	**Look where you are going.**
Shoulders	**Relaxed and the same height (level and square to the body) as each other.**
Arms	**Upper arms close to the body, with a bend in the elbow.**
Hands	**Thumbs pointing upwards towards the pony's ears with the fingers closed around the rein.**
Back	**Upright and tall.**
Legs	**Even length for both legs, knee just away from the saddle.**
Feet	**Balls of the feet on the stirrup, heel slightly below the level of the toe.**

Holding the reins

- Hold the rein between your little and third finger of your hand.
- The rein will lie across the palm of your hand.
- Thumbs should be on top of your hand and should point upwards.

The rein passes directly from the bit between the little and third fingers of your hand, across the palm and over the first index finger, the thumb can then sit quietly on the top of the hand, pointing towards the pony's opposite ear. Holding the reins this way prevents the rein from slipping or being pulled through your hand.

Figure 82: How to hold the reins correctly.

Shortening and lengthening the rein

- To make the reins shorter, you should hold the buckle end of your left rein with your right hand while you slide your left hand down the rein.
- Then hold the buckle end of the right rein while you slide your right hand down the rein. Put your thumbs on the end of the reins so they won't slip.
- To make your reins longer, open your fingers a little and let the rein slide through your fingers before closing your hands quietly around the reins when they are at a suitable length.

'The contact' is the amount of pressure from your hands to the bit. To generate a suitable contact the pony should accept the feel through the rein and relax to the pressure. This is only achieved if the pony can go with the movements of his head and neck, and in turn, this is only achieved when you can maintain an independent seat and are not dependent on the reins to keep your balance. It is the pony's responsibility to take the reins forward to secure his balance rather than using the reins for your own balance. Some ponies respond to lighter contact than others, and this is known as 'feel'. This pressure will change according to individual ponies and their level of training. The position of your hands may change and be higher or lower depending on the pony's shape, size, education, and the work that he is doing.

Moving – how to maintain your balance and position

- You should follow the pony's movement to keep your own balance.
- You should be aware of the change in the pony's rhythm when he begins to move.
- Your hands follow the movement of the neck.
- Your rein length changes when you walk, trot and canter.
- Your weight remains in your feet and through the stirrups all the time.

When you first begin to ride, someone should lead your pony until you find your balance, you are comfortable walking, and you have learned how to control your pony. The person leading you should check that you can walk, trot, turn left and turn right and know how to slow your pony down from trot to walk and walk to halt before you are ready to ride on your own.

Ponies come in all breeds and sizes; their individual shape will influence your position too. A rounder-shaped pony, such as some native ponies and cobs, may well make it necessary for you to sit with a shorter stirrup length (to accommodate the width of the pony). The opposite applies to a taller pony with a narrower frame. This shape of pony will enable you to sit with a longer leg that is straighter from your hip. Consequently, the stirrup length will vary between these types of ponies (shorter for the wider pony and longer for the taller one).

Remember, as you grow, your body will change shape. This may affect your balance and feeling of security and safety. Your age, shape and strength will influence how you can sit and maintain an independent position. If you are feeling less confident, you may be encouraged to ride a little shorter and with less contact until your confidence improves. If you ride with your stirrups too long, there is a tendency to use the reins for balance and security. Do consider that when you grow, you may need to have larger stirrups too.

Chapter 12

The Basic Paces

The Basic Paces

Walk, trot, canter, gallop

Walk

- The walk is a four-time pace – the pony moves the left hind, then the left fore, followed by the right hind and then the right fore.
- The pony always has a leg on the ground.
- There is no suspension.
- When your pony is walking, you will find that this natural movement will move your hips and seat bones forward and back.
- You sit tall and stay relaxed in your lower back.
- Your pony walks at about 6.5km per hour (4 miles per hour).

Rising trot

- The trot is a two-time pace, the pony's legs moving in diagonal pairs, with a moment of suspension (all the pony's legs are off the ground at the same time), and a moment of suspension between each pair.

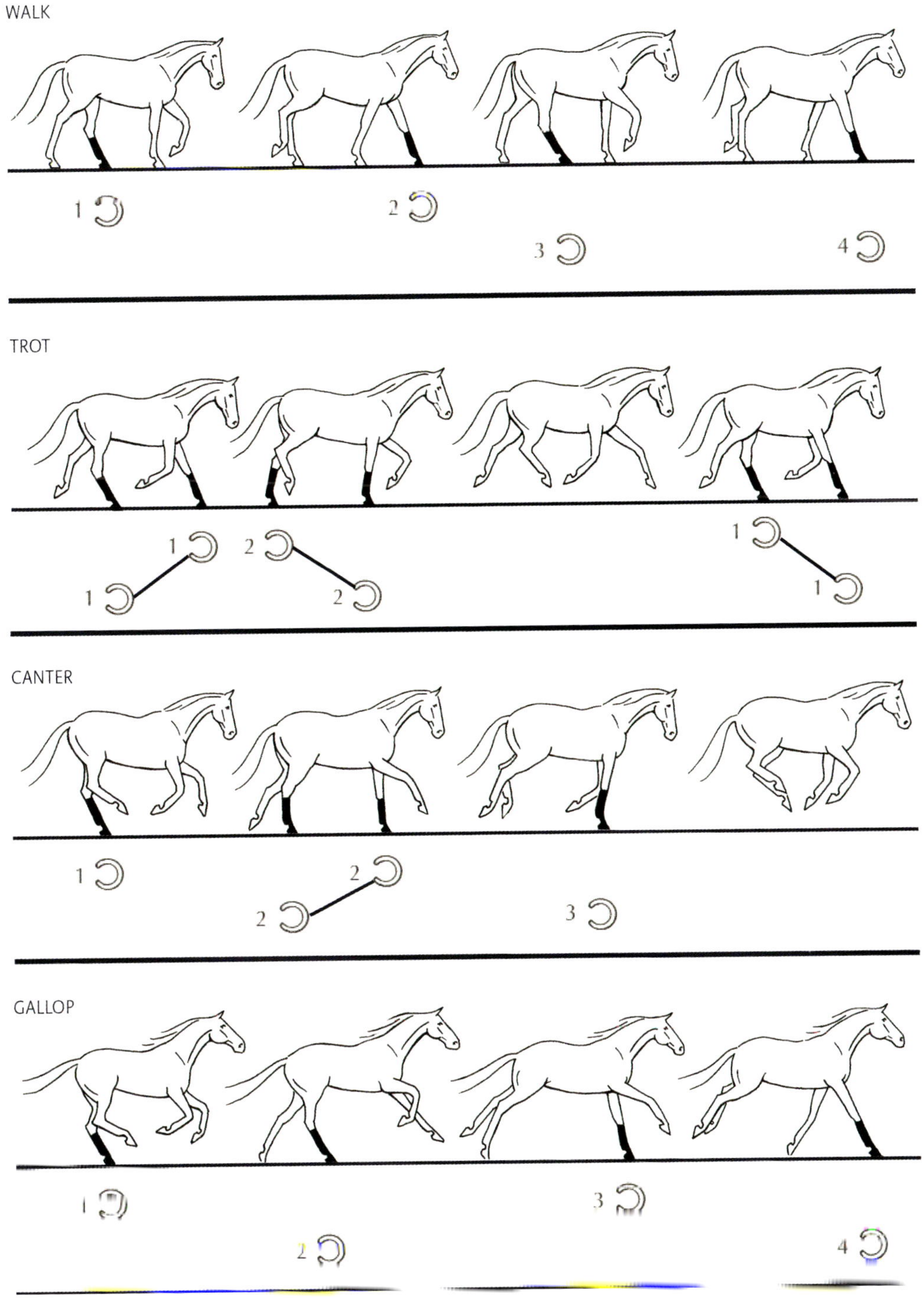

Figure 83: Footfalls for walk, trot, canter and gallop.

- You lift your seat and rise above the saddle as the pony pushes off from the ground with the hind leg.
- Your shoulders can be taken forward to start lifting the body upwards.
- Your hips are moved up off the saddle by the pony pushing you upwards and forwards.
- You should return to the saddle between rising with your weight controlled and sitting down lightly.
- Your pony trots at about 9.5km per hour (6 miles per hour).

In a rising trot, you rise from the saddle on one beat and sit in the saddle on the alternate beat. In the rising trot, your shoulders lead the movement while staying tall over your hips.

The pony's natural trotting pace provides a swinging-back-and-forward energy that enables your seat to be 'pushed' upwards and forwards. Care should be taken to allow your body weight to fall back onto the saddle gently, and unsupported (by the reins); landing back in the saddle clumsily would put you behind the pony's movement and may encourage the pony to hollow the back and rush forward to avoid the unbalanced pressure.

- You need to sit down with a light seat, staying tall (using your core).
- Your hip and knee joints should stay supple to accommodate the rising and lowering movements of the trot.
- You should keep your weight in the stirrup irons, and the contact of the lower legs should be consistent (think of cuddling the pony's sides with your calves).
- Your elbow and shoulder joints should be soft and supple, with your elbows resting close to your waist; this position allows your hands to maintain the same contact as you rise and return to the saddle.
- It is essential that a consistent contact is always maintained and that the reins are not used for support.

Diagonals

- In the rising trot, you should be sitting when the outside foreleg comes back.
- When changing the direction (rein), you should sit for an extra beat (two) and then begin to rise again.
- The diagonal is checked by looking down at the outside shoulder to ensure you sit when this leg comes backwards.

When your pony is trotting on the left rein, the left hind and the right foreleg both move as a diagonal pair and touch the ground at the same time. We call this the right diagonal, when the outside (right foreleg) touches the ground and then begins to move backwards. You are said

Figure 84: How to check your diagonal.

to be the correct diagonal when your seat returns to the saddle at the same time as the right forefoot and left hind foot touch the ground. You can learn to feel this by initially looking down at your pony's outside shoulder to check.

To change your diagonal, you sit down in the saddle for an extra beat before rising again. You should change your diagonal when changing direction and at intervals when out hacking so that the pony uses the muscles on both sides of his body equally.

Sitting trot

- This is only used once you can ride correctly in rising trot, as it can be very bouncy when learning.
- The pony must also be balanced so you can sit properly and efficiently.
- You stay sitting in the saddle all the time.
- You must keep your weight into your feet and the stirrups all the time.
- Your calves can be close to the pony's side with your knees slightly away from the saddle.
- When learning to do this, you should do small amounts as too much may be uncomfortable for both you and your pony.

At sitting trot, you sit for both beats of the trot. This is important to learn to stay in balance when riding your transitions from trot to walk and trot to canter. Remember to keep the weight on the ball of your foot, this will keep your weight down through your leg and prevent you from gripping upwards.

Sitting trot is an important skill to learn; we start to use it when riding transitions (moving from one pace to the other), such as trot to walk, trot to canter and canter to trot.

Canter

- The canter is a three-time pace. You can have left or right canter depending on which foreleg is leading.
- There is a moment of suspension when all the legs are off the ground.
- You usually keep your weight in the saddle.
- Your hips move forwards and backwards to stay in balance with the pace.
- You stay tall and straight in the saddle.
- Your pony canters at about 12km per hour (8 miles per hour).

You will learn to ask the pony to canter with the inside foreleg leading through turns and/or circles. In this pace, the suppleness of your hips is most important. Your upper body should move in rhythm with the three beats of the pony's stride. Your seat should remain close to the saddle for all three beats, with your back and hips allowing this through their suppleness. The suppleness and mobility of your shoulder and elbow joints is also very important, as there is considerable movement of the pony's head, neck and back. If you stiffen your back, you will bump into the saddle, which is most uncomfortable for both the pony and you.

Gallop

- The gallop is a four-time pace.
- There is a moment of suspension when all the legs are off the ground.
- You should stay in a light seat with a shorter stirrup length than when cantering.
- Your pony gallops at about 24km per hour (15 miles per hour).

You will need to ride with a short stirrup length, usually a couple of holes shorter than when you are cantering. There may be an opportunity to go faster when hacking (a controlled gallop). Rushing around at shows is not a good idea.

The Scale of Training

The Scale of Training comprises six steps that riders follow to prepare ponies for general riding, dressage, and competitions in The Pony Club. These steps are:

- Rhythm.
- Suppleness.
- Contact.

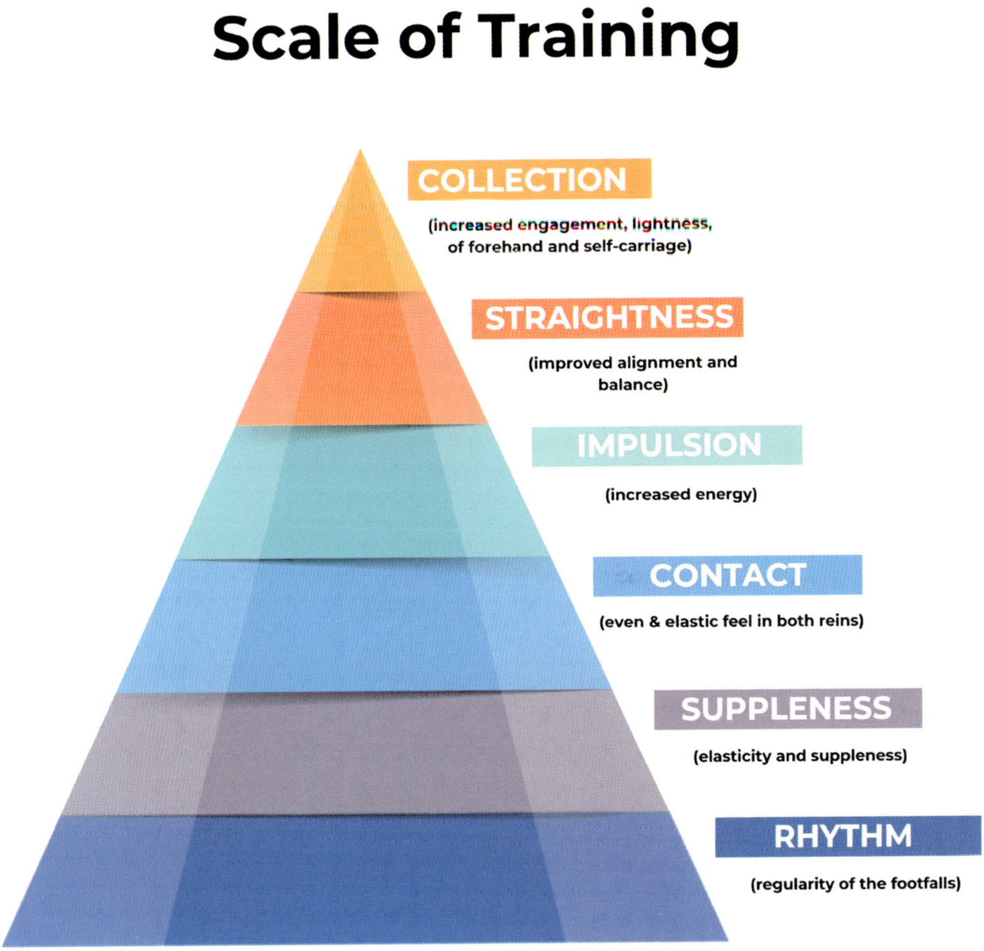

Figure 85: Scale of Training.

- Impulsion.
- Straightness.
- Collection.

The pyramid is only as strong as its base; therefore, the first three steps are the crucial areas to concentrate on.

Rhythm: is the regularity of the footfalls. Rhythm refers to the regular and repeated movement pattern created by your pony's strides. This rhythmic motion mimics the natural cadence of your pony's pace, whether it's a leisurely walk, a brisk trot, or a lively canter.

Tempo: is the speed of the rhythm and refers to the speed at which your pony moves. It's the pace at which the rhythm unfolds, whether it's a slow and steady walk when hacking or a fast canter when crossing an open field. Understanding tempo is important for you to learn so that you can adjust your posture, balance, and cues to match the pony's speed. A slower tempo may offer a relaxed ride or maybe your pony is being lazy, while a faster tempo can make the pony seem out of balance, particularly when turning.

The difference between rhythm and tempo becomes more obvious as you become more experienced. You can learn to distinguish between the steady beat of the pony's hoofbeats and the varying speeds at which those beats occur. As you become more confident and experienced, you will be able to control the tempo, through your use of subtle cues to slow down, increase, or maintain a steady pace.

Suppleness: The aim is for your pony's muscles to function correctly and to be free from resistance; his joints should be loose, and he should not tighten against your aids. The key muscles include those from his hind legs over the quarters, the loins, in front of the wither, and up to the poll. A test of whether a horse is supple and working 'through' the back and neck is that when the rein contact is eased (as in a free walk), he will want to stretch forward and down rather than trying to hollow and lift his head.

Contact: The ideal contact is a light, even and elastic feel in both reins, achieved by aids from your legs and seat rather than your hands. Your legs are applied as a forward aid, asking your pony to step under more and work 'through' his muscles along his poll, neck and over the back. When the contact is established correctly, your pony's outline and steps will be 'round', springy, and energetic. When this happens, we use the term that your pony is 'connected'.

How the scale is used

- Riders follow the scale to build a strong foundation for the pony.
- The scale helps ponies become stronger and more supple.
- The scale helps ponies respond to aids and stay balanced.
- Judges use the scale to score tests.

How the scale is applied

- Riders work on exercises to improve each scale.
- Riders think of the scale as a pyramid, working from the bottom up.
- Riders ensure that lower scales are developed before moving to the next scale.

Why the scale is important

- The scale is a guideline for trainers, riders, and judges.

- The scale is used by riders and trainers all over the world.
- The German cavalry initially devised the scale to train their military horses.

Transitions

- A transition is when a pony moves from one pace to another.
- An upward transition is from halt to walk, walk to trot or trot to canter.
- A downward transition is from canter to trot, trot to walk or walk to halt.
- You will probably find that upward transitions are easier for you to master than downward ones.

During transitions, your body should remain in balance with your pony's movement. Your body should stay quiet and supple, neither anticipating nor being left behind at the increasing or decreasing pace. You should stay tall and look where you are going throughout the transition. The trot-to-canter transition and vice versa are often the hardest to achieve.

Turns and circles, lines and school movements

Inside and outside

- The inside is the side of the pony on the inside of the movement. When you are riding on a left circle, the inside is the pony's left side.
- The outside is the side of the pony that is outside of the movement. When you are riding on a left circle, the outside is the right side of the pony.

The bend of the pony

When riding on a curved line, on a circle or around a corner, your pony should appear to bend his body uniformly from the poll to the tail to follow the curve of the circle. This is termed 'the bend' and will help him to balance and carry you more easily. This happens by the rider using their inside leg, and not via the reins.

Circles and changes of direction

- The size of a circle is dependent on its width or diameter. A 20m circle will have a diameter of 20m.
- It is best to keep slightly more weight on your inside stirrup and foot to stay balanced as the pony is constantly bending around the circle.
- Your shoulders should follow the shape of the circle.

When riding on a circle, you need to maintain your weight on both seat bones and stay sitting in the middle (or centre) of the saddle. You should have slightly more weight into your inside stirrup, helping you stay in balance. This is particularly difficult when riding in canter on a circle, as the constant turning may push you to the outside of the circle. Your hips should remain parallel (in the same direction) with your pony's hips, and your shoulders should be parallel with your pony's shoulders.

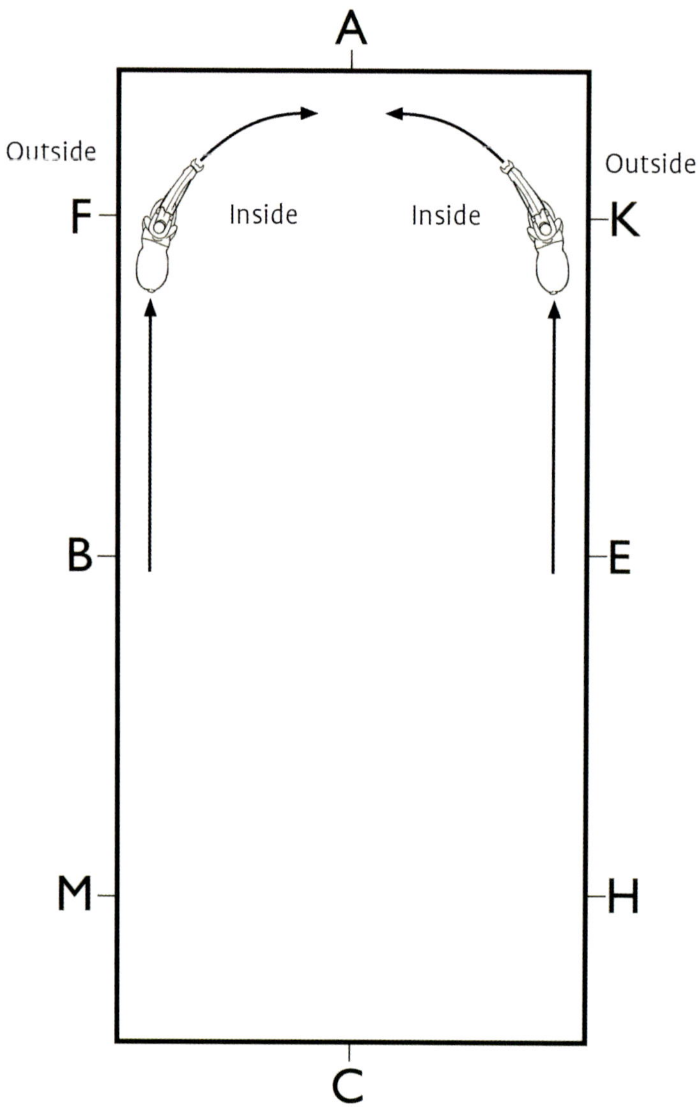

Figure 86: Uniform bend.

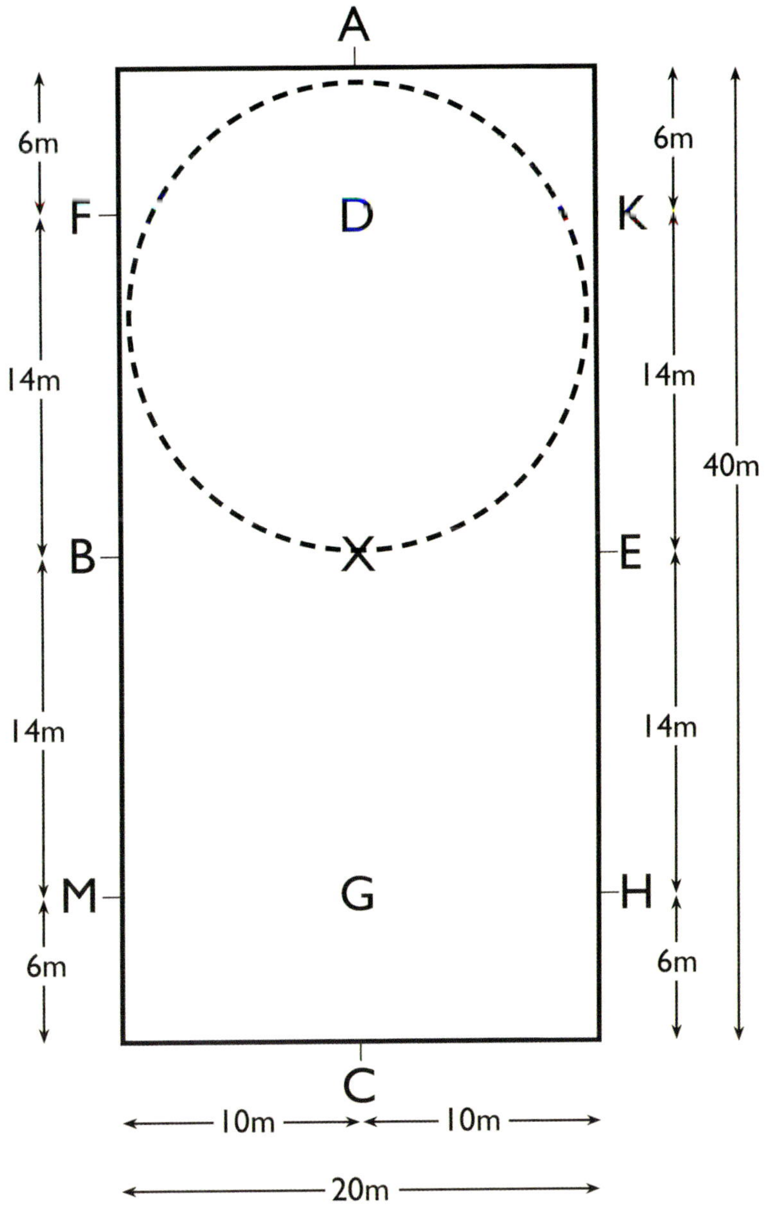

Figure 87: 20 x 40m arena and 20m circle.

Changing direction

You need to stay in balance with your pony while changing direction. You should be looking in the direction you want to go. This will allow you to put more weight into your new inside stirrup. When doing this, your pony will prepare for the new change in direction.

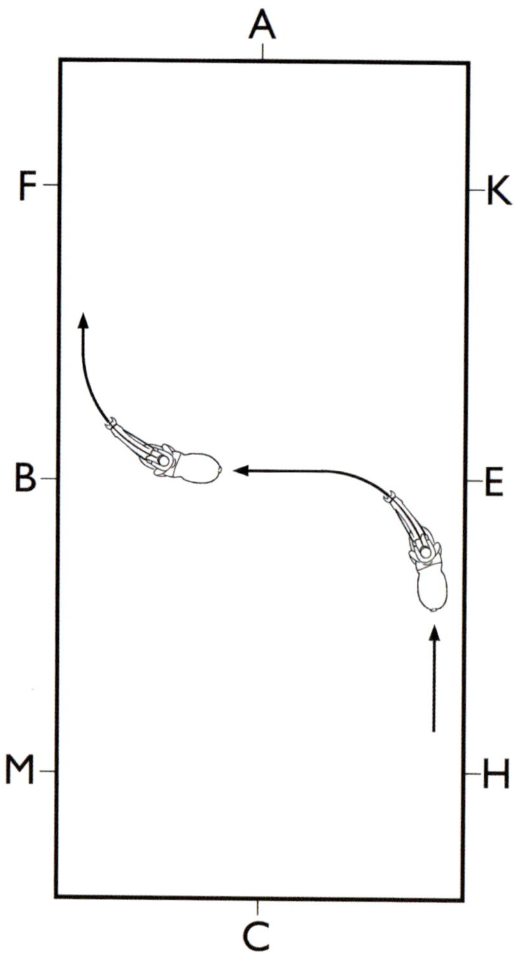

Figure 88: The arena and simple changes of direction.

Chapter 13

The Aids and How you Use Them

The Aids and How you Use Them

The aids are the method by which we communicate with the pony. Like all languages, there is a basic structure, but the principle is that the pony will react to pressure and release. It is the use of natural aids through their pressure and timing that will create understanding and desired behaviour between you and your pony. It is your responsibility to understand the use, the reasons for, and the effects of your communication and your aids. Failure to communicate with your pony in a way that he understands may create confusion and possible undesired behaviour.

The natural aids are: voice, legs, seat, hands

The voice

Your voice is classified as a natural aid by its tone and expression; it may influence your pony in many ways. Your pony can respond to the quickness of the voice, such as 'walk on' and 'trot' or saying 'whoa' or 'wa-alk' to reduce the energy of the pace.

The legs

Your legs are usually used with your other aids; their main role is to encourage your pony to move forward, and for steering and bend. When both legs are used together, they:

- Create forward movement.
- Activate the hindquarters.
- Maintain and support straightness.

As your pony has a natural flight response when pressure is initially applied to his sides, his reaction is to move forward away from the pressure. This is why you must use your leg actively with a squeeze of your calves to create this reaction, (and then take it off).

Using your leg repetitively will create a response from the pony. When your pony has responded to your legs, you can keep your leg in a quiet, soft contact against your pony's sides.

If you choose to use one leg more than the other, the pressure of your leg on the pony's side will encourage him to move in that direction. This effect can be used to move the pony laterally (sideways). If this movement is not required, the outside leg can be used in coordination to control the straightness and support the pony through a corner. Therefore, when both legs are applied, the pony will move forward.

The seat

The seat can only be used effectively as an aid when sitting correctly and in balance. You should be able to carry your weight equally on both seat bones. Your seat must follow the movement of the pony's back to maintain suppleness and the swing through the pony's back. Relaxing your seat and sitting deep and tall tells your pony to slow down or stop. If you turn your head and body to one side, your pony will know they should turn in that direction.

The hands

- Support the pony's balance.
- Indicate direction.
- Support the bend.
- Can help control the speed.
- The aim is to encourage an elastic feel from your hand to the bit, generating clear communication through the rein to your pony.
- You can also influence the contact through your hand, wrist, elbow, and shoulder, not just the hands holding the reins.
- Your hands hold the reins and should be used in a soft, light manner so that your pony is comfortable in his mouth and will be encouraged to take the rein forward.
- Your hands maintain a feel in the contact between your body and the pony's mouth/bit.

The aim is for the contact to be consistent in both reins. If you use your hands together (like squeezing water out of a sponge), your pony will slow down or stop. However, the tension in the contact may change when your pony is working on a turn or circle, and you may need to use the contact to support your pony's balance and way of going. Your hands can be used independently of each other to create specific communications with your pony. To ask your pony to move forward, both hands must relax.

Inside hand

Your inside hand guides and supports the pony's direction of movement. The contact should always be relaxed and light to encourage the pony's lower jaw to relax and accept the bit.

Outside hand

Your outside hand receives the energy created from your inside leg. It acts in a controlling manner to maintain consistent contact with the pony and the direction of travel. This is particularly important when riding a turn, a circle, or a change in direction.

Rewarding your pony

The voice is also used to praise or soothe your pony. It can be associated with a rub, scratch or stroke on the neck, which is a valuable and easy way to communicate a reward when mounted as a recognition of good work and a way of saying 'thank you'.

Coordination of the aids

Your aids should be short (quick); you should use them and then relax them immediately; a long, hard pull or squeeze will annoy and confuse the pony. To ensure your pony pays attention, give him another short aid, maybe a bit stronger than the first time, but not any longer. Sometimes, you may have to repeat this until he responds.

In time, you should aim to give aids that are invisible to the onlooker while understood by your pony. The educated rider can ride at a chosen pace using coordinated leg and hand aids. Without resistance, your hands receive the energy created by the pony's hind legs and quarters. This should give you the feeling that your pony is going forward in balance between your legs and hands, forming a harmonious partnership.

Artificial aids: baton, schooling stick and spurs

These are classified as equipment that can be used independently to either support your natural aids or stimulate communication between you and your pony. It is important to check The Pony Club guidance on the use of any equipment, as these aids and the rules regarding them are under constant review.

Using the schooling stick

Only some people need to carry a schooling stick. If you do, then this piece of equipment is used to reinforce your leg aids if your pony is not reacting positively to your aid. It is considered best practice to carry the schooling stick in your inside hand as this supports your leg pressure from the inside leg to the outside rein. Generally, when riding on the flat, using a schooling stick is best. This is usually between 0.90m and 1.2 m long so that it can be used to reinforce your inside leg without you taking your hand off your reins. This is achieved by flicking the stick across your thigh, resulting in a tickle or tap to your pony's side behind your leg.

Jumping baton

- The baton is usually no more than 75cm.
- Due to its length, the hand holding the baton must be removed from the rein when it is used.
- To do this, hold both reins in one hand and apply the baton behind your leg.

- Using a baton can be beneficial when jumping and should be carried in your hand on the side that a pony may be likely to shy or run out from.

To change the baton from one hand to the other

To change from left to right hand:

- Hold both the reins and your baton in your left hand.
- With your free right hand, pick up the baton and pull it upwards and across your pony's neck to the right-hand side.
- Bring the baton down towards your pony's shoulder and take back the right rein.

You should practise this so you can quickly change hands, as this may be needed to guide your pony to a narrow fence.

Use of spurs

These are categorised as an artificial aid, and there are many types and designs of spur. Spurs should only be used when you can correctly control and apply the pressure and release of the

Figure [illegible]. A baton and schooling stick a) baton, b) schooling stick

pressure of your legs to your pony's side. The spur should not be used to replace an ineffective leg aid. If you have an insecure lower leg, which results in you riding out of balance, then using the spur will negatively impact the pony's understanding of its application. This may result in poor behaviour through poor rider communication and harm your pony. The Pony Club has introduced a Test to assess whether a rider understands the effect of riding in spurs and is ready to use them.

The Spurs Test (2024)

The purpose of the Spurs Test is

- To educate riders on the welfare issues that might occur with spurs.
- Know that any use of spurs that compromises your pony's well-being will never be tolerated in The Pony Club.
- Spurs must only be used to give a more precise leg aid and to facilitate better communication from rider to horse.
- They are not to make the horse go faster.
- Spurs must never be used to vent a rider's anger or to reprimand the horse.
- Use of the spurs that cause injury, e.g. blood, broken skin, or a wound, is always classed as misuse.
- Misuse of the spurs anywhere at an event will result in disqualification.
- Spurs are not permitted in Endurance, Pony Racing or Mounted Games.

To pass the Spurs Test, the rider must demonstrate that they possess the skill to ride with an independent seat. If a rider's seat is stable only because they grip with their lower leg, knee, or thigh, or maintain balance with the reins, then they are not ready to wear spurs. Some may

Good. Too high. Too low.

Figure 90: Correctly fitted spurs.

be unaware that they are unbalanced with an unstable leg or that their toe points outward or downward, leading to excessive spur use.

The spur should be fitted to the back of the heel of your riding boot so that the shank is horizontal to the heel. The spur must never point upwards. A skilled rider who maintains balance with an independent lower leg can decide when to use the spur and when not to. The distance from the heel to the end point of the spur determines its length

With artificial aids, it is wise to check the permitted use and design in competitions and training events.

Application of the aids

The pony predominantly understands the pressure of the aids and the rider's weight (through their position).

You should be able to be selective in how you use the aids and be aware of the effect the timing of the aid has on the pony.

Using your aids – timings and reinforcement

Aids to walk

From the halt, you should ask the pony to walk forward by using both your legs (side by side or simultaneously, or at the same time) on the girth, asking the pony to move forward, and following the movement of the pony's head and neck with your hands. If the pony is not immediately responsive, the aid should be repeated quicker, rather than with a stronger leg.

Two types of walks are important for you and your pony to learn. Medium walk is the normal 'marching' walk for your pony. This is when you hold your reins at a suitable length and tension so that your pony can walk freely forward, paying attention, and is ready for any commands to change the pace.

Walking on a long rein is a pace where your pony keeps the same walk steps (four beat) and is encouraged to stretch his neck forwards and downwards. This allows your pony to relax his head and neck and is used for rests between work or after a dressage test. To ride on a long rein, the reins can slip through your fingers, with your pony still walking freely forwards. Your pony will want to stretch his neck forward and down to keep in contact with your rein. The reins can be shortened to return to medium walk (see shortening the reins).

Aids to trot

The previous pace must be of good quality with your pony actively walking, or marching forwards. From halt or walk, you ask for the trot by giving a quick inwards nudge with your legs, your hands going with the movement of the pony's head and allowing the pony to step actively into the change of pace. The pace is maintained using your inside leg. This naturally happens during a rising trot, when your leg naturally falls closer to the pony's side as you rise and should release the pressure when you sit.

Aids to canter

Before asking for a canter, check that the trot is of good quality. Your pony must accept the contact and go freely forward in balance and with energy in the trot. When preparing to canter, you should indicate the direction with your inside hand, then you should sit for a few strides in the trot while maintaining the energy with your inside leg; then position the outside leg just behind the girth. The pony is asked for canter by giving a definite nudge to the pony's side with your inside leg on the girth. As the outside leg is slightly behind the girth, this can be applied simultaneously to encourage the pony to step forward with the outside hind (as the starting leg for the canter sequence). As your pony strikes off into canter, you will feel the change of pace, and you must be particularly careful to remain supple, relaxed and in balance so that the pony can respond to the transition and stay in canter.

How to ride a downward transition

A good transition is created by effective preparation. Begin by deciding where you want your pony to change pace. Sit tall, look straight ahead, close your legs gently on the pony's sides and feel with the reins. Your voice – used calmly – can also be useful in helping the pony to slow. (Try, 'Whoa!'). As your pony responds to the aids and slows to the new pace, soften the rein as the reward.

Riding from trot to walk is as above, but to make a transition from trot to walk, you need to ride a few strides of sitting trot before asking for the downward transition.

Aids for canter to trot

As above, but as you feel the pony slowing into trot, remain sitting for a few paces. Once the trot is established you can begin rising again.

Learning to Jump

Learning to Jump

Safety first

Your personal equipment

In addition to your normal riding clothes, it is recommended that your shoulders are covered when jumping.

Body protectors are recommended for jumping and are compulsory when riding cross-country. Check the current BETA guidelines for the current standard. There are many types and styles to choose from, and it is important that a body protector is correctly fitted when you buy one.

When riding cross-country, a skull cap needs to be worn; this is like your standard riding hat, but it does not have a fixed peak. This is a safety design rule for jumping fixed fences. To cover your skull cap, you can wear a hat silk that matches your cross-country riding colours (a shirt or 'skin' that goes underneath your body protector in your choice of colour and design).

Getting started

When you are ready to begin jumping, having someone with you is essential, sensible and safer. Jumping should always be simple but can be challenging, and should be done progressively. It may be helpful to take a step back to re-establish the basics before moving on or to correct an error in any session.

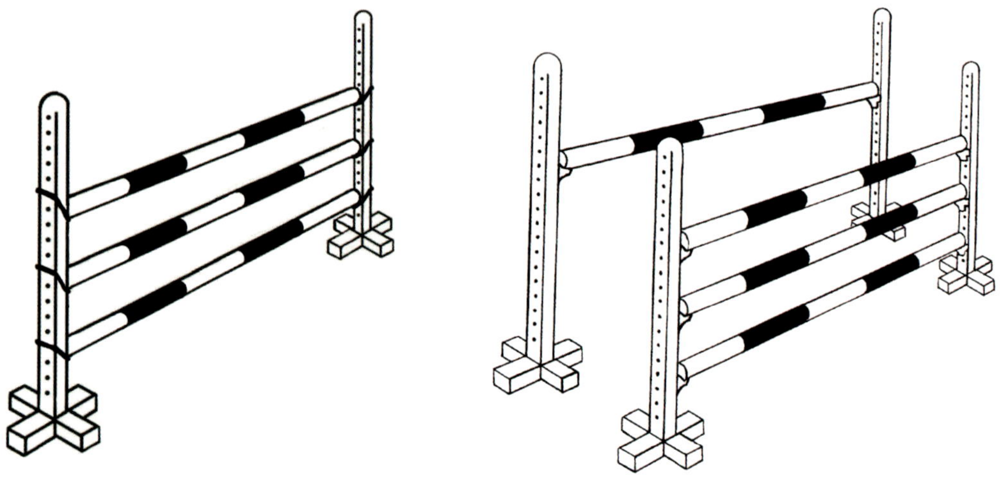

Figure 91: An upright and spread fence.

Consider the ground; this is very important if jumping outside on an uneven surface where your pony's footing may be inconsistent. Your pony needs to feel secure when he places his feet on the way to the fence and takes off to jump.

Fences should always be built with good wings and safe and sound materials. The fence structure should provide a clear ground line and be constructed of suitable materials so that the pony can see and assess the shape (profile) of the fence. Cups should be securely fitted, and the back poles on any spread fence should have collapsible cups on the back wings.

The bascule (the pony's shape when jumping the fence)

The pony jumps in such a way that he makes a particular shape over the jump. This shape will change according to the type of fence he is jumping. You would expect a pony to make a different shape when jumping over an upright fence to a spread fence and jumping over show jumps or cross-country fences. This shape is known as the bascule and comprises five phases:

- The approach.
- The take-off.
- The moment of suspension.
- The landing.
- The getaway (or recovery).

During these phases, your position needs to adapt to the change in the pony's balance. You must shorten your stirrup length when jumping, allowing your leg to bend more at the knee.

Phase 1: The approach

The direction that your pony takes to the fence is called the approach. This approach must be straight to allow your pony plenty of time to see the fence and understand how he will jump

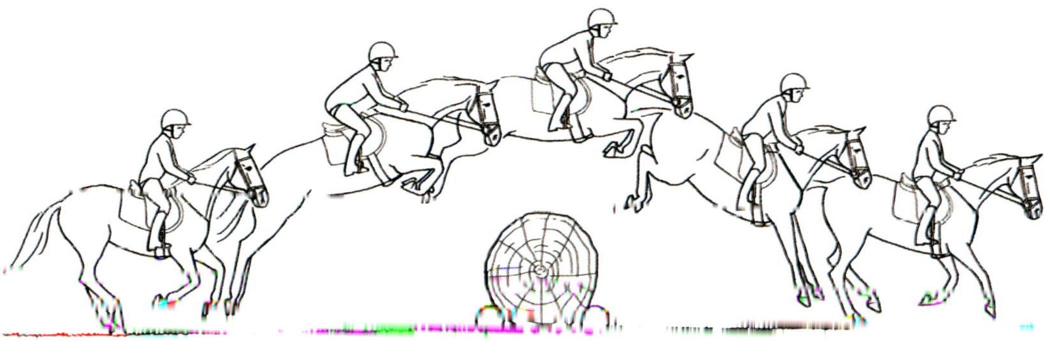

Figure 92: The bascule.

it. You must ride the approach with a forward active gait; this can be trotting, cantering (or galloping when riding cross-country). The pony needs to keep the rhythm and impulsion to the front of the fence. He may lift his head on the approach to assess the fence and then, as he gets closer, slightly lower his head and neck to determine the height and structure of the obstacle. The ability to jump the fence well depends on the line you use on the approach and the quality of the gait in which the approach is ridden.

Phase 2: The take-off

At the take-off point, the pony will lower his head and neck to see the fence's shape and size. At the point of take-off, the pony will shorten his neck and raise his head to bring his forehand and shoulders off the ground. As his forefeet come off the ground, his knees bend to fold and tuck up the forelegs. This is followed by his hind legs being brought forward and, ideally, pushing off the ground simultaneously. This enables his hind legs to be engaged and spring off the ground, pushing upwards and forward to clear the front of the fence.

Phase 3: The moment of suspension

As the pony has pushed off the ground, he is now airborne. This is known as the moment of suspension. He will stretch his head and neck forward and downward to clear the width of the fence. This allows him to stretch over his back in a round shape. His forelegs are kept tucked up, with his hind legs remaining pushed out behind him. As the pony reaches the furthest point of the width and height of the fence, he begins to lift his head and neck up and bring the hind legs back underneath him.

Phase 4: The landing

The pony will begin to lower his body once he has cleared the maximum height and width of the fence. He changes his balance to prepare to land as his leading leg contacts the ground. At the point of contact with the ground he will also lift his head and neck to rebalance his body and reduce the likelihood of tripping or stumbling upon landing. His back should be supple and soft throughout, enabling his hind legs to come underneath his body and then contact the ground as the forelegs push off in the first stride away from the fence.

Phase 5: The getaway (or recovery)

This is the first stride your pony takes as he leaves the fence; the aim is to re-establish balance, rhythm and impulsion as soon as possible. To do this, he needs to land with his hocks underneath his body to allow him to use his hind legs powerfully into the first stride. The getaway begins as soon as your pony begins to move away from landing and lasts a few strides.

Your jumping position

Riding in a light seat

- To jump safely and securely, you must adapt from your flatwork position to one ready for jumping.
- You will need to shorten your stirrups by one or two holes (depending on your stirrup leathers and your leg length).
- Your lower leg needs to rest against the pony's side to maintain your forward aids and support the pony in staying 'forward thinking'.
- Practise your light seat on the flat in trot and canter to establish your balance and coordination.
- A neckstrap should always be used when learning to jump as this helps you keep your position and avoid pulling on the reins if you lose balance, which may confuse your pony if you give him an incorrect aid.
- Practise holding the neckstrap while you are riding before you begin jumping.
- You can start jumping from a trot or canter if the pace is rhythmical, balanced and has the correct impulsion and speed for the type of obstacle you want to jump successfully.
- You will need to develop an independent jumping position that can maintain the pace for riding forward.
- Your hands should keep steady, light contact to support your pony in moving forward or guide him in keeping a straight line of approach to the fence.
- This is particularly important in the last few strides when the pony may waiver from the line if he loses concentration or focus.

Phase 1: The approach

When you start to jump, you may find it easier to ride the approach with your upper body slightly further forward (in a light seat) in anticipation of your pony jumping and leaving the ground.

Things to help you

Planning: The rider needs to be aware of the line of the track that they are riding. This can be developed by walking the course on foot when competing or simply walking the line to the fence when mounted to help you visualise the corners, turns and the distance to the fence take-off point.

Focus: For many reasons, you may lose your focus and attention. This is often seen in beginner riders, and a positive focus can be developed by thinking (or talking to a coach) about how to ride forward, keeping your pony in front of the leg, and staying forward-thinking.

Keep looking up and forward: This enables you to stay strong in your core and prevents you from rounding your back or lowering your head. Always try to look towards the top of the fence rather than be tempted to look at or into the bottom of it. If you lose your body posture, this can negatively influence your pony's balance, too.

Maintain your position: Your pony may try to influence your position by:

- Rushing towards the fence which may cause you to become left behind the movement.
- Slowing down to either look at the fence or to try and stop (refuse) or run past it (run out). In this case, the change in the pony's movement may cause your balance to be shifted forward.
- Jumping awkwardly, causing you to slip sideways or forwards.

Keep your contact:

- To maintain a consistent contact towards the fence, you must allow your pony to take the reins forward.
- It can be tempting to 'drop' the reins just in front of the fence, but this may suggest to your pony that you do not want to jump it. Consequently, this may unbalance him, and he may stop or run past the jump.
- Over-checking is when you over-use the reins (to slow down) as you approach and assess where your pony will take off from. If this happens, your pony will likely lose energy, speed, and balance.
- It is important to aim to maintain a consistent contact. If you can't keep your hands still, this is known as interfering. A constant change of rein contact causes the pony to lose confidence in you and upsets his concentration during the approach. To remedy this, you should keep your hands forward and in front of your shoulders.

Riding forwards: It's your responsibility to generate the correct amount of energy for your pony to jump a series of fences successfully, this energy should be established before you approach each fence. Your pony should stay responsive and 'in front of your leg' without requiring constant leg pressure, especially just before the fence (unless you're correcting a potential refusal). If your pony rushes in the final few strides, it will likely tip him onto the forehand, causing a loss of balance.

Phases 2 and 3: Take-off and moment of suspension

- Keep your eyes up to look at and over the fence, which will enable you to keep your head up.
- Your body should remain folding forward until the pony's hind legs have passed the highest part of the jump.

- Your hands should be in front of your shoulders, which will help you maintain your body posture and reduce the likelihood of collapsing onto your pony's neck. This will allow you to follow your pony's entire head and neck movements and limit the possibility of catching him in the mouth.
- Keep your body folded forward from your hip joints, following the movement of your pony.
- Your pony's back should be flat but with no stiffness.
- Your weight should be evenly distributed through both feet to the stirrups, with relaxed knees and ankles. If you become tight in your knees, your lower leg tends to swing backwards, resulting in you collapsing forward or leaning to one side.

Things to help you

Keeping a secure lower leg: Your security comes through the lower leg and should be your focus for staying balanced.

- Keep your weight through your foot into the stirrup, particularly at the take-off point.
- Keep your knees bent, if you grip upwards rather than step into the stirrup, your leg may straighten, causing you to tip, with your knees and lower leg swinging backwards and upwards.
- Swinging your legs back will unbalance your pony and put you in an unsafe position on landing; this is corrected by reinforcing your weight into the foot and stirrup as you take off.

Maintaining your balance: It is easy to be pulled forward (jumping before your pony) if your pony takes off later than you are expecting. This is likely to cause you to tip forward too early at the take-off phase. This will cause your pony to come onto his forehand and either chip in (take a very short last stride before jumping) or refuse. By staying focused on stepping onto the stirrups at the point of take-off, you will likely remain behind the wither and, therefore, only move forward into your jumping position once your pony has left the ground.

If you are being pulled too quickly towards the fence, you may become behind the movement at the point of take-off; this is known as getting left behind and occurs when the pony takes off before you are ready. If this happens, you can slip the reins to prevent catching your pony in the mouth and affecting his balance.

Keeping your contact: You must keep your hands in front of your shoulders throughout all the jumping phases. By following the movement of your pony's head and neck during the take-off and throughout the whole of the jump, your pony can use himself to the best of his ability. This will support your good position and reduce the likelihood of establishing poor habits, such as:

- Fixing your hands.
- Raising your elbows.
- Raising your hands as your pony takes off.
- Having straight arms, stiff shoulders, and elbows.

Slipping the reins: In case of an error by either the pony or you, you can slip the reins. This is when you quickly open the fingers in your hand to allow your pony to take the reins through the contact and allow complete freedom of his head and neck to re-establish his balance. It is best to take back the reins to re-establish the contact as soon as possible upon landing.

Phases 4 and 5: Landing and getaway

As the pony's weight is taken forward to land, you need to be able to guard against tipping forward over his shoulder. To keep an independent and safe position, you need to be able to bring your weight backwards to a more upright position. As the pony lands, you should be able to absorb most of the shock through your knees and ankles. To do this, your lower leg and the calf stay lightly in contact with his sides, ready to help him pick up the next canter stride in the getaway.

A well-ridden getaway helps your pony quickly re-establish a balanced and rhythmical pace. It can save vital seconds when time is essential, such as during a timed jump-off or the cross-country phase of a tetrathlon or hunter trials.

Things to help you

Staying light in your seat: You need to guard against landing heavily in the saddle or on the back of it, as this will result in the pony having to manage his balance and yours, too. At best, this is uncomfortable for him, causing him to hollow his back, which spoils the landing and causes the getaway stride to lose its fluency. At worst, this may result in the pony losing balance and tripping, stumbling, or falling. You must ensure you stay tall in your position to reduce the likelihood of tipping forward and losing your balance.

Developing your jumping position

Riding with your stirrups at jumping length

- Shortening the stirrups by a couple of holes from your flat work riding length is generally recommended. This will vary according to the shape and conformation of the pony, the type of stirrup leathers, the type of saddle and the build and shape of you.
- Stirrup length is a matter for the individual rider; the aim is to be balanced and independent. The ideal length is short enough to enable you to fold forward with independent balance, but long enough to use your legs effectively.

- Your hips, knees and ankles need to maintain their flexibility. Your joints are designed to absorb the shock and forces of the pony's movement, which is particularly important when the pony jumps. Any stiffness in your position/body will make it difficult to absorb the impact of the movement, especially on landing.
- Your lower leg lies in contact with the pony's sides. The ball of the foot is placed in the stirrup, with the weight evenly distributed across the stirrup bar without causing any pressure on the sides of the stirrups.
- When adjusting the stirrups, it is normal for them to feel short when standing still, but they should feel better when you canter and ride in a lighter seat.
- Your hip and heel should be along the same vertical line, with your stirrup leather hanging vertically. Once the pony begins to move, your foot may come further through the stirrup to improve balance.

Figure 93: The correct length of stirrup for jumping.

Figure 94: Light seat.

- Your rein length will need to shorten as you will be slightly more forward when they come into the lighter seat, compared with the dressage (flatwork seat).
- This can be ridden in trot but is commonly used in canter.
- Your lower leg should be secure, with most of the leg contact being with the calf or the inside of the chap (boot). This is achieved by having a soft knee, which allows the weight to come through to the stirrup.
- Your body should stay over the pony's wither and your knee. If you lean too far forward, you may use your pony's neck to lean on or overuse your reins for balance or your knees to grip.
- With an independent position, you can ride with a soft hand and apply your aids independently.
- You can develop the standing position in canter to check on your independence and effectiveness of keeping your position.

Standing in canter

- This is a balance exercise to determine that you can ride independently from your pony and the contact (reins).

Figure 95: Standing position when cantering.

- You should be able to push your hips forward to transfer your weight throughout your leg. Your hips, knees and ankles should remain soft, allowing your joints to move and receive the pony's movement.
- Your stirrups should hang vertically down with the widest part of your foot on the stirrup iron.
- Once this independence can be achieved, you can quietly lower your weight back into the saddle and choose to ride in a full or light seat.

Practising your jumping fold

This can be learnt by becoming aware of how your body needs to move as your pony jumps and takes off. It is helpful to learn to use a neckstrap so that this can secure your balance independently from your reins. You are encouraged to fold forward from your hip joint (the top of your legs) with a flat back. You can keep straight and balanced by looking forward between the pony's ears. Your hips, knees and ankles should stay soft and supple, with your stirrup leather hanging vertically. Your back should remain flat if the fold is generated from the hips. If you round your back too much, then it is likely that you are folding from your waist rather than your hips.

Contact

When you are in the folding position, your reins will need to shorten as your hands move further forward towards the bit. It would be best to practise with shortened reins, resting your hands on either side of your pony's neck or withers. The time to establish your contact will vary, and you should use the neckstrap until you have found your independence. The tension (pressure) through the contact does not change. This folding position can then be developed in the walk, trot, and canter.

Chapter 15

Progressing your Jumping

THE PONY CLUB
EST 1929

Progressing your Jumping

Poles and fences

Fence design

Fences are generally grouped into two categories: verticals and spreads. Single-wing fences are known as uprights or verticals, while oxers or spread fences incorporate two or more sets of wings to challenge height and width. Whatever the type of fence, there should always be a ground line.

Ground line

A pony is inclined to look at an obstacle from the base of the jump upwards and can then assess the point of take-off from the bottom of the fence, which ideally should be the most solid part, nearest to the ground. This is known as the ground line.

True ground lines

A clearly defined ground line will help your pony assess and see the question that the fence demands. A pole on the ground placed in front of a vertical will help your pony see the fence and the ground line more clearly and help him take off at a suitable distance to clear the front rail with the forelegs. This pole becomes the ground line for which your pony judges the distance to take off from. It is acceptable to use a pole that is placed on the ground when training at home, whereas in competition all poles must be supported from a jump wing or on little rests (known as pole pods).

For this reason, a pony will find it far easier to jump an ascending oxer, or any fence that slopes away from him as he will see the first (ground rail) and take off from the bottom point which will allow his natural jump or bascule to follow the shape of the fence.

False ground lines

A false ground line is one in which the base of the fence is or appears to be behind the vertical. False ground lines should be avoided, as they may visually confuse your pony potentially making him take off too close to the front rail.

As a false ground line creates a poor assessment for your pony to jump from, fences should always be approached in the correct direction. Fences that cause false ground lines if jumped the incorrect way are:

- Upright rails with the bottom pole, or a ground pole, pushed back behind the line of the vertical face.
- An ascending oxer built the wrong way, with the highest pole nearest to the take-off point.

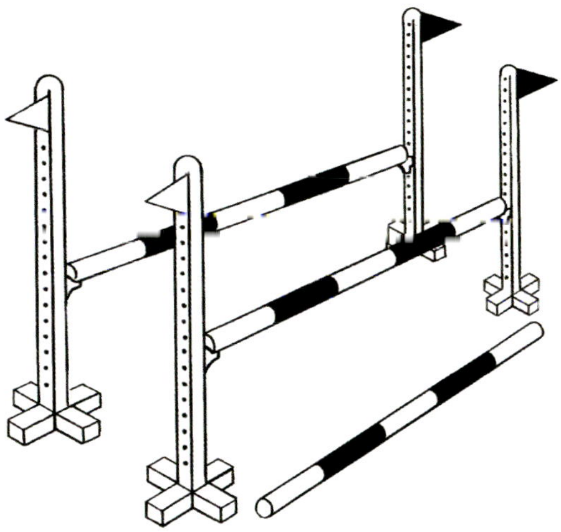

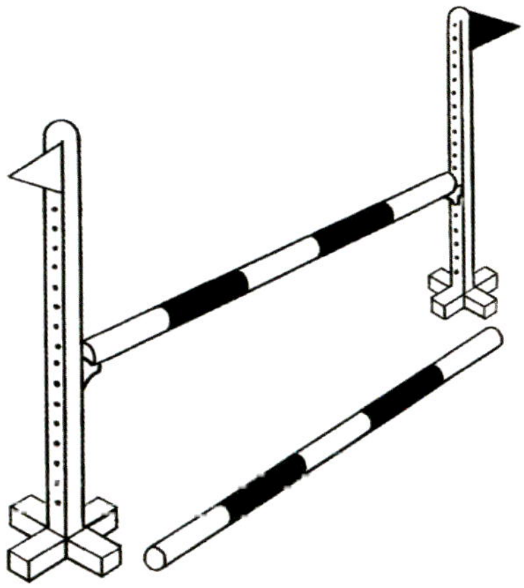

Figure 96: Correct use of ground lines.

Spreads

- **Ascending oxer**: this is when the back rail is higher than the front. This is the easiest type of fence for your pony to jump as he can clearly see the back rail and the shape of the face will encourage a good bascule.
- **Square (or parallel) oxer**: this is a parallel where the front and back rail are the same height.
- **True (parallel) oxer**: where the height of the front rail is the same as the back and the width from the front to the back is the same. For example, 1m high front rail, 1m high back rail and a 1m spread.

Building schooling fences

When training or schooling at home, it is important to build the fences as safely and correctly as possible. Fences should be inviting, with a secure and solid ground line, be solid in their appearance and safely constructed.

Figure 97: Variety of fences.

Poles

The poles may be made of wood or plastic. When using plastic poles take care to use the heaviest possible as some lightweight poles are not safe when jumping. If a pony hits a pole when jumping the pole needs to fall cleanly to the ground. A lightweight pole may be sent forward when the pony catches it with his legs, causing it to potentially travel forward rather than falling.

Poles should be at least 9cm (3½in) in diameter and be safely placed on a suitable cup. Lightweight poles (or any material) tend to create a careless jump and may encourage a pony to 'tap' the fences. Thinner diameter poles may be used when training with small ponies or younger pony riders.

Cups

Modern cups come in a variety of types and sizes. The main purpose for a cup is to hold the pole in place but not wedged in as this may cause a problem if your pony hits the fence in error and the pole cannot freely fall to the ground.

When jumping over fences, the back pole must be placed on a spring loaded (or collapsible) cup to allow the pole to fall cleanly to the ground. Failure for this to happen may result in your pony hitting the back pole as he descends through the bascule and restricting his landing. It is possible that this will cause your pony to stumble or even a pony/rider to fall if this occurs.

When using planks, fillers and any material that has square or flat design to its structure, a flat cup should be used. This allows the pole, plank or filler to easily slide off the cup and stop it from becoming lodged and restricting your pony's movement.

Building a training fence at home

An ascending fence is the easiest for your pony to jump this is because:

- The profile (shape) of the fence is very inviting and this creates a good jumping shape (bascule).
- The front pole creates a clear ground line.
- Crossed poles in the front provide a solid appearance and focus the pony's attention to the centre of the fence, supporting the straightness on the approach.
- The back pole provides the height and width, which allows the pony to take off and jump over and across the fence rather than just being higher above it.

Figure 98: Safety cups.

Adapting the training fence

The basic schooling fence can easily be adapted to:

- Single crossed pole.
- Ascending oxer.
- Parallel oxer with drop pole on the front.

Droppers

A dropper is a term used to describe where a pole is placed when it is set diagonally, with one end on the ground and the other supported in a wing-cup. It helps to visually fill up the fence, and the lower end can be pulled forward on the floor side to form a helpful ground line.

Safety considerations

- Always build a fence that is visually inviting and has a sound ground line.
- Planks and gates should always be placed on a flat cup, allowing them to freely move (fall) if hit by your pony.
- Only use round poles on the back of any spread fence with safety cups.
- A safety cup is designed to allow the pole to fall freely if a pony knocks it, so they must be used on the back rail on any spread fence.
- A spread fence as the first element of a combination encourages ponies to jump into the distance and for this reason it is advisable with novice pony and rider combinations.

- When building doubles, it is safer to initially build on two strides. This is very relevant if mixed heights (horses and ponies) are required to jump the same fence. The ponies will be more easily able to adjust their stride and if required would be able to put three strides into the distance.
- Any spare cups should be placed on the ground at the feet of the jump on the landing side. This is to reduce the likelihood of your pony stepping on them or your pony or you catching them if they are left 'empty' on the jump wing/stand.

Best practice when schooling

- When introducing your pony to a new type of fence, keep the fences small enough to jump from a trot approach. This would include the introduction of fillers.
- When increasing the height of a fence, raise all the poles and not just the top pole. This is to visually 'fill' in the distance from the ground to the highest point.
- With novice combinations, consider building the fence against the side of the school or arena to provide security and help the approach to the fence.
- Use a mixture of spreads and uprights and approach from both directions. This will encourage suppleness and an athletic way of going.
- Keep the exercises and lines simple. When this is done well, more complex lines and approaches can be added.
- The pony and rider combination should be relaxed and confident before progressing to higher or more technical demands.
- Build on sound correct distances. This will encourage your pony to develop the correct canter stride from the beginning of his training.
- When building show jumping courses, distances between individual fences are usually measured in multiples of the length of a pony's stride.
- Outdoors in good ground conditions this is usually 3.7m (12ft). For example: 14.6m (48ft), 18.3m (60ft), 22m (72ft).

Adjusting distances for jumping exercises

These distances are guidelines for training purposes. It is better to make them too long than too short; they are for a standard stride. It is important to train your eye as distance charts are no substitution for being able to see what is happening. Remember that the distances must be adjusted accordingly as the fences are raised. Distances in training depend on the following factors:

- The size of the fences.
- Your pony's length of stride.

- Your pony's education and experience.
- Your ability to establish a suitable trot or canter.

If you approach in trot, the distance between the first and second fence, may be shortened by up to 90cm (3ft).

Trotting poles

- Trotting poles are heavy poles not less than 10cm (4in) in diameter, and approximately 3m (10ft) long. If a raised trotting pole is used, they should be at a suitable height to allow your pony to maintain a consistent rhythm and balance throughout the sequence of the poles.
- This height may vary according to the education, fitness of the pony as well as the structure of the pole exercise.
- It is best practice if the poles are squared-off (rather than round) or are safely embedded in the surface or secured through blocks or a similar manner, this prevents them from being moved if the pony catches them and kicks them out of place. In training this can happen, and the coach can reposition the poles before you do the exercise again.

A useful way to prevent the poles from rolling, and to give a little height when necessary is to set each end in a scalloped log or wooden block, approximately 30–60cm (1–2ft) long.

Why trotting poles are good for your pony

- Develops the balance and rhythm by regulating and establishing the stride pattern.
- Educates obedience to your aids.
- Educates the mental and physical coordination, calmness and focus, which helps your pony to know where to place his legs and avoid touching a pole.
- Develops the correct muscles and helps to supple the pony by stretching the neck and lowering the head, rounding the back, engaging the hocks.
- Develops confidence in your pony to approach any obstacle happily and without tension.

Why trotting poles are good for you

- Working over them helps develop your balance in maintaining an independent position.
- Poles can be ridden in rising trot or a light seat and this helps you develop your feel and coordination of your aids.

A

With the approach in TROT and fences approximately 60cm high	Pony (according to size)	Horse
Between elements 1 and 2 For one non-jumping stride: For two non-jumping strides:	4.9-5.5m (16-18ft) 7.3-8.2m (24-27ft)	5.5-6.1m (18-20ft) 8.2-9.1m (27-30ft)
Between elements 2 and 3 For one non-jumping stride:	5.5-6m (18-19.5 ft)	6-6.4m (19.5-21ft)
Between elements 3 and 4 For one non-jumping stride:	6-6.4m (19.5-21ft)	6.4-7m (21-23ft)
A BOUNCE No non-jumping stride:	2.7-3m (9-10ft)	3-3.3m (10-11ft)

B

With the approach in CANTER and fences approximately 1m high	Pony (according to size)	Horse
One non-jumping stride between elements:	6.1-7.3m (20-24ft)	7-7.8m (23-25.5ft)
Two non-jumping strides:	9.4-10.4m (31-34ft)	10.4-11m (34-36ft)
Between elements 3 and 4 For one non-jumping stride:	6-6.4m (19.5-21ft)	6.4-7m (21-23ft)
A BOUNCE No non-jumping stride: Fences approximately 75cm high	3-3.6m (10-12ft)	3.3-4.3m (11-14ft)

Figures 99 & 100: Suitable distances for jumping: a) approach in trot, b) approach in canter.

- As you develop your awareness of the rhythm, you will begin to develop an eye for the distances (this is when you know when your pony is going to take the trot step from and that it is in a suitable place to clear the poles).
- This will then develop your eye for the approach to fences through riding turns and approaches to various pole exercises.
- This is an ideal preparation for jumping single fences and later course riding.

Trotting poles in rising trot

- Trotting poles should be ridden in rising trot, firstly to encourage the pony to relax and swing his back; secondly to develop rhythm for both of you.
- Sitting trot can be used when both of you have progressed in experience and confidence.
- If used too early then there is the possibility that your pony may hollow the back and become tense in the way of going, losing the rhythm and regularity.

Trotting poles in light seat

- When you can show an established independent light seat in the trot and canter, then you can begin to use this light seat position through trot poles.
- As your pony progresses through these exercises it is important that you can keep a secure lower leg.
- If this security is lost, you are likely to tip forward or to use the reins for your balance.
- Changes to your position are likely to change the pony's balance in a negative manner.

Approximate trotting pole distances

The coach should check that the trotting poles are set at the right distance to ensure that your pony's hind foot falls midway between the poles (as the perfect distance).

Pony	**1–1.35m (3ft 3in–4ft 6in) apart, depending on size and type.**
Horse	**1.3–1.5m (4ft 3in–5ft) apart.**

Using a distance of 2.7m (9ft) between poles allows horses and ponies to use the same exercise.

Trotting poles should be set just off the track so that they can be approached on either rein, or bypassed. The turn into them should be on a gradual arc of at least 15m (50ft)

Introduction to trotting poles

Stage 1: Single pole exploration, begin by walking your pony over single poles placed randomly around the arena.

- Focus on maintaining your position and balance.
- Work until your pony becomes relaxed and confident.
- Gradually progress to trotting over single poles.

Stage 2: Multiple poles, start by introducing three poles positioned 2.7m (9 ft) apart. Ideally, poles are used in odd numbers, i.e. one (1) pole, three (3) poles, five (5) poles, etc.

- Ride your pony over three (3) poles set at 2.7m (9ft) apart to ensure the spacing is safe to prevent the pony from jumping.
- Practise until your pony can step over each pole calmly and controlled.
- The wider spacing allows two steps between poles, keeping the exercise safe and comfortable.

Stage 3: Trotting with quality by introducing trot when your pony is calm walking and maintaining an even rhythm and balance.

- Practise the exercise on both reins (left and right directions).
- Approach the poles from different angles to build versatility.
- Focus on keeping the trot consistent and smooth.

Stage 4: Increasing difficulty by reducing the distance between poles to 1.35m (4ft 6in).

- Challenge your pony to take one step between each pole.
- Gradually increase to working with five poles.
- Build towards a consistent and confident performance.

Final tip

- Remember that pole distances may need to be adjusted based on your individual pony's stride length.
- Each pony is unique, so be patient and observant.

Variations of pole exercises

- When you are both confident in completing a few poles in a straight line, the poles can be placed around the school or arena.
- The poles can be placed on a diagonal or a fan on a circle.
- Placing poles in different places and shapes will encourage both of you to maintain the impulsion and rhythm around the lines to and from the exercise.
- This is the start of developing course riding, too.

Rider responsibility

Balance: You need to be able to sit and maintain your postural balance on the flat and over the pole sequences. Your balance is developed by looking forward and up to the line of the poles and then to the line of the exit from the exercise. When you can stay in balance your pony is more likely to stay in balance too.

Rhythm: Your responsibility is to keep your posture and balance so you can sit and ride in balance. Repeating out loud a jingle or a regular phase can help you to develop the feel to find and allow the rhythm.

Such exercises as the rider saying '**Mon-day**, **Tues-day**, **Wednes-day**', may help, or '**one-two**, **one-two**, **one-two**', as you approach, proceed and finish each exercise.

Solving problems/rider responsibilities

The pony needs to be working correctly in a confident and relaxed way before moving to the next stage. If any issues develop from you or your pony then the previous stage should be re-established.

Possible problems may be:

- You losing your balance and position. Re-establish your balance on the flat before working over the poles, it may be useful to check your stirrup length to help develop your lower leg security.
- Tension and resistance to the aids – pulling the contact, coming above the bit etc. Your pony needs to be ridden in balance on the flat to establish the acceptance of your aids and way of going.
- Losing the rhythm and then rushing on the approach or away from the exercise. You need to make sure you have a secure position to keep your balance and support your pony through a half-halt if the stride and his balance is inclined to change. If you can gain some experience of riding the trot in various tempos, then this is easier to feel when working through a pole exercise.
- Losing the rhythm and attempting to jump the poles. Initially check the distances and make sure that there are an odd number of poles to reduce this happening. If your pony is still inclined to do this, then the exercise should be simplified until the confidence and relaxation is established.

Heights and spreads

Small ponies and very novice riders may be more suited to gymnastic jumping with uprights through all the elements until the confidence and skill is established. Spread fences can then be introduced.

Keep your pony confident throughout the exercises by using smaller fences when schooling. When you are both confident in jumping single smaller fences, larger fences can be introduced within the second element of a related distance as this helps with establishing the canter strides between fences to a bigger fence.

In combinations, always have the proceeding element lower than the following one, this will help your pony jump with energy created from the hindquarters.

Gymnastic/grid work exercises

Gymnastic exercises can be varied using a variety of fence types such as one or two non-jumping canter strides between the elements.

The approach to the exercise may be from canter. When jumping from canter, the distances between the fences will need to be increased, allowing for the change in your pony's stride. Such variables are:

- The length and quality of the pony's stride.
- The pace of the approach to the exercise.
- The types and sizes of fences used.
- The condition of the surface.

Rider responsibilities

Gymnastic exercises should be introduced in a progressive manner. If either of you get into any problems, the exercise should be made simpler and the training taken back a stage until you are both confident and skill is re-established.

Consider your energy levels when jumping. Repetitive jumping is very demanding on a physical level and your pony can become tired through the effort of jumping and may lose the shape (bascule) over the fence.

It is better to finish an exercise wishing that you had jumped a few more fences than regretting that you jumped too many. There is always another day.

Think about how much better you are getting over a period rather than from one session. Returning to a previous stage is a positive way to consolidate and confirm a skill before moving on. This is useful if your pony has not jumped for a while or has had some time off.

If your pony is not progressing as expected, check your distances and the quality of the pace (trot or canter). Using safe and correct distances will teach your pony to jump well (achieving the required height and spread with the minimum of effort) if the approach is made in a rhythmical, unhurried pace.

Show jumping training: problems and how to correct them

A neckstrap is helpful if you think the pony may jump awkwardly or unpredictably. This narrow stirrup leather rests snugly approximately one-third of the way up your pony's neck, ready for you to hold if you may lose your balance.

The quality and success of the jump will depend on the quality of your approach, so before jumping, ensure your pony has been warmed up properly on the flat to encourage good-quality, balanced, and rhythmical gaits.

Your pony needs to be willing to approach a fence from the trot. A few canter strides before and after the jump are permissible. A forward-ridden trot is better than a pony that drops off your leg into a backwards-thinking canter.

Using another pony to give a nervous pony (or you) a lead over a fence is beneficial at the beginning of the pony's jumping education. When the combination is confident, they should be encouraged to jump without a lead.

Aim to approach your fences with a wide, straightforward approach so that your pony can see the fence quickly and with plenty of time to judge his approach.

When you both feel confident in jumping single fences (uprights and spreads, from the left and the right rein), additional fences can be added to develop your technical skills in relating fences to each other.

Tack and equipment

Your pony may behave differently when being ridden at home compared with when at a competition. It is common for your pony to require a different bit or piece of tack at an event, as your pony may become stronger or react differently in a competitive situation. If this is the case, once the desired bit or tack has been found, this bridle can be kept for the competitions, and a general bridle can be used for training. Regardless of the tack and equipment used, it must fit correctly; often, a tight noseband or a high bit will be more antagonistic to the pony than the choice of tack.

Throughout the pony's bascule (the shape the pony makes when jumping), you should be able to maintain a balanced, established position so that you can remain in harmony with the pony. To do this is easier in a more forward-cut saddle.

Jumping saddle

A jumping saddle can be used when starting to jump over bigger fences. However, a general purpose (GP) saddle is suitable for learning and developing your jumping position. You must shorten your stirrup length to maintain an independent balance when jumping and working in the light or two-point seat. A jumping saddle is a worthy investment as a general purpose (GP) saddle does not support the increased flexion of your knee and the more forward position of the knee when the stirrups are shortened.

Surfaces and conditions

Much of your pony's training occurs on an artificial surface or a level grass area, and unless you are at a significant event, the competitive show jumping phase will be carried out on grass. Knowing this, some of your jump training should be practised on grass to prepare both of you for dealing with your pony's reactions to a different and potentially variable surface.

Pony concerns

Fear – caused by:

- Your own need to feel more confidence.
- Losing your nerve due to an unpleasant memory at a previous fence.
- Over-facing your pony by asking him to jump a fence beyond his ability or stage of training.
- Lack of confidence when asking your pony to jump from a slippery surface.

Disobedience (refusing and running out). The main reasons for these are:

Pain – caused by:

- Lameness.
- Discomfort in your pony's mouth due to bad riding, over-bitting or sharp teeth and bridle fit.
- Problems with your pony's back and saddle fit.
- Veterinary attention may be needed for each of the above causes of pain.
- Lack of correct training. The basic paces from which your pony will jump lack the necessary balance and impulsion, and your pony has not been taught to respond to your aids.

- Inexperience or poor riding. Your pony has discovered you cannot control or ask him to jump.

Tiredness – caused by:

- Lack of fitness or condition of you and/or your pony.
- Avoid jumping for too long, your pony will eventually become bored or tired.

Rushing – caused by:

- Inexperience or bad riding.
- Incorrect training: your pony has never been taught to approach the fence relaxed and rhythmically.
- Fear or pain will cause a tense, or even frantic, approach.

Propping – a sudden slowing down in front of the fence or going too fast and too early in the approach – is caused by:

- Lack of confidence.
- Your pony is not going forward with rhythm and impulsion.
- Your pony's laziness.
- You may drop your contact at the last moment before take-off.
- Your pony is sore or in pain, usually in his back or feet.

Jumping with a flat or hollow back:

Your pony does not extend his head and neck or use his back correctly (in the bascule) and, therefore, cannot jump to the best of his ability. The leading causes of this are:

- Incorrect training. Your pony's basic paces have not been established, and he may approach the fence with his head too high and have a hollow or stiff back.
- You are holding the reins too tightly, which may restrict your contact, restricting your pony's ability to jump freely and use his head, neck, and back correctly.
- You lose balance, causing your pony to lose his balance when jumping the fence.
- Your pony has a stiff or an injured back.
- Some ponies naturally tend to jump with a flat or hollow back. They can be helped to overcome this by correct progressive training.

Cross-country training: problems and how to correct them

Tack and equipment

If you decide to compete in Eventing (three phases of dressage, show jumping and cross country), it is quite realistic to compete in all phases in one saddle (a jumping saddle), so this should be the primary investment of your tack and equipment to ride safely and effectively in all the phases. It would be best to always ride with your stirrups at jumping length when you practise jumping. Riding shorter than your flatwork length will establish your positional balance and help your jumping fitness. Your pony will only be able to perform to the best of his ability if your weight is balanced over the pony's centre of gravity.

Cross-country training: variance of terrain, natural obstacles

It is essential to consider the effect of your position when riding cross-country. This may be as simple as hacking out in fields, tracks and bridleways, pleasure rides, hunting or cross-country jumping.

Hacking out

Your stirrup length will be shorter than when riding on the flat but not as short as when jumping unless you intend to be trotting and cantering, too. This allows you to stay forward (light) in your position if your pony changes his balance as the terrain changes.

Cantering and fast work

You will need to shorten your stirrups more than when show jumping. This will allow a greater knee flexion (bend) to accommodate your lighter seat. When your pony is cantering or galloping, you can move your upper body more over your pony's wither while maintaining lower leg security. Your hips should remain over the seat of the saddle. This will help develop your and your pony's fitness.

You need to be able to maintain your position as the terrain changes. This may occur when your pony is asked to go across a variety of places, such as:

- Up and down hills and slopes at various paces.
- Up and over banks.
- Jumping across a ditch.
- Crossing streams/rivers and riding in lakes.
- Through narrow gaps/trees/woodland.

Ditches

Ponies and riders are naturally cautious of the appearance of holes in the ground, such as ditches that may have water in them. Ditches may also form part of a fence and be found on the fence's take-off or landing.

When introducing a new combination of pony and or rider to a ditch, it is best practice to follow a confident lead. Your pony will naturally follow another if they think the path to and over the obstacle is safe.

Start with a small ditch with a solid ground line to the take-off and landing aspect of the ditch. This will help your pony assess the width and where to safely place his legs to jump across. If the ditch is also within a fence line, it will help your pony assess his way over it rather than considering running out as a possible evasion.

Things to help you

Before approaching the ditch, it is best practice to walk your pony along the side of the ditch from the left and right directions. This allows him to see the ground line and become aware of the

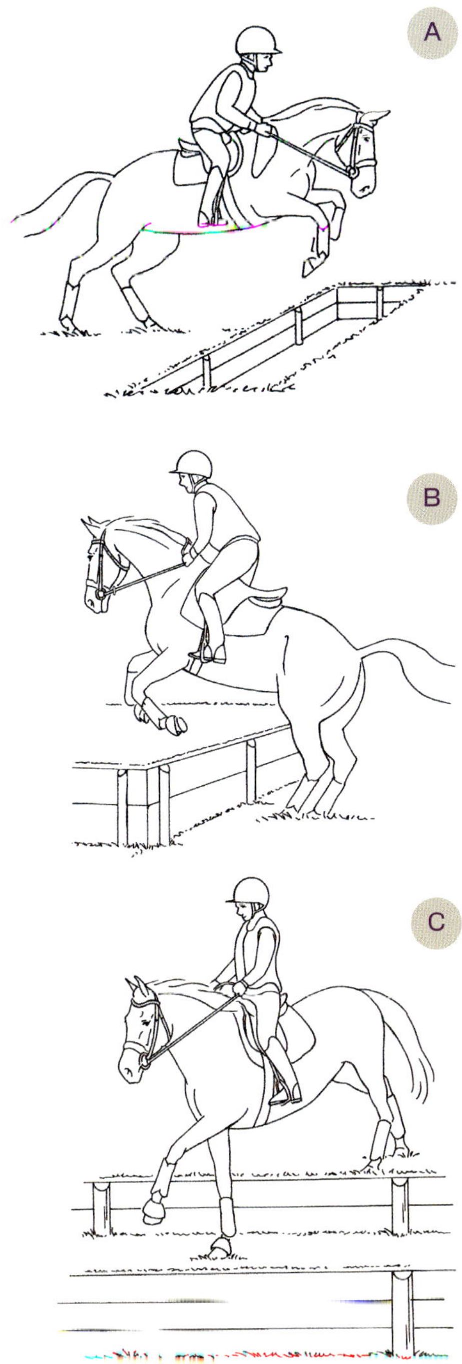

Figure 101. Cross country position a) ditch, b) steps up, c) steps down.

change in the ground. Initially, he may slightly turn his head, with the inside ear focused on the fence to assess it. When he can hold the line alongside the ditch in both directions without turning his head, he can then be asked to approach it and jump over it.

The approach to the ditch should be ridden on a forward trot, allowing your pony time to see the approach and the ground line. If he is following another pony, there should be a couple of lengths between the lead pony to allow both ponies to be safe when jumping.

When you and your pony are confident in jumping the ditch in both directions with a lead, your pony should be encouraged to jump on his own. The lead pony can initially stand on the landing side before you ask your pony to jump away from the lead pony.

You should keep your eyes up and look forward, like jumping a spread fence (looking over the fence) and towards the ride away. This allows your position to stay secure and upright and reduces the likelihood of being pulled forward and down if your pony should lower his neck on the take-off point to assess the ditch.

Once you and your pony are confident in jumping small ditches, you can ask him to jump a ditch with a fence behind the ditch (see Figure 101). This is a safe and kind fence profile, as the ditch acts as a ground line to the fence being jumped (hedge, rails, etc.).

If a ditch is on the landing side of a fence, you need to ride forward to the fence to encourage your pony to jump across it and land further out on the ride away. Ideally, you would think of jumping the fence as a spread to help your pony make a good bascule (rather than jumping too high and landing too steep on the landing side of the fence).

Water

Your pony may have to go into the water for various reasons:

- Crossing a wide ditch with water in it.
- Streams and fords.
- Crossing lakes, large ponds, and the sea.
- Jumping into and out of lakes.

Most ponies initially question walking or crossing into the water as they cannot see the bottom of the base and, as such, are cautious about stepping straight into the unknown. Your pony should be introduced to walking into the water, like approaching a ditch for the first time. It is best practice to have a confident pony and rider as the lead. As your pony only needs to step into the water, the approach can be from a positive marching walk rather than a trot. Your pony should be able to see the ground when he is first introduced. Artificial water jumps or shallow fords are ideal for this when out hacking.

Things to help you

When introducing your pony to water, it is best practice to walk into it, allow him time to work out where to place his feet, and then quietly turn around and walk back the way you came in. This allows your pony to understand the importance of going forward into the water in a relaxed and confident manner rather than rushing through it to get to the other side.

Once your pony is confident in going in and is quiet in leaving the water, he can trot in and out. When crossing water and exiting where there is a step or jump, your pony should be encouraged to stay in trot. This is because trotting produces less splashing than a canter and, therefore, less spray. Too much spray can make it difficult for your pony to see and judge the correct take-off point, and it is easy for him to make a mistake and trip when leaving the water.

Banks and steps – up and down

This may be something that your pony comes across naturally when out hacking or on a cross-country course. Banks can be a simple single natural obstacle out hacking or be part of several jumping efforts when riding across country and combined into steps.

As negotiating steps involve your pony jumping (upwards or downwards), you must maintain your independent position to remain in balance. You can practise keeping your position by riding up and down steep inclines, ensuring control of your position and supporting your pony's balance.

Things to help you

Jumping up

When your pony must go up a steep incline or jump up a bank, you must ensure you have your weight in the stirrups and stay in a light seat. This allows your pony to use his hindquarters to push his body upwards. If you sit heavily on your pony by becoming behind the movement, he cannot step upwards and may trip when negotiating the bank/step, and this is very important where there is a series of steps. This will likely cause your pony to run out of impulsion and stop before completing all the steps.

Jumping down

When the pony is asked to step down a steep incline or off a bank, he is likely to be a little cautious, like when jumping a ditch for the first time. You should present your pony as if you are approaching a ditch and can take a lead from a more experienced pony.

Your pony should be introduced to a single step for the first time. It would be best to allow the pony to assess the change in the ground line by quietly riding forward, keeping your eyes up and forward to the landing, and riding away. It can be tempting to look down the step, but this can unbalance your pony, causing him to come onto the forehand and hesitate. As your pony takes the step off the bank, keep your weight in your lower leg with a soft, flexed knee. Your upper body should stay tall and upright. This will allow you to stay behind your pony's wither and his centre of balance when he lands. If you come in front of the movement, you will likely tip forward and may fall forward as your pony adjusts balance on the ride away. If your pony takes a bigger-than-expected jump off the step, you must be prepared to slip your reins to keep your balance and allow your pony the freedom of his head and neck to adjust his balance on landing. More steps can be added when the pony is confident in jumping single steps up and downwards.

Chapter 16

Riding on the Road and in the Countryside

Riding on the Road and in the Countryside

Road safety and etiquette in the countryside

Being seen

When leading or riding on the road, you must wear suitable clothes so that other road users can see you and your pony. These include:

- Jodhpurs or leggings.
- Current standard hat.
- A long-sleeved jumper or coat done up.
- Gloves.
- Riding boots or jodhpur boots and half chaps.
- Body protector (if required).
- Being seen: you must also wear hi-vis equipment when riding or leading your pony on the road. Fluorescent equipment is bright, and reflective equipment reflects light.
- Ankle light (riding on the road).
- Ensure your pony is in a bridle and can be seen too (leading on the road).
- Charged mobile phone if you have one with emergency numbers saved, check where this is placed on your person so that you are not harmed if you fall off onto it.
- Any emergency first aid such as EpiPen or inhaler.

The Countryside Code

Most riders love hacking in the country and enjoy exploring the great outdoors on horseback. We all need to respect each other, and this is explained in the Countryside Code.

Figure 102. Correct clothing for riding on the roads.

- The Countryside Code is a set of rules and guidelines for all countryside users to protect livestock, property, and wildlife.
- All riders need to respect the countryside and understand it well.

Respect

- Close gates: If you open a gate, close it behind you. This helps keep animals safe and prevents them from wandering onto roads.
- Stay on designated paths: Know the signs for bridle paths and byways so you ride along the correct path. When you meet other riders or walkers, ask before you pass them and only walk. Do not canter up behind other riders.
- Ask permission: If you want to explore private land, always ask for permission from the landowner first. Respect their property and follow any rules they may have.
- When someone in a car slows down or stops for you, thank them by smiling, nodding, or mouthing thank you.
- Respect other people: Always be considerate and helpful to others when hacking. Consider the local community and other people also enjoying the outdoors.
- Passing etiquettes: When passing other riders or walkers, slow down and announce your presence politely. Give plenty of space as you are passing.
- Control your pony: Always maintain control of your pony, especially when passing other trail users or encountering unfamiliar situations. Be considerate of other riders, walkers, and cyclists.

Figure 103: a) Public footpath, b) Public bridleway.

- Respect farming: Familiarise yourself with local regulations, etiquette, and guidelines for riding in the countryside. Understanding the rules and expectations can help you navigate trails safely and courteously. If you see farmers working in the fields, give them space and don't disturb their work. Farming is an important part of countryside life.

Protect the environment

- No littering: Always take your litter home with you. Leave the countryside as beautiful as you found it for others to enjoy.
- Protect livestock: Animals in a field with a bridle path should be avoided, especially ewes lambing. If you find an injured animal or (damaged structure) see any damage while riding, alert the landowner if possible.
- If you must pass through a field of crops (and it is permitted to do so), stick to the paths to avoid damaging the plants.
- Protect wildlife: Remember that animals and insects live here too. Watch them from a distance and never disturb their homes or nests.

Learn and appreciate: Take the time to learn about the countryside's plants, animals, and history. It's a fascinating place with a lot to discover.

Riding in the countryside: gates and shared access

Plan your ride

Planning a few things before setting out is sensible when you decide to go on a hack.

Time of day: Make sure there is enough time to go out and come back in good daylight.

The weather: Check the forecast before riding in heavy rain, high winds, or other poor weather.

Your pony's fitness: Is your pony fit enough to manage your planned ride? This may vary from a short hack on easy tracks to hunting for several hours.

Be safe: Stick together with friends or family, wear appropriate clothing for the time of year.

Before leaving: Always tell someone where you are going, even when you ride in the fields with friends and let them know what time they should expect you back.

Mobile device: Carry a fully charged mobile device with you so that you can contact someone in case of an incident or problem. Your parents can track and locate you if necessary.

What3words: This is a service that divides the world into 3m by 3m squares, each with a unique three-word address. For example, The Pony Club Head Office is ///grazes.weekend.shimmered.

- **Finding and sharing a location**: You can find the three-word address for a specific location using the what3words app. Once you have the three-word address, you can easily share it with others, making it simple to direct people to a specific spot.
- **Navigation**: The what3words app can be used to navigate to a specific three-word address, often integrating with other navigation apps like Google Maps.
- **Emergency services**: Many emergency services, including over 85% of UK emergency services, accept what3words addresses. This allows people to quickly and accurately communicate their location to emergency responders.
- **Why use it?** Traditional addressing systems can be inaccurate, especially in rural areas or new developments. What3words provides a more precise and universally applicable way to pinpoint locations.

Here's a guide on what to do if an incident or accident occurs when you are out riding.

Stay calm: It is important to remain calm to assess the situation and provide appropriate help.

Check for injuries: Check that you are okay and have not hurt yourself. Get immediate medical attention if needed.

Secure your pony: If the incident hasn't spooked your pony, check that you have control and dismount if safe to do so. If not, try to seek help from someone more experienced.

Move to safety: If possible, avoid any immediate danger, such as busy roads or other ponies.

Call for help: Don't hesitate to ask for help. Call emergency services or notify someone nearby for assistance if the situation warrants it. Anyone coming to help you will need to know where you are and how to get to you on a track or the nearest road.

Comfort and reassure: Comfort the injured rider and reassure them that everything will be okay. Offer them support and encouragement.

Report the incident: Depending on the severity of the incident, it might be necessary to report it to a responsible person, such as a coach or Pony Club official.

Review and learn: After the incident has been addressed, take the opportunity to think about what happened and learn from it. Consider what could have been done differently to prevent it in the future.

Remember, prevention is always better than cure. Sensible route planning and choosing your ride partner can go a long way in ensuring safe and enjoyable pony rides.

Lead by example: Set a positive example for others by demonstrating courteous behaviour and good hacking and countryside etiquette. Your actions can influence the behaviour of others and contribute to a positive riding experience for everyone. Following these tips can contribute to a positive and enjoyable riding experience for yourself and others in the countryside.

Know when you can access fields and when you cannot

The land that you ride on is often owned by someone else and we need to respect that there are tracks and bridleways for us to access.

Permission and access: Always ensure you have permission to ride across fields. If the land is privately owned, you need permission from the landowner. Signs indicating private property, or no trespassing should be respected. If the land is public, be aware of any regulations or restrictions regarding where you can ride. Look out for bridleway signs and check the local map.

Weather and ground conditions: Pay attention to weather conditions and ground stability. Riding across fields when the ground is wet or muddy can cause damage to the land and increase the risk of accidents, such as slipping or getting stuck. Avoid riding in fields that are waterlogged or during periods of heavy rain.

Crop growth and livestock: Be aware of the presence of crops or livestock in the fields. Riding through fields with crops can damage the plants and impact the livelihood of farmers. Additionally, riding near livestock, such as cattle or sheep, can spook the animals and potentially lead to dangerous situations. Look for signs indicating the presence of livestock and avoid fields where animals are grazing.

Know when grass becomes a crop.

Observation of field activity: Keep an eye on the fields that you ride in throughout the year. Fields used for grassland usually get mown or grazed by livestock. If you notice changes in activity, such as ploughing or planting, the grassland has likely been converted into a crop field and you should not ride across it.

Be sensible: If you need more certainty about the crop in a field, then you should avoid riding across it.

Opening and shutting gates

If your pony has been trained at home and is obedient to the aids, this is comparatively simple. A young pony is often anxious about going close to a gate and finds it hard to stand still. A little time and patience is usually required.

When opening a gate, it's crucial to position the pony correctly. Ask your pony to stand still, parallel with and close to the gate, with his head facing the latch. Use your hand nearest to the gate to unfasten the latch. Once the latch is unfastened, you can pull or push the gate open and pass through.

To shut the gate, turn your pony round, transfer your reins (and baton) to the other hand, and either pull or push the gate shut. Again, ask your pony to stand still, parallel with and close to the gate, while you lean down to fix the latch with your hand.

If you and your pony are not accustomed to opening and shutting gates, it's important to be aware that you may encounter some challenges. When passing through a swinging gate with a group of other riders, prevent the gate from slamming in front of the person following you. Push it well back so that you can catch it easily. Hold the gate until you can reach it if it is a self-shutting gate. If there is livestock in the fields, it is vital to prevent them from escaping, so the last person through the gate must ensure it is shut. Never gallop off, leaving someone else to shut the gate alone.

A

Figure 104: Opening a gate: a), b).

Glossary of Terms, Credits, and Index

Glossary of Terms

Above the bit Head position avoids accepting the contact by putting the head forward and upward.

Action How a horse moves.

Activity Energy and the liveliness in the hind legs.

Against the bit Horse pushes mouth against the bit with rigid neck/poll/jaw.

Basics The correct foundation of progressive training of the horse: all the criteria of the training scale.

Behind the bit/aids/leg An evasion in which the horse retracts from the bit/contact; avoids working forwards from behind into an accepting rein contact.

Behind the vertical The head position in which the nose line comes behind the vertical.

Bone A term used in conformation referring to the circumference of the bone below the knee. If the measurement is generous, the horse is said to have good or plenty of bone; if it is not, the horse is short of bone.

Bounce When landing over an obstacle, the horse immediately jumps the next one without taking a stride.

Breaking out Starting to sweat again after exercise, having previously cooled off.

Cast, to (a shoe) A horse is said to have cast a shoe when the shoe comes off by accident: i.e. is not removed deliberately.

Cast (in box or stable) A horse lying down and unable to get up: usually due to rolling over too close to the wall, or getting his feet caught under the manger.

Cheek (on a bit) is the straight side part of some bits.

Circuit breaker A safety device fitted in a wall socket. When electric clippers, for example, are plugged into it, the power will instantly be cut off if there is a fault in the machine or its cable – thus preventing an electric shock.

Clench The part of the nail which, during shoeing, is left projecting from the hoof wall after the nail's end has been twisted off. The metal is then bent over and hammered in to secure the shoe to the foot.

Cold hosing The use of a gentle stream of cold water to reduce inflammation.

Concussion The jar caused to the feet and legs of a horse when working on hard ground – also, a brain injury.

Contact Works from behind through a supple swinging back into a consistent, elastic contact.

Double bridle A bridle with two bits and two sets of reins.

Falling in This occurs when, to compensate for stiffness or loss of balance, a horse turning on a circle or around a corner moves his shoulder in and comes off the true circle.

Flexion Lateral/Longitudinal flexion at the poll.

Gait/regularity The sequence of footfalls in a pace.

Gamgee Cotton wool encased in gauze.

Going, the The condition of the ground.

Hacking exercising (i.e. going for a ride), as opposed to working.

Hacking on riding to or from a venue without making excessive demands on the horse's energy.

Half-halt A momentary increase of collection, or an effect of the aids which increases the attention of the horse and improves its balance.

Hollow back Horse comes above the bit dropping the back away from the weight of the rider to give a 'hollow outline'.

Hot up, to A horse who becomes unduly excited, particularly when ridden, is said to hot up.

Impulsion Increased energy from hindquarters. Forward thrust, pushing power. Hind legs swing forward with supple swinging back.

Irregular Unlevel or uneven which may or may not be due to unsoundness (not unsteady tempo).

Keepers Fixed loops which keep the ends of bridle straps, etc., in place.

Lateral To the side as in flexion, bend, suppleness or direction of a movement. Incorrect walk sequence.

Longitudinal Lengthwise dimension front to back or back to front.

Long and short sides differentiate between the sides of a rectangular arena, or school.

Near and offsides The near is the left side of a horse, the off is the right side.

On the aids Willing, confident and immediate reaction to the rider's aids.

On the bit Supple, quiet acceptance of the contact with lateral and longitudinal flexion.

On the forehand Longitudinally poor balance, too much weight on the forelegs for the task.

Over bent Behind the vertical with too much longitudinal flexion in the poll or upper joints of neck.

Over-face, to To ask a horse to jump an obstacle which is beyond his capability or stage of training.

Over track The hind foot is placed in front of the print of the forefoot.

Pointing A horse standing with one foreleg stuck out markedly in front of the other. This usually indicates discomfort in a foot. The same action with a hind leg is normal and is referred to as resting a hind.

Pulling (mane or tail) Removing hairs from the underside of the mane and sides of the tail to improve their appearance.

Quartering A quick grooming, to tidy up a horse before exercise.

Resistance Physical opposition by the horse against the rider.

Rhythm The evenness of the footfall and regularity of the beat.

Roundness The convexity of the profile of the horse's topline.

Run up a stirrup iron Slide the iron to the top of the leather.

Scope Athletic ability.

Self-carriage The horse carries itself in a balanced and unconstrained manner without taking support or balancing on the rider's hand.

Set fair, to To give the horse a light brush over, remove droppings, and tidy up bedding.

Short side (of arena) *see* Long and short sides.

Skip A strong basket used for removing droppings.

Stale, to To urinate.

Staring coat A coat standing up and looking dull instead of lying flat and looking glossy. It is usually a sign that the horse is cold or unwell, or both.

Stiffness Inability to flex the joints or stretch the muscles to the required degree for the task.

Straightness Forehand is in line with hindquarters on curves and straight lines. Horse is able to bend equally on both reins.

Strike-off The first step of the canter.

Suppleness Ability to adjust the carriage (longitudinally) and the position of bend (laterally) without loss of balance and fluency. State when the horse is relaxed mentally and physically. Horse works over the back and through the neck with elasticity.

Tempo The speed of the rhythm.

Top line The horse's outline from the ears along top of neck and back to its tail.

Tracking up The hind feet step into the tracks of the forefeet.

Turn out, to To put a horse out in a field (out to grass).

Turnout The general appearance of horse and rider, grooming, trimming, saddlery, dress, etc.

Uneven Unequal in length of steps.

Unlevel Unequal in height of steps or unequal bearing of weight on both sides.

Uphill The horse's longitudinal balance; higher forehand relative to the croup.

Wide behind Hind feet travel further apart than forefeet (an evasion of engagement when lengthening trot or in halt).

Wind A horse's breathing or respiration when working.

Wings Extensions to the sides of a fence which are generally higher than the obstacle itself. They are used to discourage a horse from running out. In show jumping they also provide support for the fence.

Credits

Illustrations

Carole Vincer

Figures 1, 3, 6, 7, 13, 14, 15, 16, 22, 24, 26, 30, 31, 32, 33, 34, 35, 36, 37, 40, 42, 44, 51, 52, 54, 55, 56, 58, 59, 60, 61, 62, 63, 64, 65, 67, 68, 69, 71, 72, 77, 79, 83, 84, 86, 87, 88, 91, 92, 93, 94, 95, 96, 101, 105.

Photography

Pete Morris Photography

Figures 4, 5, 17, 18, 19, 20, 21, 25, 28, 38, 39, 41, 50, 57, 70, 73, 74, 75, 76, 80, 81, 82, 89, 90, 102, 103, 104.

Organisations

Blue Cross – Figures 47, 70
British Equestrian – Figure 8
Jump4Joy – Figures 97 & 98
World Horse Welfare – Figure 9
Worshipful Company of Loriners – Figures 64 & 65
SupaStuds – Figure 45
Kent and Masters, Frank Baines, Zilco – Figure 53

Index